# Artie Shaw

ALSO OF INTEREST
AND FROM McFARLAND

*The Pacific Northwest: Growth of a Regional Identity*
(Raymond D. Gastil and Barnett Singer, 2010)

*Maxime Weygand: A Biography of the French General
in Two World Wars* (Barnett Singer, 2008)

*Brigitte Bardot: A Biography*
(Barnett Singer, 2006; paperback 2013)

# Artie Shaw
*Icon of Swing*

BARNETT SINGER *and*
JESSE READ

McFarland & Company, Inc., Publishers
*Jefferson, North Carolina*

LIBRARY OF CONGRESS CATALOGUING-IN-PUBLICATION DATA

Names: Singer, Barnett, author. | Read, Jesse A. author.
Title: Artie Shaw : icon of swing / Barnett Singer and Jesse Read.
Description: Jefferson, North Carolina : McFarland & Company, Inc.,
    Publishers, 2024. | Includes bibliographical references and index.
Identifiers: LCCN 2023043375 | ISBN 9781476689708
    (paperback : acid free paper) ∞
    ISBN 9781476650258 (ebook)
Subjects: LCSH: Shaw, Artie, 1910-2004. | Clarinetists—United States—
    Biography. | Jazz musicians—United States—Biography. | Composers—
    United States—Biography. | Conductors (Music)—United States—Biography.
Classification: LCC ML419.S52 S55 2023 | DDC 788.6/2092 [B]—dc23/
    eng/20230918
LC record available at https://lccn.loc.gov/2023043375

BRITISH LIBRARY CATALOGUING DATA ARE AVAILABLE

ISBN (print) 978-1-4766-8970-8
ISBN (ebook) 978-1-4766-5025-8

© 2024 Barnett Singer and Jesse Read. All rights reserved

*No part of this book may be reproduced or transmitted in any form
or by any means, electronic or mechanical, including photocopying
or recording, or by any information storage and retrieval system,
without permission in writing from the publisher.*

Front cover image: Artie Shaw publicity photograph
from the author's collection

Printed in the United States of America

*McFarland & Company, Inc., Publishers
    Box 611, Jefferson, North Carolina 28640
        www.mcfarlandpub.com*

# Contents

*Acknowledgments*     vi
*Preface*     1
*Introduction*     3

ONE. Reaching the Top in the Swing Era     21
TWO. Shaw at His Apex: 1939     43
THREE. The Second Great Shaw Orchestra: 1940-41     74
FOUR. More (and Less) of the Same: 1941-42     99
FIVE. Bringing Music to the Troops     109
SIX. Swing Sunset and a Last Great Shaw Band     113
SEVEN. Toward Musical Retirement     141
EIGHT. The Long Coda     158

*Chapter Notes*     173
*Bibliography*     181
*Index*     185

# Acknowledgments

This book's primary author wishes to acknowledge, and warmly, the vital help and contributions provided by his co-author, Jesse Read, and by (you will know who you are) Charlie, Elaine, Sharon, Ruth, Mary, Ray, Susan, and my daughter Alexandra. I also acknowledge the great contributions of previous giants in this field, particularly Vladimir Simosko and Tom Nolan, and the time a retired Artie Shaw once gave me for long conversations; and I obviously take majority responsibility for all infelicities here.

Jesse Read acknowledges the aid and support of Samantha Wright, in particular, and of his wife, Rapti, along with a number of others with whom he corresponded on this project.

Both of us thank Susannah Jayes for invaluable advice on pictures permissions and Cindy Coan for her work on the index.

# Preface

Briefly put, this book may be considered several in one on a remarkable musician and person. The main part reflects our title and treats Artie Shaw's brand or brands of swing, when he was indeed an American icon. But there are also memoir swaths here, reflecting how the book's primary author got to know Shaw and his thinking well after he had retired from his original career, and preoccupation in life.

Elements of biography also figure in this treatment, because Shaw certainly had an interesting, often turbulent life story, and his own character formation greatly impacted the quality of his extensive, often unique musical output, including his one-of-a-kind clarinet. Additionally, one might consider this a contribution of sorts to fields like American studies, and of course musical history, too, especially the history of jazz. We hope that it will complement much fine work that has already been done on the great Artie, and that it will appeal to a variety of readers, young and older, those new to the subject or the many already possessing much prior knowledge in this field, including acquaintance with Shaw's old recordings. What Artie Shaw music, and there was a great deal of it, should people today listen to and savor? This is a fundamental question we try our best to answer here. Enjoy!

*Note: All references to "I" or "me" are to Singer; references to "we" or "us" are to Singer and Read.*

# Introduction

One initial matter that needs to be addressed in an introduction to this book seems to be: how did I first become interested in Artie Shaw, then remain obsessed with his music made in the high Swing Era, and for many years? A mini-memoir of sorts will help answer that question.

It all started with the fact that I was extremely musical from early childhood. And was then impelled paternally into a huge amount of sports activity, at which I acquitted myself pretty decently; but in the process also covering up or tamping down too much of what I loved most.

I did select a music option in high school, starting on violin in ninth grade. But after a week I pleaded to my mom that the instrument required more dexterity than I possessed. (I was also terrible in courses like shop or industrial arts.) She quickly took me out of the orchestra part of the course and into band, where I was awarded the same difficult instrument on which Shaw once astonished the world.

One day my parents and I were at the home of some friends of theirs, and I mentioned that I played clarinet; so the hosts dutifully put a Benny Goodman LP on their stereo. And not just any Goodman, but the absolute *crème de la crème*—a selection of "air checks" from his greatest band of 1937-38 (featuring Harry James, Gene Krupa et al.), i.e., live performances of great Fletcher Henderson or Jimmy Mundy arrangements from hotel engagements and such, heard on radio broadcasts and taped. The best of these tapes (via modern engineering) became LP cuts in the late '50s, and I was wowed by the powerful band ensembles and by James' solos, and by Goodman's clarinet scampering so adeptly over the powerful mix of brass and reeds. Was I also bowled over in part because I was discovering the era of my dad's youth back in those Depression days? Perhaps.

Anyway, I had to hear and buy more of those LPs, better by far than the original recorded versions of these arrangements. Why was that? In Goodman's case many of these records were made at the Swing Era's dawn, circa 1935-36. After so many times playing them live, and with such great sidemen brought into the band, the '37-'38 performances chosen for these albums mainly worked much better, Goodman's clarinet work included. They also outdid the famed recording of Goodman's 1938 Carnegie Hall concert or the soundtrack to *The Benny Goodman Story*, both of which I also acquired.

I'm a bit rough in a number of spots below on Goodman, mirroring Artie's own often damning-with-faint-praise views there; but there is no question that there was—and had to be!—great influence on Shaw's bands from swing's first king, and especially from the finished standards of those remarkable Henderson arrangements, which supplied something of a template. Why shouldn't Artie have done some sipping at the same trough? And he certainly did. These stellar arrangements and Benny's clarinet and band-welding on "Down South Camp Meeting" or "When Buddha Smiles" were so powerful and riveting that I listened to those air checks (on these LPs) over and over, compulsively so. No one in the field back in the '30s could ignore them, either.

Meanwhile: around 10th grade, and when I had my 14th birthday or so, my mom decided on an interesting gift that would open up a world for me. Without any fanfare and hardly any words at all she handed me an Artie Shaw LP titled *Moonglow*, a potpourri of his great work made during the period 1938–41 and drawn from two of his greatest orchestras. At first I caviled, saying something like: "Isn't his stuff just like Kostelanetz?" I.e., musical cotton candy, fluff, elevator music? To which my mom said nothing. The proof would be in the proverbial pudding.

I then put the LP on our Hi-Fi built into a cabinet in the living room, and I was absolutely floored and moved by Shaw's inimitable, buttery, melancholy tone on the licorice stick, so seemingly effortless in all registers, and downright gorgeous! And with a certain saxophone-like thickness and sensuality to it like no other. I loved, too, how his entire orchestras (with and without strings) sounded polished, compelling, dramatic, and fresh (even on old standards), due to Shaw's enormous self-demands I couldn't yet grasp.

But through the years I kept acquiring more of his old recordings on various albums, and in the '70s, on a series of LPs called *The Complete Artie Shaw* (on RCA), beginning with his first two waxings for them in 1938, originally released as a 78; and ending in 1945, when he had a wrangle with company executives. And when public tastes were changing markedly as well. Shaw then moved from RCA to another, less important label, working in 1946 with upcoming talents like Mel Tormé. This was when the Swing Era (and Shaw's popularity) had clearly waned. The only sub-period unaccounted for in *The Complete...* was due

***Introduction*** 5

to the fact that his fine Navy band working in sometimes dicey swaths of the Pacific theater made no records at all for part of 1942 and through '43.

From the summer of 1968 I lived in the Pacific Northwest, and during the subsequent "Me Decade" of the '70s (when AM radio played hits by Carole King, Elton John, and so forth), I taught courses in history at the University of Washington, Seattle, where I'd gained my Ph.D. (1971). I also worked at a nearby think tank (one result being an eventual, co-written book called *The Pacific Northwest: Growth of a Regional Identity*). And in that period I decided I wanted somehow to get in touch with Mr. Shaw, the once famous clarinet-playing bandleader, now in his 60s and long retired from his primary calling. Of course in the '70s there was no internet to help me along in this regard. However, I did procure Shaw's home address in Southern California, where he was then residing, after living in numerous other places (New York, Connecticut, Spain, Bucks County, Pennsylvania, etc.). This address was surprisingly listed at the end of his entry in *Who's Who in America*, a copy of which I found at the university reference library circa 1976. I sent a letter or two to Shaw, but received no answer.

Remaining decidedly quixotic and maybe naïve, I then decided to take that address as a starting point, and one day got out L.A. area phone books, also housed in the reference part of the university library. I pored over huge lists of Shaws and located no Artie. But finally I did come upon an A.N. Shaw on Outpost Drive and knew this was it. Eureka!

My then-wife and small daughter remained quiet that evening while I hesitantly dialed the number, stupidly (or ignorantly) neglecting Paul Valéry's advice to the effect that it's never a good idea to meet one's idols. (This despite Tony Oppedisano doing so in mostly beneficial fashion with the iconic Sinatra, who became a close friend.)[1] I did expect a voice on the phone with roughly the same romantic sweetness and emotion as in Shaw's copious, so often marvelous swing recordings; instead, I got a jolting splash of something very different, rather like the water of an icy mountain lake that shocks you when you first enter it for a dip. Shaw's "Hell-o" was an accusatory, almost paranoid boomer! He quickly asked, legitimately puzzled, who this was (at first thinking it was one of his sons, Steven Kern Shaw). I knew he didn't suffer fans or fools gladly, and so I rapidly identified myself, then said hesitantly and even apologetically, "I ... I just wanted to know what you're now into, Mr. Shaw." (I knew that since his abandonment of popular music-making and most tragically for many, his clarinet during the mid–'50s that that included much reading and writing.)

Shaw replied gruffly that he was "into" the philosophy of history, and I believe he added nuclear chemistry or another scientific field. I shouldn't have been surprised, but I was! Especially by that almost scary timbre of his voice, so much at odds with his old music, a shattering contrast indeed. In a rich New York accent (though he'd migrated to New Haven, Connecticut, during childhood), Shaw proceeded to rattle off a number of books by Louis Halle, such as *The Cold War as History* and *Out of Chaos*. Within days I would take them out of the university library and peruse them carefully.

For some psychological reason (and not because I was then planning a book on him), I kept calling Shaw every month or so for years on end, always in the afternoon (so as not to disturb his mornings, which I eventually knew to be reserved for a sprawling autobiographical novel he tentatively titled *The Education of Albie Snow*; nor his evenings). Amazingly, unless busy, Shaw took many of those calls, then proceeded to talk my ear off, for up to 45 minutes on end. He was not only an ex–jazz star who'd practiced and played endlessly, but also a champion talker and intellectual. He kept telling me what he was reading, and I'd generally go and get those books, too, taking a course of sorts (of the type he'd already given luminaries like Ava Gardner, though why he foisted *The Brothers Karamazov* on her, or worse, Mann's *The Magic Mountain*, I'll never know). As an example of what he recommended to me, I asked one day what he was reading, and he told me he'd been devouring Hemingway's letters round the clock. He emphasized with obvious feelings of kinship that Hemingway truly detested ambition. And "so do I," Shaw earnestly

The great and handsome Artie Shaw in his musical heyday (Getty Images/Michael Ochs Archives).

declared. I remonstrated with some astonishment that he'd certainly been ambitious back in the day. "None more so!" he replied.²

Among many other books, he also mentioned an early and elegant self-help offering by Wendell Johnson called *People in Quandaries*, and Lewis Thomas' *The Lives of a Cell*, both of which seemed pertinent to the way Shaw's own turbulent life and career had unfolded. Quandaries? He'd had more than his share, especially the fact that he loved contributing so beautifully and uniquely to the Big Band era, but simultaneously hated so much about that life that he kept thinking of trying his hand at something else. (Even in the music itself, one can detect some of Shaw's ambivalence, strong and soft often commingled and almost jousting, it seems, one reason so many have considered him *sui generis*.)

I could certainly see why he was drawn to Thomas' *The Lives of a Cell* along with Halle's *Out of Chaos*, because both those books emphasize how periods of coherence in nature or biology and in historical eras, too, are the healthiest ones. And yes, Shaw's own aggregations of the swing period were so marvelous in good part because he patiently and doggedly welded his players into a smooth organization of parts, all contributing to the whole, and to superb, finished products, mirroring exactly what the bandleader desired—and which he so often obtained. (Many of his old sidemen agreed entirely on this.)

Aside from things intellectual, did Shaw also discuss that old music with me? Not nearly as much, but a little. One time he chided the late Glenn Miller for not picking up his singer Helen Forrest from his first great orchestra, after Artie shocked the world by junking it in late November 1939. Using a term of contempt, he derided Miller's taste. In addition he'd sometimes use a musical song title such as "Pick Yourself Up" to rally me from a comparative case of the blues. He didn't like singers that well, so he said nothing nice about his old romantic rival, Frank Sinatra; but instead commented derogatorily on that icon's personality, calling him a would-be "pope," and much worse.³

How long did we talk? I'd have to estimate it as about seven years, i.e., from the late '70s through 1984 or so. I clearly remember that in early January of the latter year we spoke, and Shaw mentioned a *Newsweek* article on his astonishing re-formation of an Artie Shaw orchestra playing the old arrangements, with a Bostonian, Dick Johnson, anointed as its bandleader and lead clarinetist. Artie even read from the article, obviously glad for the attention. And I remember (also near the end of our conversational days) him telling me about the reissue of some of his last small-group recordings of the '50s by the Book-of-the-Month Club, work that was astonishingly progressive and modern in tone, and where his clarinet more than kept up. I immediately ordered those records, and was wowed.

Fortunately or unfortunately (or both?), I never took down notes of these many conversations with Shaw, or precise dates; but in a Proustian manner, and also the way Tony O. did in his book on Sinatra, I still recall a lot of what Artie told me over those years. (Speaking of Proust, Frederick Morton, who had known Shaw in Spain during the '50s, asserted that he ploughed through all the volumes of that author's masterwork, *Remembrance of Things Past*.)[4] To repeat, I remember much of what Artie told me on the phone. His apothegms poured out aplenty, such as "You have to act as if you don't have the neuroses." (He must have retailed that one a good deal in different ways, including with heavy drinkers in his employ, like the great drummer Dave Tough, among others who worked in his bands.) Or: "You do the most good being selfish." Or: "You have to write what obsesses you." (Play musically, too?) Or: "A band swings when it doesn't try to swing." As for his clarinet work that stood out so much in his heyday, he would emphasize that everyone's thumbprint is different. And finding that difference in yourself was what really mattered in such a field.

From the books he mentioned I derived a lot as well. For example, in the edition of Hemingway's letters I took out of the library, I came upon a fascinating line from Ernest H. to the effect that the artist hates himself and loves the world. Obviously this wouldn't be true of every artist (Renoir, for instance, seems to have had a mostly happy existence). But I feel this view really did pertain to Artie's musical standards and greatness, and particularly, why he went beyond that other Swing Era heavy, Goodman, especially in terms of his frequently melancholy, poignant, and complicated clarinet sounds (and those of his bands) on those lovely old recordings. Did Shaw indeed hate himself and love the world (the latter especially seen in the copious, soulful, marvelously honed work he gave to it)? In part, I'd say, owing at least somewhat to a difficult, unhappy childhood he'd endured as an only child of two immigrant, constantly bickering parents.

Partly due to an ear injury sustained during World War II, that voice of his on the phone kept shocking, but enlightening me, too. Meanwhile, I still played Shaw's old records over and over, though at one point he called that pure laziness! He really did want me to pursue and offer my own "thing," as did another of my idols of that era, the novelist-intellectual Saul Bellow. À propos of this, I wrote a memoir on Bellow, claiming an entire periodical, called "Looking for Mr. Bellow" (1982),[5] and sent a copy to Shaw. And he appreciated what it said about me in particular, rather than simply about my heroes (he was discussed in there, too, as at one point I put on some Shaw records for a visiting Bellow and wife). In conversation the novelist mentioned Artie dragging him off to Birdland in Manhattan, but Shaw couldn't remember or corroborate that. And according to Bellow, when Artie tried to crack into the New York intellectual scene circa 1950, he kept mentioning a therapist and ethnographer, Abram Kardiner. Abe Kardiner this, Abe Kardiner that.... He was undoubtedly trying to impress and be accepted. And one intellectual, pretending not to hear the name "Abe Kardiner" very well, snapped: "Ava Gardner? I never knew she was such a deep thinker!" (Thankfully, Shaw didn't seem to mind such things pertaining to him in this memoir.)

When I much later (January 2006) met Dick Johnson in suburban Detroit, where the reconstituted Shaw orchestra was appearing, he said in a grave voice that Shaw must have liked me, or he would never have taken all those calls and divagated so extensively on the phone all those years. Well, this much is indisputable: I certainly took the man's intellectual or philosophical proclivities seriously. And at the same time I was also super-immersed in his old musical *oeuvre*, probably more than most anyone—helplessly so, I'd say. Meaning, for example, that as I went off to teach this or that class, I'd find myself whistling uncontrollably in the stairwells, making for a kind of microphone effect, as I laid on the earthy sweetness derived from this old Shaw record, that one, the other. When classes were done and I was alone again, I was back to that activity once again. The music was deep in me with all its subtleties and contrasts, warmth and power; and yes, I was good and bitten. But I was also biographically empathetic re how difficult Shaw had found the intrusions that came with being a celebrity, and the problems, too, of melding art and entertainment (and money-making), concerns he retained during his long life, and which he mentioned in many of his interviews almost down to his death.

Of course like any great jazz player who did so much of it, starting in his early teens, Shaw was all themes and variations; and with these variations, certain opinions I got from him have naturally turned up in different spots and ways, and could easily be located once the internet took hold. I.e., I was far from unique in what I culled orally from Artie, though some of what I heard seems not to be found elsewhere, and will help flavor this particular treatment of such an unusual, popular musician.

But really, why do we need another book on Shaw? There have been some fine secondary treatments on him, notably Vladimir Simosko's *Artie Shaw: A Musical Biography and Discography*,[6] which is superbly researched and an invaluable source for our own work or any other on

Shaw; and John White's *Artie Shaw: His Life and Music*.[7] But both are in part biographies, and in the case of the latter, too slim and full of long quotations; while the former also has a lot of extended quotations, including from old periodical articles. However, it is also an exhaustive reference book replete with a lot of amazingly thorough and useful information and lists. All books on Shaw's music, however, become a bit too much like extended lists. They don't give you a good enough sense of the music itself, and why one ought to listen carefully to this or that recording in order to derive different kinds of enjoyment from them.

I concede of course that there is a major problem for anyone trying to describe the content or flavor of those records, given the fact that music is an entirely different language from the verbal, from explication and so forth, all of which are bound to fall short. I never found it enjoyable to read this or that "expert" telling us that Shaw was more "lyrical" than Benny Goodman, and so on. But even in our own effort, in no way, shape or form can we entirely surmount such a pervasive problem, not by a long shot; and yet readers will hopefully get a tasteful guide here to the plethora of music one can pick up from Shaw's high Swing Era contributions of 1938–45, helping them (maybe most particularly, comparative neophytes) savor his substantial, astonishing evolution in that field.

The best biography of him to date is Tom Nolan's *Artie Shaw, King of the Clarinet: His Life and Times*,[8] and it is certainly readable, drawing on quite a variety of interviews and other primary sources. But it also owes a good deal to Simosko's earlier book, and like that one and White's, too, to memoirs by such as Helen Forrest, Ava Gardner, or Evelyn Keyes; to long, informative articles like Robert Lewis Taylor's "Middle-Aged Man Without a Horn," in *The New Yorker*;[9] and naturally to Shaw's own autobiography of the early '50s, *The Trouble with Cinderella: An Outline of Identity*.[10] Part of our problem here (and it would be the same for others well acquainted with Artie's full, turbulent life) is that much of this material had already been known, almost too well known. A good deal of it had already surfaced in a great number of published interviews.

The main point: none of the fine secondary works mentioned above, nor Shaw's memoir, really do what we try to do here. In this introduction I've been sketching what drew me to Shaw. And it was the music that mattered most, and still does, rather than the life history, including Shaw's much-married personal resumé, about which he himself said virtually nothing in *Cinderella*. In conversation, too, I never introduced the matter nor pushed him on it either, though he did confess to me that he was being pestered to the tune of advances of a couple million dollars or so (equivalent to much more in our era) to produce a kiss-and-tell tome on the subject. Maybe out of a certain *pudeur*, he always refused.

So for us, and undoubtedly for many listeners, too, the music Shaw created during his greatest, most popular period remains central. And there again we hope to provide a real guide of sorts. Which means we won't try to duplicate the other secondary treatments by being nearly so biographical, especially by repeating a good deal found there on Shaw's fraught, disorderly life with the eight women he married (including Lana Turner, Ms. Gardner, Jerome Kern's daughter, Betty, the novelist Kathleen Winsor, and Ms. Keyes). Nor do we accentuate Shaw's relationship with his two sons from two of those wives, whom he definitely treated quite badly. On the latter subject, may I intrude an anecdote you probably won't get elsewhere? Shaw told me that one day his son Steven came to him with a guitar in hand, obviously wanting to be another Willie Nelson, as Artie put it. He asked the great clarinetist and bandleader (and very intermittent father) whether he had any musical talent, and Shaw replied, probably gruffly: "Well, I'm your father and Jerome Kern's your grandfather, so you ought to have some."

Will such anecdotes pop up intermittently in this account focused on the old records, and the best of that generous output which today's listeners of all generations can still relish? No question. But again, the main emphasis here will be not on the biographical or anecdotal (and/or prurient!); but instead, on those records which Shaw made so memorably, especially between 1938 and 1945, our central chronological limits here. If we may say so, our takes on this recorded *oeuvre* will unroll in a mostly less technical and more "felt" manner than one finds in other books or articles on this Swing Era genius.

At the least there should be two pluses in the present offering. One, I suppose, is the fact that I talked to the man for so long and have retained a good deal from those conversations. The second is that our highlighting of this or that Shaw tune will help younger people locate his work via YouTube and so forth, now handily available on their computers. And it may help older fans, too, who have given away frayed old albums and even CDs or put them in storage.

We will also avoid duplicating the story of what constitutes a long professional preamble to the point when Artie began recording for RCA's Bluebird (originally conceived as a budget label), and really hit the top as a swing icon. We will be much briefer here on that upward course than are the standard biographies, along with Shaw's own memoir.

That previous musical life must certainly include the effects on his psyche of his difficult growing-up period, which started in New York, where he was born Arthur Arshawsky on the Lower East Side, May 23,

1910. There his constantly bickering parents struggled in their dressmaking business (his mother, Sarah, a seamstress, his father, Harold, a tailor with other ambitions, including mounting a portrait photography studio that unfortunately went bust). One would have to emphasize both how Artie tried to skirt this loud, boisterous father, but also pitied him in a way for being held down by a domineering, more practical wife. One would have to zero in on the family's intermittent poverty, including a bankruptcy, and its move to much more WASPy and back then, anti–Semitic New Haven, Connecticut, when Artie was seven. This reflective, bookish boy felt out of place there, owing to his penchant as well for music (at first the ukulele and the piano, learned via lessons his mother pushed on him), and from being no physical match for tough guys in the streets or schoolyards. He was a lonely only child, with parents who spoke in heavy foreign and to him, shameful accents. His alienation and sense of utter instability continued with four jarring familial moves to other New Haven addresses. Getting away from what already felt to him a broken home of sorts, and which eventually became a literal one, seemed ever more imperative.

The first way out came when the boy started frequenting Poli's Palace, a local vaudeville haunt featuring a well-clad sax player who entranced him, and beautiful ladies parading on stage. The 13-year-old decided to put all his energies into mastering a used saxophone, one he bought with his summer deli wages for the sum of $40, and on which he received two lessons from the fellow who made the sale.[11] Blowing away *ad nauseam* and even making his mouth bleed didn't bother this teenager; but it made his father scream even more frequently and stridently, both by day and in the middle of the night at his wife, continuing to terrify the young Shaw.

One must then move on to Artie's apprenticeship with quite a variety of groups and bands: first, after many hours of saxophone practice, with a friend who had a banjo, and then with three others in something called the Peter Pan Novelty Orchestra, playing weddings and other such events around New Haven. At least Shaw's bumptious father got so put off by his son's "blower" and increasingly, by life with his spouse that he finally solved an oedipal problem of sorts by taking off to California, never to return, and making Artie's earned cash necessary to keep him and mom fed and lodged. What made the boy ambivalent and sometimes angry, however, were his mother's inveterate attempts to stick close to him wherever he went, including much later in life.

The young man's peregrinations began via his first truly professional assignment with an older bunch in Johnny Cavallaro's New Haven–based band, one that also traveled, and sometimes far away.

## Introduction

In a well-known anecdote, Artie, the callow autodidact, was shocked when Cavallaro insisted on him reading, which initially the teenager thought to be books. Once he understood that Cavallaro meant musical sight-reading, Artie promised that within one month he'd learn that art. (Naturally, he kept the promise.) By age 14 or so he was cutting high school, listening to records by much greater instrumentalists, and playing not only with Cavallaro but on days off, with other regional bands.

Down in Florida with Johnny's group, and only 15 (his dad and school now gone from his life), and using the more "American" last name of Shaw, the teen received another tough assignment. He had to quickly learn what was par for the course when it came to sax players (i.e., to "double" on clarinet); but even this lifetime self-starter found it hard to master the new fingering and embouchure involved, including adequately closing that instrument's open holes, which otherwise could produce squeaks, in contrast to the sax with all its keys covered, constituting a simpler fingering system. Eventually (via more hard work) Shaw did learn what was a *sine qua non* for playing professionally in any orchestra. He also graduated to different kinds of saxophones, including the large and growling baritone. And he kept on moving toward better and more challenging assignments that should have been well beyond someone of his still tender age.

In 1926 he migrated to Cleveland. There he joined Joe Cantor's band, becoming its lead alto player, and with his mother in tow to take care of him at an apartment they rented. He would later call her the typical showbiz mother of the era. Shaw also began learning—still as a teen—the art of arranging, taking that skill to another band headed by Austin Wylie, the most important one in Cleveland. He was nothing if not precocious, not only because of "talent" (a word he always detested), but more, a prodigious capacity for concentrated labor. In all, Shaw lasted three years in Cleveland, and then on an impulse entered and unexpectedly won an essay contest, which got him a free trip out to La La Land, a.k.a. Hollywood, still in its gilded youth. Quite predictably, the young man was blown away by these sunny environs, but he also kept his career moving forward there, linking up with Irving Aaronson's Commanders and still hoping to keep imbibing knowledge from the more seasoned players with whom he rubbed shoulders.

Finally he got to join the Commanders for good, and when the band made it to Chicago, Shaw went slightly mad by playing with all sorts of greats on the side, like the pianist Earl "Fatha" Hines, or watching and hearing other clarinet virtuosos, such as Jimmie Noone, on what was becoming his own preferred instrument. Noone was an influence as well on a young Chicagoan named Benny Goodman. Artie also encountered someone he'd much later recall in a documentary as a "god" to him, the pioneering and nonpareil trumpet player Louis Armstrong. Watching Armstrong gig in Chicago and play tunes such as "West End Blues" in his own inimitable jazz manner was a heady experience for the young Shaw.[12] He also bumped into legends with whom he would one day room, such as Bix Beiderbecke and Bunny Berigan, both grand trumpet and/or cornet artists, but alcoholics slated to die young. In sum, this vibrant and thriving Chicago jazz scene was a kind of university for the young Artie (still generally known back then as "Art").

When the band roosted in New York, he had to leave Aaronson due to the after-effects of his car killing a pedestrian there, an accident eventually deemed the unfortunate walker's fault. But till the matter got sorted out, it made for a difficult hiatus. At least Shaw formed some lasting friendships in Manhattan, especially with the pianist Claude Thornhill, a kindred spirit of sorts. And he certainly got to jam! Up in Harlem for solace but also more musical education, his extensive noodling there by day and night, meaning sometimes till dawn, shaped him far more than teachers could do, as he emphasized in his autobiography and various interviews. And this was especially true when he jammed with an idiosyncratic jazzman and stride pianist extraordinaire, Willie "The Lion" Smith. Smith enjoyed it when this determined youngster kept diving in on his "axe" beside him, and for extended periods. "The Lion" was Black, but also part-Jewish in origin, and with the gaudy real name of William Henry Joseph Bonaparte Bertholf Smith. Here was a jazz artist who could also play Bach, plus work as a cantor in Harlem (and speak Yiddish, too!). With "The Lion," Shaw kept his chops in shape and his technique advancing by leaps and bounds. This was still his M.O., i.e., to keep learning his musical craft from players with far more experience and accomplishments. And finally the gigs came back, as he signed on with Red Nichols' orchestra, and then more lucratively, and as lead alto, with Freddy Rich's ensemble, which appeared regularly on CBS Radio. Shaw also played as a New York freelancer in a variety of other gigs, raising needed money in the midst of an unprecedented Depression.

But the radio work also had its downsides, and Artie started to rue the drudgery of giving in to commercial needs and playing music that didn't really interest him. Much more exciting was sitting in with such players as Tommy Dorsey at a Princeton University bash in 1931. He also played with Dorsey at CBS, as well as other top brass players like Manny Klein, but became increasingly irked by the limitations there. In 1932 he took a break to play with Roger Wolfe Kahn's band for a time, and then it was back to radio work and its cloying boundaries. Finally, he decided to give up the job and the wonderful Depression-era money it brought him. If, as he notes in Brigitte Berman's 1985 documentary, he always wanted more, especially in the musical field, a part of Shaw also wanted less, too. Or at the least, very different things.

So in the early '30s he decided to acquire a farm in Bucks County, Pennsylvania, a pretty spread by the Delaware River, where he sold firewood as one way to make money. He also read omnivorously and tried unsuccessfully to put together a novel on the great and tragic Bix. A year of all that gave him peace of sorts, but not nearly enough income, and Shaw intermittently went into Manhattan to play and bring in cash. By February 1934 this musical work started to beckon again as his sole option, and fully so by the fall of that year. In the Big Apple he beheld Goodman's beginnings as a bandleader and both the Dorseys' too, though they would soon split into rival contingents; and all that had at least some influence on Shaw's own eventual direction. Mainly, he was back to giving his all into honing his clarinet technique and evolving a sound that would eventually be like none other. But he also kept playing for money, too, both on radio and as a sought-after sideman for the next couple of years, and was heard on quite a number of recordings.[13]

We are now approaching a real turning point in Shaw's upward course toward a great bandleading career during the Swing Era. But we need to linger a bit longer on the key elements in his background that contributed mightily to the creation of this remarkable and eventually very popular musician of that period. One was the melancholy quality that worked so well in his mature work, and which went back in good part to this vulnerable only child experiencing his parents' bouts with poverty and their constant, sometimes terrifying arguments. We should highlight as well the boy becoming a target of other boys in New Haven, Connecticut. Even if one hasn't read Shaw's *The Trouble with Cinderella* in many years, as I hadn't when beginning this effort, certain parts, particularly from those early days, stay with the reader. One is when Shaw was hooted and derided as "Columbus Arshawsky" for exulting over his youthful "discovery" of ants streaming out of a (to him) miraculous anthill, along with other such incidents. In sum, this kid who skipped a grade without much study was both super-intelligent and sensitive, and Jewish, too, in a milieu that overwhelmingly wasn't; and therefore received plentiful slings and arrows to help produce the poignancy and sadness so often heard in his later bands and clarinet solos.

Readers of *Cinderella* will also recall with no difficulty another major part of Artie's formation: learning by doing, and not at all from formal musical instruction; but rather from records, including both the jazz and classical fare that he obsessively devoured, and from other experienced types in the field with whom he played. All this obsessive work allowed him to hone his arranging skills (far beyond those of most other future bandleaders) and especially, his celebrated, inimitable clarinet sound and technique—again, like no other. In *Cinderella* some of the most memorable and significant passages are on the young Shaw bleary from nocturnal jamming with other marvelous players, not least that unique jazzman Willie "The Lion" Smith. Artie played and learned so compulsively that he could allow his instincts to take over, leading to fingering and embouchure innovations that eventually helped send him to enormously difficult places on the clarinet, but always with an amazingly pleasing, silken tone. And yet one can never discount the psychological and heuristic effects on his often-poignant musical quality from those numerous childhood difficulties and hurts.[14]

All this then constitutes a long prelude (if briefly sketched here) to Shaw's fitful period of trying to put together an orchestra that would please both him and audiences. Many already know the story of how he graduated from being a well-known sideman, working both on radio and with Berigan et al. into becoming a bandleader. It began with his appearance at "New York's First Swing Music Concert," to benefit the American Federation of Musicians, Local 802, helping the many artists who weren't making much during the Depression. The event was held at the Imperial Theatre, May 24, 1936. Luminaries like Tommy Dorsey, Teddy Wilson, Berigan, and Armstrong were on hand, with big bands given priority, and small groups such as the one Shaw formed given 10–12 minutes tops with their chosen sidemen during intermissions of sorts. Glen Gray and his Casa Loma Orchestra started the evening off in suitable style for the era. But Shaw brought in an unusual, home-brewed group with strings, along with a rhythm section. They played his own chamber music cum jazz-type composition, "Interlude in B-Flat," one he'd tossed off quickly and which only came to some four minutes, featuring his own clarinet against a far different background than the norm. However, it was an unexpected smash! The place erupted in fierce applause at this strange offering, and with no other tune to play, and Artie also having unfortunately to visit the bathroom, he was nonetheless impelled to do the same piece over again as an encore. And that led to him being unexpectedly attractive to agents, urging him despite some misgivings to start up an orchestra of his own.[15]

Perhaps it shouldn't have been such a surprise that Artie wanted to include elements of a classical music background in such a composition, nor that he would do so later as well. He would always maintain that composers like Debussy or Stravinsky, and more particularly in this case, Ravel, had as much influence on him as did jazz players like Armstrong. He also learned a good deal from Guy D'Isere, who was a classical clarinetist Shaw got to know well and whom he admired as a kind of role model when the latter played with the Columbia Broadcasting Symphony in the early '30s. Although Gunther Schuller, originator of the term "Third Stream Music," i.e., music melded from different genres, would later be condescending toward Shaw's efforts in this regard, Artie was certainly on the road here to that breaking-down of boundaries that were then clearly in place.[16]

So when Shaw gave in and decided to sign with the Rockwell-O'Keefe Theatrical Agency and start up his first professional orchestra, he included strings, which made him something of a misfit for the period when Goodman, the Dorseys et al. were first soaring to national prominence. This initial AS edition began recording for Brunswick several weeks later, but with a group that was decidedly less imposing and powerful than the usual swing complement. Those recordings started with two violins, one viola, one cello, but only one trumpet, one trombone, and one sax player, plus the normal rhythm section. And of course Shaw on clarinet. Eventually there were two trumpets, but this kind of aggregation obviously felt on the lean side to some listeners and dancers. Violinist Jerry Gray, who would stay with Artie and make a great contribution to his future successes, helped craft arrangements. A New Haven buddy, Tony Pastor, came in to play tenor sax and sing for "Art Shaw and His Orchestra," and a Bostonian singer named Peg La Centra joined as well. Shows began at the Silver Grill of Manhattan's Hotel Lexington, August 21, 1936; but despite some good reviews, a heartfelt reaction from a teenaged fan named Judy Garland, and radio broadcasts (now a big part of Goodman's success and that of other bands), not enough people filled the seats at the hotel venue. Shaw's efforts in this new enterprise pleased him, but didn't make sufficient cash or attain enough popularity, eventually drawing the philistine ire of the grill's manager, who blew up at how this kind of music made little financial sense. Even Artie had to keep supplementing his income with his own sideman gigs in order to survive as a bandleader.

After a month and a half there, the group moved to New York's French Casino for roughly an equal swath of time, starting in early October and ending November 20, 1936. There were more Brunswick recording sessions, some useful changes in band personnel, and then another move early in January 1937 to a hotel in Dallas, a good place to be in winter. And thence to New Orleans at the outset of February, where cancellations began. Short of cash, Shaw and his group blessedly got into New Jersey's Meadowbrook Ballroom at mid-month, and there were still broadcasts; but the whole endeavor came to an end in March, with Artie deciding to be more practical and to mount a second band that was closer to expectations in the now wildly popular Swing Era, ditching the "longhair" element, painful as that was to him.[17]

His final broadcast with that first contingent occurred on March 9, 1937, and all through that month he was busy as a bee auditioning numerous players and taking what he could get for his second kick at the can, a group called Art Shaw and His New Music, hatched as a larger, louder, more down-the-middle, and emphatically stringless musical organization. This second band of his marched into a Boston ballroom at the beginning of April with an ever-burgeoning library of new charts that made it increasingly better. Raiding personnel from other bands like Tommy Dorsey's or later Berigan's, and also learning why their scores worked, made Shaw's outfit improve, too.

In addition to working in the Boston ballroom a couple nights a week, the band began an onerous round of one-nighters, traveling in a rickety bus (memorable pages on this are found in Shaw's autobiography), which he'd acquired from T.D. But recordings from radio broadcasts (made with the Thesaurus Transcription Service) and later, "real" ones for Brunswick starting mid–May were still too often based on offbeat, little-known tunes and a bit too stilted as well to hit big.

That May of '37 the band moved from Beantown to Washington, D.C.'s Capitol Theatre, but with a trip back to New York for those Brunswick sessions; then from May 21, still fighting to be financially viable, it started a relatively extended stint at the Willows near Pittsburgh. And thence to another month-long, oceanside gig in New Jersey in late June. Taxing one-nighters continued, too, and Artie kept tinkering frantically with and fine-tuning band personnel through the fall of '37 and into the winter, and while still having difficulty paying the freight, remained on a mission of sorts.

By February '38 Shaw courageously decided once more to kick over the traces and abandon this band's focus, too, dropping a lot of his (and/or Gray's) painstakingly crafted arrangements that hadn't resonated in a major way with the public. Moving into Si Shribman's Roseland State Ballroom in Boston on March 22 gave Artie more stability to reshape his band all over again. What became basically another one already bore key players like trumpeters Chuck Peterson and John Best, trombonists Harry Rodgers and George Arus, guitarist Al Avola and drummer Cliff Leeman, and far from least, lead alto man Les Robinson and tenor sax player Hank Freeman, both of whom gave Shaw great and enthusiastic credit for teaching them phrasing, so vital to what became a band sound that could really score.[18]

There were regular broadcasts from the Roseland State, and this whole period into the early summer became a crucial one for Shaw and his arrangers to recreate the band's overall feel and make it stronger and more polished; and also to have its members play on largely more well-known numbers, including quite a few show tunes, in new or recrafted arrangements. For all that, one cannot discount the legacy of "Art Shaw and His New Music" of 1937 to early '38. Recordings of better-known songs by that bunch like "All Alone," "Blue Skies," and "Someday Sweetheart" (though the latter was not up with Goodman's marvelous aircheck version) will be enjoyable to listeners who unearth them. And Artie's clarinet was already more than worthy on them, and definitely distinctive, if a bit more hesitant and definitely thinner than it became later in '38. However important, that ensemble still constituted a kind of prelude to the constantly improving (and improved) big band that first "made it" in the summer of '38, becoming what can then be called the 1938-39 Shaw band; and the one where our emphasis here begins.

Other secondary authorities (particularly Simosko), plus Shaw in his autobiography, have already done fine, extensive work on those earlier AS aggregations. And Max Kaminsky, who became a Shaw sideman on trumpet in the fall of '37, has a colorful chapter in his own memoir on Artie's efforts at finding a band orientation that could really work well and lucratively. However, Kaminsky takes inordinate, almost comical credit for what began to gel for Shaw and his players, and one can see why he and Artie, old friends as former sidemen in New York, finally split acrimoniously before Shaw got to the top. Kaminsky's book is an enjoyable, if idiosyncratic take on the bandleader's transition from "Art Shaw and His New Music" toward what becomes our main focus here: the first of what we deem Shaw's three truly great musical organizations of the Swing epoch. What became a two-edged sword for this cerebral bandleader started when Artie ceased to record with Brunswick and took time off through that spring of '38 and into summer in order to put together both personnel and a book of arrangements that he felt would do his bidding, forming an orchestral ensemble he could truly live with; then, when he and this much-improved organization first, and unexpectedly (to him), hit the top of their métier in the summer of '38, when the Swing Era was itself at its peak.[19] All this via a little-known Cole Porter tune arranged and performed so uniquely in Shaw's big band version that it really stood out and apart, to the point where it became one of the top-selling records of the '30s, and still remains an enduring masterwork from that classy time. As many will already know, we mean the Shaw interpretation of a tune called ... "Begin the Beguine."[20]

ONE

# Reaching the Top in the Swing Era

Despite Artie Shaw's intellectualism and garrulous, analytic brilliance, he also had the yin of simplicity to go with the yang of complexity, which, we feel, amounted to a certain genius at his musical calling. One could even say that he had what the French call "l'innocence des purs" (the innocence of the pure). The purity of a true artist? Though that word ("artiste") is bandied about too frequently and sometimes frivolously, Shaw was, indeed, an authentic artist on his clarinet, if that implies masterful uniqueness and a deep, personal sense of musical beauty on the instrument. But he was also a now seasoned and formidable hand at welding bands together. In the latter department, and just for openers, he knew a variety of instruments and their exigencies well. (In addition to clarinet, he also played other reed instruments to a high standard, as well as piano.)

But one common element is found in many true artists: they often don't know which of their products will eventually catch on and gain great popularity (think Van Gogh in that regard, and many others, too). That was pretty well the way Artie felt when he was awarded a prestigious recording contract with RCA's Bluebird label in 1938 and decided not to opt for safe items on his first two-sided 78, like, say, a version of a standard such as "Body and Soul," or various hits of the day. Instead he selected that generally ignored Porter tune noted above, and in the most credible version of various stories on the subject, made a decision on how to shape it when in a Boston hotel with the sidemen in his band, along with Jerry Gray, who, with Artie, crafted many of this band's arrangements. Awaiting their engagement in Beantown, they decided to monkey with "Beguine," and then tinker some more. But when Shaw and band finally cut the disc (in a recording session of July 24, 1938), Artie felt that a cute, pulsing, almost comedic version of "Indian Love Call" on its A-side (78s of course containing only two numbers) might do good sales for Bluebird; but emphatically not "Beguine." (The comedic parts of "Love Call" came from several guys in his band doing a send-up of Tommy Dorsey's chorus in "Marie," and especially via Shaw's pal Tony Pastor providing a scat singing solo on a tune that was better known in the earnest Nelson Eddy–Jeanette MacDonald rendering.) But despite the lighthearted tone on this piece, we also have elements here that would be common to so much Shaw work of 1938-39: his own quintessential fluidity on clarinet; the sax section cum clarinets and then the entire reeds section using the same style of vibrato and with similar intensity as in Artie's solo work; and just plain high standards in the entire orchestra, which truly jumps here, exuberantly so. Finally, there's a concluding Shaw glissando on "Love Call," a well-paced, dramatic, signature soaring which lands perfectly in time with this well-honed band's last full entry.

But neither Shaw nor those in his employ could see ahead at all to the far greater impact that would come from the B-side of that 78. And yet, when one listens even today to this first Shavian offering on Bluebird, one realizes that in "Beguine" one is still hearing a seamless masterpiece, no matter how many times it's been previously heard. Right from the clean snap of the intro (contributed by Gray with dancers in mind), and thence into the warm, melancholy clarinet sound that was now entirely Shaw's own, and with the marvelously controlled, reined-in punch of saxes and brass behind him, this is a tune you can't switch channels on, so to speak, even in today's super-impatient society.

The entire orchestral sound in "Beguine" was pure Shaw, and again, those in this first great musical aggregation of his would always agree that he was the major reason it belatedly gained that distinctive flavor. The way he blended question-and-answer woodwinds and brass certainly went back to Goodman and his key Black arranger, Fletcher Henderson, as much as Artie later criticized BG and was on the tepid side, too, re Henderson's massive contributions and influence. However, the gorgeous, crisp, romantic "bending" of the notes (which is how his players and Shaw himself put it) was entirely his band's trademark, and truly distinctive. Nothing in "Beguine" is at all wasted, and the drama that comes from the unexpected reigns supreme here. Simplicity of genius? Or let's say, the apparent simplicity? Making the hard ones look easy (as a great Yankee centerfielder was then doing in the Big Apple)? Absolutely. Joe DiMaggio certainly had that quality, and so did Shaw, and it's fully on display in "Beguine," so much so that the true artistic originality here would astound a nation of listeners back then. And this in a fortunate, heuristic period of sorts, when Shaw benefited from the fact that both the public's sense of good material and his own cohered far more

## One. Reaching the Top in the Swing Era

than would later be the case, especially near the end of World War II and into the '50s.

On "Beguine," Shaw's sidekick Tony Pastor, originally Pestritto, with whom Artie had really grown up musically, contributes a tenor sax solo that's also simplified Italo-American, and as "right" as any meal you could get at many of the fine Italian restaurants in cities of the Northeast. Over the ensemble Artie darts high twice (having started in the lower, moodier chalumeau); then comes the main tugging refrain that even now feels nostalgically evocative of something we've all lost, the romance, the deep feeling, call it what one will. Trombones take over near the close of the recording, then Artie, ever dramatic and always the astonishing performer, teases with a high clarinet "tweep-tweep"; and finally there follows a super-warm clarinet glissando, starting with a difficult C# (or on clarinet, D#/Eb), a sweeping, upward, smooth and expressive arc on the licorice stick that we defy anyone who plays the instrument to match. Never had such a thing been heard in this manner chez Goodman, or really from any clarinet player, including classical virtuosos. And with that final flourish, Shaw concludes this masterwork of popular swing. And then did the roof fall in? And right onto this sensitive, obsessed professional? To a great degree!

Shaw still sounded sensitive and relentlessly interesting when recalling the making of "Beguine" and its impact in a fine documentary. He emphasized that back in the day songs often contained no more than 32 bars, but this one had over 100! From our point of view, making such a tune melodious and memorable, and on his first recording as an "unknown" for RCA, was truly a creative feat extraordinaire in the annals of popular American music.

The story would have remained a sweet one if only a sort of Greek tragedy hadn't then transpired, given that Shaw lived almost entirely for making lovely and often unusual music, and not at all for being a celebrity. But thanks to "Beguine," which again, became one of the biggest sellers of the era, Shaw's crowds after its release and the precipitous onset of national popularity suddenly grew raucous and overflowing. In addition, this reflective and at times reclusive man was now renamed (by RCA) a more mellifluous Artie Shaw (from Art); and henceforth this "Artie" was tracked constantly by autograph-hungry fans. Many weeks, the count of letters to him reached over 10,000. The man who probably felt too guilty not to take *my* later calls also showed his generous side by initially trying to wade through them all. But it got far worse when people followed him in the streets, trying to pull out chunks of his hair, etc. Those constant intrusions—the same sort that would affect later stars like Bardot and Monroe, and in Shaw's realm, Elvis and the Beatles—became ever more onerous and repulsive to him. So did increasing business demands he didn't enjoy either, but which he had to deal with incessantly. Just choosing which gigs to accept and which to beg off took a large amount of his time and energy.

On the brink of all this change Shaw hadn't seen coming, he and his band members were traveling around the country to play dates, including taxing one-nighters. But when "Beguine" made it into record stores and jukeboxes and became insanely "in," it impelled people to demand more and more from him and his aggregation, altering his life in a more than major fashion. It was a night-and-day sort of change that began with a huge roar in St. Louis, where the band was then appearing, and in no way was Shaw prepared for this onslaught, just as many aren't prepared for the figurative curves life unexpectedly tosses at them.

Trumpeter John Best was an AS band member who experienced that unexpected delirium in the city of baseball's Cardinals, quickly realizing that "Beguine" had now come out and made it big. He visited a record shop to buy a copy and was flabbergasted to find it had sold out. Very soon it was played constantly on the radio, and Bernie Privin, another fine trumpeter who had moved from Tommy Dorsey's band to Artie's, beheld his new boss suddenly grappling like a drowning man with all the turbulence sketched above, which goes with becoming a sudden and massive celebrity.[1]

Of course people like to have it all ways, to get the clichéd cake and eat it too; and Artie would often plead guilty in this regard as well. For post–"Beguine," the money started pouring in aplenty (eventually, with variations, to the tune of a good $30,000 to $60,000 per week in the Depression!).[2] Which would allow him to hire better band players to do what he desired, but also to buy fine cars, snazzy, expensive clothes, and so forth. Shaw had grown up in tenements, but as he once told me in conversation, "we didn't know they were tenements." To many observers, this fellow from humble origins was now living the ballyhooed American dream; but simultaneously, it became a terrible trial or series of trials, as his breakout band was compelled to appear constantly on the road or in hotel gigs, on radio programs or movie lots, and made plentiful swing records in New York and Hollywood, which will get extended analysis from us here.

Against the odds and working harder with that first great contingent of his than ever he would do in the future, Shaw continued to make wonderful music. Both competitive and not, he also dethroned in quite short order the original King of Swing (Goodman) as the most popular bandleader in America, during that poignant era when Hitler was causing war clouds to loom over quite a number of European countries.

**All of Artie's swing bands were his own unified creations and made to sound the way he wanted (Getty Images/Bettmann).**

And before other bands, preeminently Glenn Miller's, began coming on strong and overtaking this Shaw edition in popularity.

Playing round the clock grew draining but also made Artie's band ever more unified and cohesive, and his own playing even more remarkable, too. But prices continued to be paid. In one example among many of gigs rapidly foisted on him, the manager of the Ritz-Carlton ballroom in Boston, where the AS band was opening, decided on his own to hire them for a live event as well, to be held at the Boston Common the next day. Only very reluctantly did Shaw comply, and then paid big time! On the day of the Commons event, a huge crowd followed the limo where he was ensconced with the mayor of that city. The crowd eventually pushed the car over, and Artie escaped on his two legs, but with his face lacerated from people's avid fingernails, and his clothes tattered as well. Only after much persuasion did he come back to the ballroom engagement that night. All this repetitive mayhem constituted and remained a huge shock to him; as he says in his autobiography and elsewhere, he could no longer be the same person he'd been before this tidal wave of celebrity hit.[3]

Just the fear for his own safety began to consume the famed bandleader, and did so right through almost all of 1939. Getting stabbed in the leg or arm by importunate autograph seekers' pens, or finding his clarinet bashed into by groupies while on stage, threatening his super-vital teeth, went with the territory. Kids cutting school in the thousands to attend his daytime concerts, forcing ever more law enforcement and security types to intervene—all this and much more became a serious set of downsides to him. Commenting on this to Brigitte Berman some four and a half decades after the explosion of this "Shaw" insanity, he still seemed pained, as if it had all happened that very day.[4]

Artie found it perplexing and even baffling that while he hadn't essentially changed, so many he'd either marginally known before or not at all were suddenly treating him reverentially, trying to get far too close and familiar. Society types he'd previously meant nothing to now crowded around him, and this also shocked him. Shaw kept trying to get his head around this phenomenon, but it was hard for him, as there was always a modest element about this cerebral musician, deeply averse to press agentry and the whole publicity machine that goes into high gear when someone becomes celebrated in the mainstream. Suddenly being ubiquitously deemed "important" and getting placed on a pedestal felt daunting and even surreal to him.[5]

In addition, there was more particularly the women issue, to be intermittently discussed throughout our treatment. Artie would often maintain that another byproduct of overwhelming fame was that it drew a lot of beauties into his orbit, beguilingly so. In an interesting, stream of consciousness–type series of articles, Gene Lees cavils somewhat with this Shavian estimate; but we believe there's something to it, as long as one adds that the sensitivity and sheer beauty Shaw put into his music (and later into his talks at music schools and such) also helped bring quite a few pulchritudinous and/or good-hearted women to his attention. Which meant a series—and we mean series!—of complications Shaw could scarcely have foreseen in his youth. This was partly due to having been a poor, somewhat withdrawn and alienated Jewish boy suddenly besieged by lovely goddesses and feeling perhaps a bit like the proverbial kid in the candy shop. But these complications would also stem partially from a severe "mother" issue Shaw had and always would—with a mom who lived through her son's achievements and even threatened suicide when he'd try to leave or abandon her. And from the memory and example of a brutal father as well, one who had simply left the family during Artie's early teens, and whom he hardly ever saw again.[6]

Moving back to the music, in addition to "Beguine" and "Love Call," this AS breakout band made four other sides on that initial recording date for Bluebird; and several were Artie's own songs, written wholly or in part by this man who was both spontaneous (often minting tunes on the bandstand) and very dogged concerning final results. "Comin' On" (entirely by Shaw) is comparatively forgettable, though not even close to bad; but "Back Bay Shuffle" (by Teddy McRae and Shaw and hatched as the last train back to New York was set to leave Boston) shows again, and on an upbeat tune, how marvelously Shaw had gone beyond the givens of Henderson-Goodman to create his own band sound. Part of that first remarkable batch cut for Bluebird, "Back Bay..." is simply spectacular both in what it does and doesn't do.[7] Crisp saxes lead in with typically terse but decisive power, the brass starts out compact and muted in response; and the whole orchestra has a sweetly draggy, legato flavor that again, distinguished it greatly from the more hard-driving Goodman band. And yet it swings! Artie's first solo on this "Back Bay..." is also "draggy," slow but not slow, utterly warm and scampering, but not à la BG; instead, more in a way that Ava Gardner insisted became an influence on Sinatra's deliberately drawn-out way of singing, as much an influence as the trombone playing of Tommy Dorsey, for whom Frank worked early in his career. In Shaw's "Back Bay..." everything in the ensemble is a prelude to those riveting clarinet solos (he comes in several times on the number). The other soloists keep things short and sweet, as Shaw would advise them to do, including Les Burness on piano, to be turfed within months but more accessible than Goodman's Jess Stacy; and Pastor, before he got upstaged as the band's main tenor soloist by Georgie Auld. The entire effect in "Back Bay..." seems pared down yet full of surprises, including via complex syncopation and Shaw's swooping entries on clarinet, all driving toward a denouement that feels totally right. Do we have another masterpiece here, one that remains listenable even now? No question, and the public made it a hit as well back then.

When he cut this record, Artie was not yet dubbed "King of the Clarinet," but aware listeners could already detect his idiosyncratic lightness, sweetness and almost drinkable fluidity even in the highest register, plus his effortless use of descending chromatics and more generally, voicings and colorations like none other. Above all, the man during this period was super-subtle and multi-hued in his work, fully capable of supplying (along with the entire band) dramatic, surprising embellishments and U-turns; but also of keeping to the required rhythmic structures and punctuating exactly when needed.

Still part of that first batch of six songs that Shaw recorded before the onset of his celebrity travails was another Artie original, "Any Old Time." Unfortunately, it was the only Shaw record his singer Billie Holiday made with him before her imminent departure. And unfortunately, too, it wasn't released to the public at that time, though Artie had specifically crafted it with Holiday in mind. Like others, Billie knew that Artie was often in his own private realm, or at least seemed to be; but that deep down he was also caring in his way. However, having to fight both literally and figuratively for her right to eat at restaurants or stay in hotels, especially down South, became eventually too distracting and exhausting for Shaw and his players; and after Holiday departed, Helen Forrest stepped fully into the breach as the band's female vocalist.[8] And she would surpass Holiday's mostly positive view of Artie as a boss, to the effect that he treated female singers like herself royally, compared to what usually obtained back then.

Some, however, have alleged a rivalry between the more jazz-oriented and mature Holiday and the 21-year-old Forrest; but when she came to Shaw's band, Helen recalled, Billie was thoroughly encouraging and quite maternal with her. Forrest also felt deeply guilty about Holiday's departure, but she really did click with Shaw, whom she adored not only as a bandleader, but as a kind of friend, and a mentor who could talk intelligently to her of much besides music. Above all, his laissez-faire approach to her vocals would absolutely astound her. Forrest would be heard on about 40 recordings for him on Bluebird, plus a number of others that weren't cut back then but which survived as "air checks" taped from remote broadcasts and later collected on LPs. The band's only other singer was now Pastor, who by and large did novelty tunes in an offhand, but enjoyable manner. Hard as it may be to believe, especially given her later involvement with a future musical employer, Harry James, the young Forrest had no romance with any of Artie's sidemen, nor with Shaw himself. All were super-protective of her as they traveled around, sometimes overly so, in her view.[9]

By contrast, Forrest's stint of some 20 months with Goodman after her time with Shaw seemed to her like a "life sentence." We will be alluding quite a few times below to Artie compared and contrasted to Benny, both of course the top swing clarinetists of their time. But regarding that and other matters, we will keep our amount of quotation on the slim side, and purposely so. However: one can't read Forrest's memoir of the early '80s when it moves to Goodman and not quote!

Here is how she starts her initial chapter on the King of Swing: "Benny Goodman was by far the most unpleasant person I ever met in music." According to her, he hardly engaged with his musicians, rarely complimented their work, and though by far the most affluent person

**Billie Holiday with the great Count Basie. Artie fought a losing battle to keep Holiday in his own band, particularly on the road (Alamy/Album).**

in his bands, would consistently dodge checks at restaurant tables! If one was unfortunate enough to have him pull up a chair, he'd read the paper while eating, and meanwhile, "he slurped his food. The food fell all over him. [The man] was a slob. And he never talked to people, even if they talked to him." And should his sidemen somehow get stuck in a taxi with him, Goodman generally slipped out first and left them with those bills, too. On the stand at this or that venue, he also had a disconcerting habit of hampering vocalists and instrumental soloists by "noodling" near them on clarinet. And he almost never used any band member's first name, including Forrest's: most everyone was indiscriminately called "Pops."[10] In sum, Helen felt much better treated by Artie, not least as a woman, than by Benny.

    A parenthetical aside might be in order here: One time on the phone with Shaw around 1979, I put on my then four-year-old daughter, who complimented his music (especially his recording of "A Table in a Corner," made in 1939 and which we discuss below). And he told me when I took the phone back that he would have rather had a daughter than all those wives! This was an odd thing to say, but an avowal, I suppose, that relationships didn't always bring out his best with women. We do know that he was good in this period to the young Judy Garland, treating her as a kind of "sister" figure, which is what he considered her to be. However, marriage (which he thankfully eschewed with her) was a different story!

Are there obvious paradoxes here? For certain. One is that Shaw's very complexity as an individual helped make his music so different from that of the entire Swing Era pack. A more linear and predictable type would never have created such an *oeuvre*. In the main, one can declare with some certitude that he didn't treat wives very well, not to mention sons! And yet, Shaw was much more considerate toward associates in his band than ever Goodman was. The latter, married but once, and apparently quite happily, was super-difficult not only with his female warblers, but with the men who played instruments for him, too. One of those was Gordon "Chris" Griffin, who had a trumpet chair in Goodman's greatest contingent during the middle and late '30s. Griffin played beside no less than Harry James and Ziggy Elman, completing Goodman's stellar trumpet trio of 1937-38 that Duke Ellington called the best of that era. He much later got to work for a short time with Shaw. In any event, Griffin once told me, and similarly to Forrest, that the four years he spent with Goodman felt more like 40![11]

But back to Shaw's music, where the charts he crafted for this great band, often with Gray, whom he'd schooled in the art of scoring, were key elements. (Like Pastor, Gray was Italian in origin, a violin player from Boston originally named Generoso Graziano.) On the arrangement of "Any Old Time" Shaw's legato saxes weave a leisurely, sweet lead-in to the main refrain, and the brass engages in the usual "call and response," but again, with more awesome and stately class than ever the Goodman orchestra possessed. The final musical product and its effect meant everything to Artie, versus a mere series of techniques on display. Sticking with the same record, his warm, leisurely clarinet on this slow number, utterly romantic and right for such a context, makes one see again why Ava (who knew both Artie and Frank well) saw a DNA line here leading in part toward the great crooner's own imposing musical footprint. Shaw's interpretation of melody on his instrument is characteristically vocal-like here. But the entire band on "Any Old Time" stands out, providing a fine background for Billie, neither beneath her nor hampering her savorous, jazzy rendition on the number. That singing interlude is followed by Pastor's compact tenor sax, leading to an ensemble finish one easily forgets being this good (if you've put it down for a while). Even the brass in unison vibrato contributes a

# One. Reaching the Top in the Swing Era          31

Helen Forrest sings in the late '30s with Artie Shaw's band, backed as well by three fine reed players, Tony Pastor, Les Robinson, and Hank Freeman (right to left beside Shaw) (Library of Congress Prints and Photographs Division, Washington, D.C. [cph 3c34895/LC-USZ62-134895]).

lifelike breathlessness that most other such sections of the Swing period weren't able (or asked) to do. The articulation of notes both in Shaw's solo work and in the band's is simply more subtle and soft than in Goodman's outfit, despite superficial similarities (such as the opening here with an augmented pattern on the dominant chord, which those who know the intricacies of swing will also locate in BG's work).

The last of Shaw's first, pre-celebrity batch of late July '38 is "I Can't Believe That You're in Love with Me," a real pacer, where again, the band and arrangement are central, rather than just a series of soloists on parade. It's hard to feel how much Shaw put into making his entire contingent sound exactly the way he wanted, given the fact, too, that some of his players were not even 20 and quite inexperienced before putting themselves in his hands. He makes it all look easy, including his own buttery clarinet contributions (in "I Can't Believe..." he saunters in three different times with octave leaps, bluesy "swoops" into notes, and fine sound control even in an alpine range). However, he is matched here by reed section jazz "solos" (as certain sidemen would call them), where Shaw made the players collectively into a kind of single instrument. But all of it constituting utter sophistication in an era that so valued it. No wonder so many women of the time wanted to marry this accomplished, debonair bandleader, including Garland, soon to become herself a great victim of celebrity. But again, one of our main points needs to be emphasized: the music in this high Swing Era was always more important to Artie than women or anything else in his life; and being ever the fine performer and really, giver, he makes his various numbers work exactly as he wished, marching seemingly ineluctably to appropriate, satisfying conclusions. But only following one musical surprise after another!

Shaw liked his band to play both originals and good show tunes done up in his own fashion, and less so, pop offerings of the day, which (despite what he then felt) were generally much better than our current ones. Back then these pop tunes were often foisted upon him by primping song-pluggers, whom he found it ever harder to resist. But in his next clutch of records, cut September 27, 1938, and now in the period of palpably jarring, post–"Beguine" celebrity, came another of his own compositions and also the band's theme song, "Nightmare."[12] It deserves extended treatment here. Typically "Shaw" in its searing melancholy, this lead-in for his concerts, etc. makes a stark contrast to the upbeat, perky "Let's Dance" theme his rival Goodman used. À propos, Shaw would later frequent a psychiatrist (near the end of World War II) to find out why he hated himself, as he declared. And you feel all that angst in the recorded version of this theme song, transmuting what Jews of Shaw's generation would call "tsooris" (or worries) into grandly haunting, marvelous music.

Shaw had composed "Nightmare" late one night in 1936 before his initial band was set to open, and he'd made a Brunswick recording of it, too. But the much-improved, marvelous quality of this Bluebird version of '38 stemmed in part from present conflicts he had to deal with, and his still trademark melancholy, along with higher and higher standards. With earlier bands Artie had already been traveling aplenty, and it was onerous even back then, playing one-nighters here, there, and everywhere; but if anything, that whole routine had grown worse as the demands and distractions of fame came to the fore so hugely. Shaw's 1938 "Nightmare" amply reflects these problems for a man who could be so warm yet so cold, so open and so closed—all of that. Hence Shaw exploits here what feels like quite a number of colors, tempos, and moods, including the use of the Hungarian or "double harmonic" minor scale, plus a subtle, relaxing, yet dramatic slowdown to the ending.

But one must again highlight, and quite emphatically, the fact that this theme song of his totally stood out from the rest of those selected by other bands of the time, including Tommy Dorsey's "I'm Getting Sentimental Over You," Glenn Miller's "Moonlight Serenade," and even Ellington's "Take the 'A' Train." And as a real difference from many other Shaw records of that period, the ensemble work on this '38 "Nightmare" doesn't figure at all in the front line here. The number is much more Shaw alone, exploring away and pleasurably on his inimitable "axe," truly showing off the virtuoso he'd become, and in a manner that was getting former Goodman acolytes to worship at his feet. (As an example, Mel Tormé, who would later sing with Shaw after World War II, was a teen in Chicago who definitely found himself back then in the "Shavian" group, rather than the Goodman one, albeit that the latter clarinet master also hailed from the Windy City.)

Shaw's moody clarinet work on "Nightmare" certainly showcases all the scales, arpeggios, etc. that he'd had to learn and assimilate over the years and could now use to advantage as a self-made musician extraordinaire. Where in his youth Goodman had taken formal lessons from Franz Schoepp, Shaw, as seen, learned clarinet on his own, but in his typically super-committed way that made him that rare kind of autodidact who could "bring it" professionally, and now of course lucratively. He had reached this summit by imbibing everything necessary to his trade (as he later would at quite a number of other challenging pursuits), putting in work far above and beyond the norm. So here on this recorded "Nightmare" with RCA was the virtuoso on compelling display, clear and warm in every register, going up and down, down and up, as on an escalator or staircase, and magnificently holding the listener all the way. Just searching and searching, or so it feels, and speaking like a voice,[13] rather than simply parading his superb clarinet techniques. No wonder marriage couldn't compete with this kind of one-track devotion to recorded beauty and mastery. And no wonder that after he quit music in the fall of 1954 Artie wouldn't just pick up his instrument for fun, as many exhorted him to do; it simply took too much to make things look so easy and natural, as they do even today on this utterly beguiling and affecting "Nightmare."

But the two standouts in this 9/27/38 group of recordings are the AS band's rendering of Jerome Kern's "Yesterdays," a tune thankfully not much sung by the simpler crooners who followed the Swing Era, and which may therefore be new and fresh to those who pick up Shaw's 1938 version on YouTube, etc.; and the original flip side, on which more will be offered below. There was certainly a congeries of great composers like Kern to provide fine material back then, many of them Jewish and still close enough to their hereditary Weltschmerz to put it in their songs, as is no longer the case. And in the crooner department as well, we might also ask where the Italian-American Deans, Franks, Damones or Vales have gone? And yes, the Tony Pastors.... Now spitty-bearded nobodies prevail? So it too often seems.

Jerome Kern (with credit for "Yesterdays" and of course many other better-known songs like "Ol' Man River") would later become Artie's father-in-law. But well before that, we know that he very much appreciated Shaw's take on this particular tune, as he would the stirring AS version of his "All the Things You Are" in '39, which we discuss in the following chapter. Kern saluted Shaw's jazz talent on his instrument, even if "talent" wasn't a word Artie much liked, preferring ones like "work," reiterated as work, work, and more work! Or persistence (at a trade). Or following and learning from other greats' techniques. Nonetheless, people would often ask him silly questions about how he had inherited his musical "talent," and one thing he'd reply, among others, is that neither of his parents had an ear for music at all. And that he was therefore a kind of rose who had emerged from a pile of manure!

In any event Kern was definitely impressed by this band's lovely interpretation of "Yesterdays," because it's another Shaw masterpiece, and still relevant and resonant today. Exactly as it was in that fall of 1938. When of course the fateful Munich Conference was set to get going as well (only three days after this particular Shaw recording session), and when an insouciant America was still trying to ignore those brooding, ever more dangerous war clouds looming over European and British horizons.

If you go right to this "Yesterdays" on YouTube or wherever you locate it, you'll encounter another crisp band ensemble at the top, but only as prep for a long, remarkable passage in the limelight by that moody, commanding Shaw clarinet—clear, clean, and marvelous again in all registers, searching and searching, it still feels, and never quite enough to its "author," or so one senses. But for the pampered listener it certainly *is* enough, a solo that's still classically gorgeous and which makes this Kern tune much more soulful than had it been merely sung. Once again, Shaw, like DiMadge or a more contemporary Derek Jeter, makes the hard ones look almost effortless on this "Yesterdays."

Following his marvelous, extended solo here are the pretty and emphatic Shaw saxes (like none other), jousting beautifully against the brass, but again, a brass section much more restrained and classier than in the Goodman manner that blazed a path in the Swing Era. And then the gorgeous reeds take over completely alone, carefully shaped by Shaw, and almost soloing jazz-style as an ensemble. All of it remains to this day tasteful in the extreme! And all preparing for and driving toward Shaw's final "gliss," which in its seamless, dramatic verve became his "signature" of sorts. And even magical, as in conversation with me he'd describe such innovative efforts to be. And certainly eliciting deep and real feelings in the listener.

Oddly, however, as a bandleader at live venues Shaw didn't outwardly emote too much, and was even likened by someone who wanted him to do so to a dead lox in that department! But he saved the feelings for what really counted, and as much as he would rue over and over what he didn't do musically (while in retirement from the mid–'50s to his death in December 2004), what he did do was plenty copious and major, and still emotion-provoking. And as so little is today—one reason YouTube is facilitating such a rich, posthumous Shaw renaissance, a computer afterlife for much of what he recorded, and which he could never have predicted even in the early 2000s.

Returning to "Yesterdays" and others from the same batch shows that Shaw had different ways to skin the musical cat. For in that same group of 9/27/38 recordings we get another, very different masterpiece, Shaw's version of a ditty that is more widely known than "Yesterdays," or at least was: "What Is This Thing Called Love?" This A-side makes an almost total contrast to the super-moody version of Kern's tune analyzed above. Shaw would often excoriate the comparative sameness of Glenn Miller's output, and in interviews would say that he himself didn't have one particular style, but a number of them in this first great band of his. And he was totally correct on that score. All of it was calculated to surprise and compel the listener (many such), which, as this swing band drove to number one in the *Downbeat* poll and became wildly popular, seemed ever more imperative in order for that contingent to maintain its standing.

So the "Yesterdays" flip side is anything but a lachrymose and slow "What Is This Thing Called Love?" Instead? From the start it's unexpectedly bang-bang and upbeat, a true surprise, starting with a brass-and-reeds call-and-response, clarinets together, then the fine saxes alone. Which are, as usual, Shaw-disciplined, precise, yet full of feeling. The trombones buoy up proceedings, and then we get an ebullient Artie on clarinet, flying up to the heights, but also slurring and making the rapid runs seem paradoxically easy and even slow, sounding a bit like earlier clarinet virtuosos like Noone, but much warmer and more fluid in those fast, but not so fast-sounding passages. (He would liken this ability of his to play 16th or 32nd notes "slowly" to the great boxer Joe Louis, punching fast but simultaneously not fast in the ring.) Even Artie's highest clarinet notes on "What Is This Thing" seem simple, clear and warm. This is why Dick Johnson much later said that if you could play 15 solos from Artie's heyday, you were some clarinetist! Johnson himself could do that when he helmed a reformed Shaw band from the early '80s; but not (as I can attest from hearing him live) the way Shaw made everything on his instrument sound so thick and natural, no matter how high up or how lightning-quick he was playing. But then again, Artie would indeed tell me a number of times, and doubtless many others, about everyone's thumbprint being different. And his difference from all other swing leaders and players here is so palpable that it's again a species of genius.

Returning to "Thing...," after Shaw's first solo in the stratosphere, the brass and reeds come back toughly and assertively, as if in a sweet, music-making marital fight of sorts. Then comes a trumpet solo by Best (soon to be displaced by the more featured Privin), and one on trombone by George Arus, neither at all long-winded, as Artie advised his soloists never, or at least rarely, to be. And then follows the plush ensemble, Artie scampering alone over tom-toms, and a marvelous ending that always (in his great work) feels inevitably concluded, pleasurably so.

The rest of that recorded group of six from September 27 contain two pop songs, featuring a Pastor vocal on one (often Louis Armstrong–like and slightly comedic), and Forrest on the other. Was the latter a good band singer of her time? Absolutely, and Artie's favorite, too, though she was later bypassed in the female vocal department, which obviously evolved greatly over the next several decades. Both of these pop tunes are well done, but we will talk more about Ms. Forrest's efforts anon.

The following group of six records made November 17, 1938, saw Shaw's band still at its acme in terms of popularity (increasingly a two-edged sword for him, to say the least). But on the plus side, he could use the great gobs of cash he was now earning to improve an already wonderful band by new hires—and of course fires, which didn't really please him, but which he deemed necessary. All his players knew that Shaw wanted his orchestra to cohere in a certain way and that its demanding leader would do anything to get that final result.

This November 17 session contains several little-known songs, featuring Forrest on four of them ("Between a Kiss and a Sigh," "Thanks for Everything," from a movie of that title, "Deep in a Dream," and "Day after Day"). And yet few listeners, particularly those with a romantic bent, will feel unrewarded by them. Forrest was always a warm, effective band singer who was totally right for the era (that warmth later working well for her alongside Harry James on a number of wartime hits they made together). But again, singers and singing have obviously gone through huge transmogrifications in subsequent years through to the present. One can only judge Forrest for and in the period during which she sang, not by later ones (against, say, Diana Ross, Dusty Springfield, Linda Ronstadt and other such stars to come).

But the Shaw record from 11/17/38 that stands out is one in the minority, i.e., sans Forrest and featuring just the band itself. It's an absolutely moving interpretation of Sigmund Romberg and Oscar Hammerstein's "Softly, as in a Morning Sunrise." Here was a product from that poignant period (given a European Holocaust just about to occur) when America had many worthy first- and second-generation Jews crafting so many wonderful songs, while their unfortunate brethren across the Atlantic were soon to be slaughtered in their ghastly millions. This AS version of "Softly" is a marvel all the way, and one where his solos have more stirring beauty in them than anything Goodman ever did. Soul? You obviously can't buy that quality. Techniques? Those one can obviously work up, including via the interesting key changes Shaw uses here, plus his chromatic dancing to a top G and the like; but the two—soul and technique—coming together in a player like Shaw made him musically unique, and they are both amply on display in this version of "Softly...."

In fact, when Saul Bellow and his fourth wife, Alexandra, visited the Northwest in the early '80s, and I and my lady friend of the period had them over to dinner the night before their flight back to Chicago, I opted to play this 1938 Shaw recording for them. And when the first clarinet solo approached, I peremptorily shut down all conversation, urging the couple to listen carefully—"so Jewish!" I exulted. And even vaguely klezmerish? Perhaps. But above all, characteristic Shaw melancholy on display, even a kind of wailing, sobbing quality here, exaggerated as that may sound.

The ensemble contributions on "Softly" are marvelous, too, particularly from those bent-note saxes led by Robinson on alto, contrapuntally so effective against the stronger brass. But all of it preparing the table for Artie, the unmistakable star and virtuoso here—both for his first solo and a second, too, which I so nervily told the Bellows to hush up to savor! And again, there is nothing here that Goodman or any other clarinet-playing bandleader could duplicate.

The superb band work on this "Softly" grows punchier and louder, and then there's a Pastor tenor solo, a role he'd soon cede almost completely to Georgie Auld, who, according to Artie, played differently from what he initially thought would fit in the band, but who paradoxically made it even better. Then comes a trombone solo by the fine Arus. The composers? They must also have loved this Shaw version of their soulful ditty.[14] "Plaintive" and "gorgeous" are the adjectives that come handily to mind as this "Softly" sweeps up to Artie's own final climb to the heights, ever the dramatic performer who knew how to create a compelling, vivid listening experience. And in this case, yet another masterpiece.

Last of that batch? Entirely, and almost shockingly contrastive to

"Softly," in the form of a snappy, pared-down, but wonderful jitterbug version of "Copenhagen" (not to be confused with "Wonderful Copenhagen"). Of course Shaw increasingly loathed jitterbuggers, but he also knew he could attract both listeners and dancers via his work; so here is one arrangement where he could really do that. He certainly never became or wanted to become formulaic or expectable, even if his efforts from that pre-war period occasionally seemed to tend that way (particularly on the romantic pop songs featuring Ms. Forrest); but really, there are at least several discrete varieties of Shaw recordings in this era, ones where "vive la différence" seems to have been his guiding motto.

On "Copenhagen" Shaw's clarinet easily keeps up with a rapid dance tempo, where he himself plays very fast, too, but still in characteristically earthy fashion, and whether high up or down low. In his solo work here, Shaw is both incredibly light and inventive, using unexpected interval movements and chord changes; but in other spots tough and deliberate, employing insistently repetitive notes to grip the listener. Jazz clarinetists might well consider his work on this '38 "Copenhagen" among his finest, most awe-inspiring examples of up-tempo playing. As Shaw would put it of that first era of widespread recognition and demands on him, he was working so much back then that he felt he could do pretty well anything he wanted on his instrument.

That seemingly effortless mastery is borne out not only on his recordings at this apogee of the Swing Era; but on tunes he never put onto wax back then, yet played at hotels and broadcast on radio, where air checks or transcriptions later made it into a number of LPs, which still legate some of these offerings (miraculously so) to the internet. By this time, one plus for Shaw was a certain stability wrought via his band's nightly residency during the week at the Hotel Lincoln's Blue Room in Manhattan, with a feed to NBC that got the outfit heard nationally on radio. That engagement basically lasted to the beginning of February '39, with a few short hiatus times. Even longer-lasting was the band's tenure with the Old Gold *Melody & Madness* show for CBS with Robert Benchley, a well-known humorist of the era. This assignment also produced plentiful transcription tapes that are now found on the internet, and it endured till early October of '39.

How does one generalize about those "air checks" or "transcriptions" that could later be heard on LPs, and which I've sampled in fairly great quantity? In the main Shaw's results were quite opposite to those I've heard by Goodman. Benny's band would have a year or two to polish arrangements after first recording them, and those live versions we later got on record collections seemed even better than the original discs. With Shaw, it was mostly the reverse. I've heard quite a few "covers" of his recordings, which were taped live at the Lincoln or on the Old Gold show, and they are all good, no question. But not quite up with the recorded versions. Some that weren't recorded (and for good reason) were more forgettable, such as "Who Blew Out the Flame?" featuring a Forrest vocal, or "Shine On, Harvest Moon," both of which were played at the Blue Room. More interesting, but also unrecorded by Bluebird due perhaps to length requirements, is the AS band's "In the Mood," predating Glenn Miller's iconic hit so made for dancers. The Shaw "Star Dust" you can get on internet from that 1938-39 era was also unrecorded by RCA, partly because the arrangement seemed to be grappling for a final form. It's not to be confused with the very different and stellar Shaw recording of that chestnut in 1940, which most swing fans will know more readily. But the AS "My Reverie" transcription from the Blue Room (where you can even hear the clinking of glasses or dishes) is just gorgeous, partly due to Artie's lovely clarinet and Helen's fine vocal; and yet it, too, failed to make it onto Bluebird. About another unrecorded, live Shaw standout, "At Sundown," where his clarinet goes amazingly and immaculately everywhere, more will be given a bit later.

His last batch of 1938 closed out a dizzy half-year he himself couldn't fully navigate, forcing him now to take strong medicine for the many headaches that came literally to him, and figuratively as well. On these records made 12/19/38, Shaw had several new sidemen to replace terminated ones, players who brought a lot both to the group sound and to their solos, including the trumpeter Privin, tenor saxist Auld, and trombonist Les Jenkins, who sometimes made even Tommy Dorsey envious jazz-wise. They gave the band a somewhat peppier sound, but the jump element never took precedence over its slower, moodier offerings and never would. Thus the December 19 group of six includes an ultra-romantic, typically Shavian "A Room with a View," featuring Forrest singing it midway through. As most know just from films of the time, this was a much more romantic era generally than ours; but even then Shaw's bunch led musically in that department, compared to other swing bands of the period.

Speaking of comparisons, Artie was supposed to be super-competitive with BG, as exemplified in numerous interviews that came after his retirement. And indeed, some of his opinions proffered there did sound downright snide, as when he'd call Benny stupid or simply more fixated on the clarinet than on music, including the romantic-type music that Shaw and his organization did so well. But it's undeniably true that Artie always felt himself more of a music-maker of different varieties than simply a clarinet virtuoso. And that he wanted above all to convey pleasurable feelings from whatever his band played.

Objectively put, there is no doubt that Shaw was more romantic in his Swing Era work (and in life, too) than Goodman. He also expressed more pathos in his *oeuvre*, which obviously increases romanticism, and which again, partly went back to Shaw's difficult, isolated growing-up period in a turbulent family and milieu. When he finally went into psychoanalysis near the end of World War II and told his story, the analyst declared that it was as sad a one as she'd heard! Of course such an estimate was more than a bit exaggerated, given the terrible tragedies occurring in much of Europe during that era and not least, befalling the many American soldiers wounded or dying abroad; but still, Shaw did put his own sadness and plenty of it into his work.

And this recording of "A Room with a View" amply shows that melancholy bent of his. It's simple, but beautiful, and can still stick with a modern listener feelings-wise.

In that same end-of-the-year studio session, Shaw included three more tunes featuring Ms. Forrest. An easy way out of sorts? To a degree. By this time the suave bandleader did feel overloaded and heavily pressured by those insistent, cloying song-pluggers, and of course by a skein of gigs that didn't relent. So that whatever made his recording sessions a bit easier at times was obviously welcome. And yet, Artie never stood pat, or remained in one familiar furrow. He kept mixing things up, memorably so, and to close this batch of late '38 we have a full-band instrumental version of a standard, "It Had to Be You." And would one doubt it? Shaw does very well by that well-known tune, with his own melodic clarinet solo lasting about a minute and contributing strongly, via elements like triplet slurs that were so typical of him. At the end of the piece, he enhances the entire effect with short "conversations" (between clarinet and band) that are truly delicate.

But delicacy was only one element, if a key one, of this bandleader and his aggregation. By this point Auld, in particular, was starting via his tenor contributions to move the band in a somewhat different, more forthright direction. So even more so when he came on board did Buddy Rich, as ebullient a drummer as there ever was, though only a couple decades old at the time, and first heard on Shaw recordings at the beginning of '39. These cuts would show from the get-go what an aggressive, vivacious Rich could do to help swing a band. He's also heard to advantage (including with a bit of yelling issuing from his enthusiastic maw) on unrecorded tunes marvelously preserved from those hotel and radio gigs, like the sensational, but probably overly long (for recording) "At Sundown," mentioned above. As noted, this remarkable piece of work includes absolutely superb solos from Artie and from Auld, too. (It's now a YouTube marvel, a truffle that was once nearly lost from view or hearing, though it did appear on an old LP or two.)

In any event Shaw mainly liked the perkier, "pushier" effect he was getting via these new players he'd engaged. Even slightly more than he did with his break-out band of 1938, he would often call his '39 aggregation (an extension of the "Beguine" one) the greatest he ever had, the one that despite all the pressures he faced, stemmed from more obsessive work and care on his part than ever he'd devote to later orchestras.

Shaw likened himself to a good newspaper or magazine editor when it came to arrangements and such. Beyond the arrangements he always wanted, as stressed, to assimilate his sidemen into a cohesive whole that was much greater than the parts. Only one of those players through '39 would be a bit of a problem there, becoming (and considering himself) an increasing star. And this was of course the one-off Rich, always a larger-than-life personality and drummer. He had been a child prodigy performing in vaudeville with his parents, then with his dad alone, from a very early age, and utterly used to being a star even at age six. When vaudeville got clobbered by the stock market crash, and with a resultant Depression fully in place by the early '30s, as well as the new "talkie" films, Rich moved toward band work alone, becoming a fixture in the clubs that proliferated on New York's 52nd Street midway through the decade. And he learned from other fine drummers like Chick Webb, Tony Briglia, Sid Catlett, and of course Gene Krupa. Rich had his first major gig with Joe Marsala, then moved to Bunny Berigan's band in 1938; but when Berigan broke his foot and in a bad temper reamed out Auld, Georgie went right over to Shaw, and soon hyped his good friend Rich as a topflight drummer, even though he couldn't read music. Auld knew very well how fast Buddy could digest and master charts. Shaw gave him a tryout at the Blue Room, and either in December of '38 or just after New Year's (there are at least two versions of the story here), Rich entered the AS band, bringing a slew of unique techniques with him—more bass drum than was usual, an ability to reach all sorts of places on his equipment that others couldn't match, delicacy on the brushes, unexpected rim shots and stick use, and an ability to modulate and adapt to soloists, and yet... Going too far was also Rich's stock in trade, and thankfully, Artie helped refine his work so that he would fit well in this very popular swing organization. In that, we could call Shaw as a bandleader not only an editor of sorts, as he'd put it, but also similar to an adept baseball manager.[15] Artie really did know how to bring out the best in his players for the common good, and for the final product, and that included even this mercurial, temperamental great that was Rich, or "Traps, the Drum Wonder," as Buddy had been dubbed early on.

Was his new employer authoritarian? Not nearly so much as Goodman, and more prone to pick up on his sidemen's ideas and even quirks. But he was the band's firm leader, no question about that. Helping to account for the band's extraordinary and varied output, the human paradoxes in this musical contingent's *chef* and key soloist remained stubbornly intact: most obviously, Shaw's own tenderness and sensitivity combined with the toughness I encountered in my phone calls to him; not to mention impulsive, improvisational verve along with dogged thoroughness and incredible organizational skills. Put another way, this popular musician had gossamer-sweet artistic qualities, but also mathematical, even scientific exactitude. These paradoxically clashing traits helped make Shaw the pace-setting player and bandleading master he became in the era under discussion. Does one forgive that "master," that Swing Era icon, for at one point tossing Lana Turner's spaghetti on the floor, food she'd offered his friends and which somehow didn't pass muster? Or for later snapping at Ava Gardner about his paying utilities and other bills, and generally taking care of all business? Or for thundering at Evelyn Keyes in the late '50s when she forgot passports in Spain that he might very well have remembered himself to bring?

Some, in fact, don't want to forgive all that, despite how much Shaw gave to so many through his lovely, well-crafted, and truly unique brand of popular music. In his biography of Bellow, the late James Atlas psychologically took that master to task for his own apparent character flaws; but there again, the same thing holds true: incredible and satisfying artistic results, though produced by less than perfect humans, are what have vouchsafed so many people so much pleasure. This then remains our main focus (as distinct from gossipy tidbits) in this study of Artie Shaw; i.e., the music itself. Onward we can now move to the peak he reached in that realm during 1939, and at the very apogee of the swing craze, too, when Shaw both fit in and thankfully didn't, surpassing norms in a truly unusual and satisfying manner. (At least as long as he could stand to do so!)

# Two

# Shaw at His Apex

## *1939*

The title of this chapter again reflects Artie's own viewpoint, and also the level of public adulation, which remained red-hot (and in the entire country) for this bandleader's group. By this time Shaw had gotten designated as "King of the Clarinet" (not that he much liked such publicity-driven monikers); while Goodman's greatest bands—particularly his superb aggregation of '37-'38, driving toward a concert at Carnegie Hall—were behind him, in good part due to the departure on bad terms of his star drummer, Krupa, and in the same era, of a great trumpet soloist, Harry James, along with other noted players. And Glenn Miller hadn't quite reached his own summit yet. So the Shaw band of 1939 was both his most popular, as well as the one he thought his finest, and on which he lavished (in his own estimation) the most care and labor, and against increasingly steep odds.

However, this band can still be properly called the 1938-39 aggregation, too. Yes, there were some different and wonderful soloists, preeminently Auld, and an exciting new, 20-year-old drummer almost instantly on the road to greatness; but Shaw's clarinet sound was not significantly different here than it was in the summer and fall of '38. The sections were still giving out roughly the same flavor as previously. In future orchestras Shaw's clarinet work would change quite dramatically to adapt first to strings, then to a bop-oriented bunch. In addition, the orchestral brogues of those organizations, particularly the ones with classical-type instruments, would feel almost foreign to those who only knew the "Beguine" sound that essentially lasted through most of '39.

However you want to designate this band, Shaw and his sidemen were absolutely at their most polished point in the period leading up to the outbreak of World War II, September 3, and a bit beyond. But despite all the cash he was bringing in for himself, the record company, his agents, lawyers, etc., Artie found himself increasingly exhausted from round-the-clock demands on his time, and his own conscience-driven sense that he must keep doing the near-impossible.

The band's recording session of 1/17/39 featured a Romberg and Hammerstein show tune, "Lover Come Back to Me," which I would call (after "Softly...," also by them) Shaw at his most Jewish in that band, to be followed later by one more of the same ilk. I'm talking of his reflective, "draggy" mood, prepared at the outset on this "Lover..." by a soft piano intro, and with Rich unwontedly restrained on drums. Then we get Artie's clarinet lead, with its heartfelt pathos like no other, and offering two choruses that are almost like tangled, beautiful spiderwebs. Pastor contributes sweetly with his tenor solo, as do those pathos-driven, well-blended saxes, with their trademark "squeezed notes" neatly arrayed against brass that's only demi-strong at most. That gorgeous, extended-passage sax work reflects Artie's own voice, exactly as his clarinet solos did. Privin on trumpet is also discreet, and the saxes come back with their distinctive sound for a third go-around—lovely, almost thinking reeds here—followed by the held-in trumpets and trombones, and a slow-down coda that couldn't have been easy to negotiate.

Buddy's powerful fills, saluted by others in the orchestra if not always by Shaw (who sometimes wanted him to give less), are more prominent on "Rosalie," cut in the same session with a gravelly Pastor singing stint; and on "My Heart Stood Still," both listenable today. And then, barely a week later, Artie's band recorded another clutch of sides on 1/23/39! No wonder he felt himself on a treadmill, an uncontrollable, misery-inducing treadmill! One, as he repetitively noted, in which he was pushed in many different directions, and where intrusions kept coming from agents, attorneys, and of course dancers and autograph seekers, people who weren't his preferred dish at all.

In the session of January 23 there follows a third truly Jewish-sounding AS item (to go with "Softly, as in a Morning Sunrise" and "Lover Come Back to Me"), especially on clarinet but also in the ensemble work. Here was the second Shaw piece I chose to play for Bellow and wife, and with another "shhh..." at its outset, as I carefully put the needle on the record. We are speaking of a great Gershwin standard, "The Man I Love," and some might cynically want to step in on this, asking, in effect: "How can one do badly with such a tune?" Exactly as one might say of "Body and Soul"—which, by the way (and inexplicably to this observer), Shaw never recorded with his three greatest Swing Era organizations—because it, too, had all the requisite melancholy that so appealed to Artie's musical instincts.

So there I was in early '82, shutting down the Bellows again with perhaps cheeky omniscience when Shaw's moody clarinet took the initial melodic spotlight on "The Man...." His work here flows almost like a gliding violin, and he slurs up to notes to increase the poignancy, minimizing use of the tongue for articulation (very different from Goodman in that regard). Afterward, Alexandra Bellow exulted as to how much she liked this one, despite being (or perhaps because she was) a mathematician by trade. I do recall noting to the Bellows how Shaw's work simultaneously mirrored Pascal's "esprit de géométrie" (though apparently no clarinetist had a better sense of time than Goodman) and "esprit de finesse." I remember how with a slight smile Bellow seemed to appreciate that humanistic reference. But this '39 "Man I Love" seems far more on Pascal's "finesse" side emotionally and/or artistically, rather than just the mathematical one. Bellow did counter his wife in her unqualified enjoyment of something so supremely natural (Rich would say that this Shaw band was indeed so natural it was hard work keeping it that way). The great American writer conceded that he, too, liked the clarinet here, but "not that 'kiss-ass'" ensemble. Which would hurt anyone knowing how much Shaw put into creating the 1939 band's particular sound. It could be that Bellow, having gotten to know Shaw in the late '40s and early '50s, when Artie tried to be part of Manhattan's intellectual scene, was still acting as a kind of derisive gatekeeper here.

But I'll give him and many other honest listeners this: that Shaw clarinet stint starting this wonderful "Man I Love" is indeed a stunner, drawing out all the longing and Weltschmerz of a great Gershwin tune, and more than was usual. One can see Shaw in the spotlight playing this in some packed venue of the time and almost massaging the crowd with such dramatic sweetness on his instrument. Re this recorded version, different adjectives come to mind on that clarinet work heard there: sad, reluctant, and even humble! Artie Shaw humble? Absolutely. When I saw him on *The Tonight Show* in the early '70s and he parried Carson's usual question on why he didn't play anymore, he seemed definitely and even supremely humble. The reluctant part? That, too, seems a relevant adjective here. Without the deadlines of these studio sessions, nothing would have been quite good enough for such a man. And yet, he does stay within boundaries, and his playing on "Man" is again simple but not simple, and above all, romantic in the extreme. As in "Lover..." the saxes on this one play a key role with their remarkable, Shaw-shaped phrasing that's simply beautiful and heart-tugging. And Pastor's solo is simple and right for this interpretation, too (with Auld more of a jazz technician on tenor). As for Privin's trumpet improv, it, too, seems linear and uncomplicated. But again, the yearning reeds, which seem to be talking along with Shaw's warm "axe," are a major reason for the poignant mood we get on this "Man I Love," along with the original nature of the tune itself.

But from the same studio session there's an entirely contrastive version of "The Donkey Serenade," a Rudolf Friml tune that became a vehicle for opera-trained Allan Jones, Jack's father. And whereas Buddy found himself constrained on "The Man...," necessarily so, here he really indulges the tom-toms in several extended solos, against Shaw's own tough, clean, and insistent articulation in the upper register. Artie's clarinet regains the opening motif throughout the arrangement, but the band's contribution is primary, too, and plenty swinging, till later in the piece, where unwonted Shaw frivolity takes over. This includes Artie's purposely "off," donkey-like clarinet wails, especially at the end of the recording. But there are deliberately mocking grimaces throughout, and in fact, this is almost several kinds of numbers in one, with Rich authoritative all the way as the drummer who felt he could propel an entire band.

Shaw sometimes had to tamp down that star drummer, and on a number of occasions and in fits of pique would even fire, then quickly rehire him! (Tommy Dorsey would do the same thing, too.) Shaw also didn't appreciate Rich's practical jokes, such as when he gummed up the piano at one point and no solo came out. But he always thought of Buddy as a real artist on the hides and superior even to the great Krupa, who gained fame in the Goodman band. And Rich truly reveals that uniqueness on this effervescent version of "Donkey...."

By contrast, Jerome Kern's "Bill," cut at the same session, is a much more sedate and melodic piece, including via Helen Forrest's vocal. It's still beautiful, but not nearly so sad as "The Man..." or as exuberant as either "Donkey Serenade" or from the same studio stint, "The Carioca." Shaw's own playing on "Bill" is smooth and sweet, and, especially in his second solo, he's quietly tasteful in his use of slight bends in the held notes, as if figuratively begging, then wanting to put things right. Music aficionados will note him landing at 2:21 into the piece on a deliberate, slightly flat C# (or Db), in order to set the table for a crisp move back into perfect tune. Making invidious comparisons avails little here, though this "Bill" isn't nearly as arresting as either the '39 "Man I Love" or "Donkey..."; but it's pretty, and worth a contemporary listener's time.

All these Shaw discs were recorded in New York, a different one from today's, and where those demands on Shaw's time and energy became ever more onerous, driving him to the point of a nervous breakdown. And again, an enormously tight recording schedule (RCA obviously wanting to milk this cash cow as quickly as possible) played a key role there, too, because his next session of six sides came a mere eight days after that of January 23! This is hard to believe, and one can only try to imagine how much Shaw put into rehearsals in order to make the band "right" on each and every record he chose to cut.

Those long, painstaking rehearsals were crucial for Artie, and would continue to be through the entire Swing Era. In his autobiography, *The Trouble with Cinderella*, Shaw strips away the glamour of it all, showing how hard and in what difficult circumstances he'd worked his groups in order to blend them so well. Especially before he hit big, the picture is often one of drafty or boiling halls, with his players working over and over on this or that number under dim Stalinist-like bulbs, and late into the night; then traveling hardly in style, on crummy buses and in terrible heat or blistering cold, before comforts finally came with success. But those onerous rehearsals continued. And meanwhile, this bandleader also used keys or ranges that wouldn't needlessly ask too much of musicians who had sometimes started out as quite callow hires. Yet he always demanded that they learn and keep on learning how to work together as a seamless unit.[1]

In the January 31 studio session, "Alone Together" (from the musical revue *Flying Colors*, when there was a super-thriving Broadway in the Big Apple) is a tune worth learning—and one many won't automatically know. And that's another plus of discovering so many old Shaw recordings, such as this one; i.e., learning many good songs that have sadly fallen into oblivion. Now that there's no more AM hit parade radio to make one want to hear the latest offerings over and over, as used to be the case, you'll find that numbers like Shaw's '39 "Alone Together" will keep reverberating inside, especially for the truly musical. In a way Shaw's substantial *oeuvre* constitutes a marvelous series of idiosyncratic takes on "The Great American Songbook," and by an emphatic member of the Greatest Generation, a mostly industrious one with little time to waste.

This "Alone Together"—the very title connoting a romantic, brooding quality Artie obviously loved—starts in slow, morose and certainly moody fashion. That's exactly the way Artie wanted it on his two initial choruses of clarinet work, his inner sensitivity, sense of beauty, and dissatisfactions, too, fully displayed here. On this one, his clarinet is typically thick and buttery in the lower register, but so seemingly simple in that first part that an amateur clarinetist, as I can attest, will play along with that swath of the record sans great difficulties, which would rarely be the case. Then come those talking, searching, disciplined saxes that Artie had molded, followed by the strong, full ensemble, and those masterful reeds returning a couple extended times more, with the brass happily discreet and held down. (Shaw's trumpeter, Bernie Privin, was grateful for this, saying that Goodman's arrangements, by contrast, could be very rough on that section.)[2] This AS "Alone Together" (there would be another with a different orchestra of his) has a seemingly effortless quality to it, but again reveals Artie's lofty standards to get that effect, and the deceptive simplicity that is often, or so it seems, a trait of genius. The record's start-out is quintessential Artie on his "axe," and not complicated; but when he's back in at 2:36, those who play that instrument will hear him make a descending glissando sound easy (in this part, the amateur may indeed decide to take a break!). However, the team band so many of his sidemen recalled as central more than contributes throughout, making this a wonderful collective and again, romantic effort.

For certain Artie must have loved this melancholy tune, because rarely did he record the same number later and differently with a subsequent aggregation (not counting his "oldie" reruns circa 1950). However, in this case he did and it's marvelous, too, and will be discussed below. He also cut another fine version of "The Man I Love" with his 1945 band. These constituted the type of poignant, even lonely tunes Shaw obviously favored in his own playing and that of his bands.

I noted that a tune like "Alone Together," so wonderfully done by this great '39 band, would be relatively unknown later on. Not so, I suppose, among jazz players, and in fact, we have an album of the late '50s that's titled "Alone Together," featuring the cool, "progressive" trumpeter Chet Baker on that number, and pianist Bill Evans, along with such stellar contributors as flutist Herbie Mann and Pepper Adams on baritone sax. They also do it well, if far less romantically (which seems to be the tune's essential trait).

And then for those with the original 78, one could flip from this ponderous "Alone..." to an utterly contrastive "Rose Room" on the B-side! Artie was of course always proffering musical surprises, not least in his *sui generis*, masterly contributions on clarinet. (He would say that playing all the time in that heady, thronged period of '38-'39, his instrument almost became an appendage, and that egotistical as it might sound, he could do pretty well anything on it that he heard inside.) And does he ever do so on this remarkable and beautiful "Rose Room"!

A short, unassuming band intro sets the stage here, and then on this arrangement Shaw crafted himself, comes the star's entry, making an extended, up-to-the-rafters-and-back passage a *chef-d'oeuvre* of big band clarinet. It's a number where he plays fast and emphatically, and in a way that no jazz artist on that instrument could ever rival; and yet it feels—due to his legato phrasing and rich, sophisticated timbre—that he's again going both fast and not fast all at once. And behind him in that marvelously extended early going is an ever more assertive Buddy, buttressing but not overwhelming the warmly dexterous Artie at his finest. To reiterate, Dick Johnson, who took the clarinet parts in a reconstituted Shaw band from the early '80s, asserted that if one could play 15 of these old solos, one was some player, indeed! But the notes themselves are far from all there is here. Again, it's much more the mood that moves a listener. This masterful Shaw solo in the initial, but drawn-out swath of "Rose Room" would be super-difficult for most on his instrument; but even those who could more or less negotiate these flying passages successfully could never at the same time replicate Shaw's reliably lush tone and persistently stirring quality here. And all on something so hellishly difficult as this '39 version of "Rose Room"!

After the clarinet star has drawn things out and pulled listeners deeply and firmly into the piece by his awesome virtuosity, the saxes eventually take over in their masterly way, too. And as they do, careful and curious listeners might find it hard to believe how Shaw the player also did such great scoring here (as "Rose Room"'s sole arranger). He even uses high, Glenn Millerish clarinets at the end to replace those saxes, and yet it all feels "right" and anything but derivative. Once again Shaw and band give the illusion here of a certain ease and ineluctability, but which would be impossible to duplicate. Other swing bands or small combos could play this chestnut, but none would be remotely in this league. (In fact, I heard Goodman play "Rose Room" with a small group circa 1964, but in a starkly contrastive, overly technical manner.) The relaxed, almost sluggish tempo in the AS version creates a kind of dreamy mood throughout. But Shaw's playing in particular—with such effects as cookie-cutter descending thirds to prepare a huge, explosive leap to the high register, and thence into more descending thirds, all lacquered with his own finish like no other—constitutes some of the most arresting clarinet work he ever put on record.

From that jazz peak Artie completes the session by resorting more to singing interludes—partly as a kind of respite?—using Forrest, including on "I Want My Share of Love," with another moody feel that's a giveaway from the very title. Here Shaw's clarinet is rather easy to play along with, as on the first part of "Alone Together" (and emphatically *not* "Rose Room"). When he blows languidly and methodically here, all that stands out beneath is the thumping bass; and Artie's intelligence is displayed even on such an ephemeral, little-known, but again, romantic tune of the day. And as the piece gains more power and strength, so does Buddy, remaining a key ingredient in that great band both on pacers but also on these ballads.

Artie keeps demonstrating in this swing work how he could be both complex and at the same time elemental. And he was recording like mad through almost all of '39, often without multiple takes. Not only would the vocal interventions help keep things easier, but so would introductory clarinet parts played in the low or chalumeau register, which on this instrument is easier going than higher ones above the octave key. Of course amateur or beginning clarinet players generally use a soft reed, which works well in that lower region but not so easily as one mounts higher. How Artie did both (i.e., the very high and very low) so well remains one of the positive aspects of his playing on virtually all his records of this era. (It would be interesting to know if he changed reeds, depending on the song and its range.)

From that same session of 1/31/39, "It's All Yours" and "This Is It" also feature Forrest, and the band seems to be ever more crisp and machine-like, but in a pleasing way, as if Shaw were implying something like: "There's much more here we could provide, and look out—on other numbers you'll get it!" Of course he felt pushed against his will into cutting some of these songs that never lasted; but in the main, he and his band did so creditably and marvelously, and with Buddy ever more apt in under-girding the ensemble's feel on different numbers. Above all, a careful listener can see how much work Shaw devoted to making an entire contingent of different players cohere exactly as he wanted. The unity, particularly in the sax section on a side like "It's All Yours," playing as if one instrument, and with the same nuances of vibrato matching Artie's, is simply astounding.

Another record from this session, "Delightful Delirium," also gives the band some break time of sorts with Pastor's pleasing, gravelly vocal in the middle, and the band now sounding—especially the brass—utterly mature and anything but bubblegum-like, despite some of the players still being very young. Shaw here remains characteristically melodic and in great control on his instrument, even up on the rarefied peaks.

And then came a break in the recording action as the band did other things in Shaw's now heavily busy career—super-busy, given that this was about as popular a musical contingent as any, much like the Beatles were in 1965 or the Eagles a decade after that. There was still the band's regular tenure on the *Melody & Madness* radio show, if no longer at the Hotel Lincoln. On February 3, 1939, at the Strand Theatre, where the band was now booked, the irritable Artie, as breakable as a rubber band, began noticing a large difference between the sedate atmosphere at the Blue Room, and the more raucous, unhinged one which was drawing stage-rushing youth at the Strand. And then came more mayhem at the Paramount in Newark from February 17, and worst, at Philadelphia's Earle Theatre for a week near the end of the month, where mobs of students who had cut school got completely out of hand, police or no police. The band then went off to play for a week at the Stanley Theatre in Pittsburgh, starting March 3, and thence to a number of colleges, which also had a lot of young, over-the-top listeners and dancers. By then Shaw was plain exhausted and on the verge of potentially life-ending health problems, and there were still many other gigs to come that we haven't space to enumerate here.[3]

Given just those dates noted above, there was no more recording in New York till the session of six sides made March 12, with Artie, despite so many trammels and problems, still making memorable music with his band, but trying to make things a bit easier on himself, too. Thus one in this batch is another "Any Old Time," basically the same as the earlier one, only with Ms. Forrest's vocal replacing Holiday's; and with the band sounding more authoritative, providing the sense that much more could be possible. And there's still a Pastor tenor solo here, soon to be a rarity in this greatest of Shaw's contingents, given the presence of the more jazzy Auld on that instrument.

Shaw uses Forrest again in "I'm in Love with the Honorable Mr. So and So," a little-known Sam Coslow tune on forbidden love in Gotham high society, long before the sexual revolution hit in America. It was probably a number Shaw felt pressure to record. But the band does this one up in reliable, listenable fashion, and it sold quite well.

With "Prosschai" from this 3/12/39 gaggle of discs, Pastor provides an upbeat singing stint on a song about a girl having to say goodbye to her beau in Russia, which of course was Stalin's grisly if still too often admired Soviet Union back then. Unusually, Pastor then sings more snippets against Shaw's clarinet riffs, with only percussion behind (at one point Tony even calls out as though on a ball field, "Play it, Arthur!"). The first half of the record is simply fun, but the second becomes unbuttoned swing, with the band initially and almost deceitfully minimal, but then a freed-up Buddy leading the way as he guns into several drum breaks. Rich's last drum roll here almost begs the band to amp things up even more, and that they do; then Artie flies high over this controlled but ever more complex mayhem, as the ensemble drives things to a close. Shaw's altissimo verve and general playing here seem somewhat reminiscent of the Johnny Dodds/Louis Armstrong style of the '20s, helping to create an unusual and worthy "Prosschai," indeed. Professionals may note Artie's somewhat shocking entry into the second solo on F, clashing with the Eb major chord; then his "twisting" to wring out as much tension as possible, with the chords alternating quickly between

Eb and F, all again revealing the paradoxical series of opposites in the character of this great musician.

The standout of that March 12 session follows, and makes for a real contrast to the one we've just discussed. "Deep Purple" is by far the most serious, gorgeous, and surprising cut of the batch, arranged as almost all these '39 AS offerings were by Gray and Shaw (with the latter often starting with a sketch of what he wanted, then refining and editing the final result).

The surprises on "Purple," perfectly tasteful and emotion-producing, include the fact that Helen sings this Peter DeRose song from the start of the piece, which was unusual for her (she generally comes in around the middle). And her big band sweetness is well displayed, unaffectedly warm and romantic on this sweet American standard. She's "Purple"'s initial and apparent star, but when she's done, Shaw follows with one of his finest solos (hard of course to rank them and really, one shouldn't). But he, too, is a major contributor to the astonishing and thoroughly arresting quality of this 1939 version of a once well-known song.

**The great but sometimes over-the-top drummer Buddy Rich, who made a major contribution to Artie's swing band in 1939 (Library of Congress Prints and Photographs Division, Washington, D.C [LC-GLB23-1481/William P. Gottlieb Collection]).**

That clarinet solo immediately following the warm Forrest is leisurely, beautiful and facile-sounding—again, rather like the Yankee Clipper making the hard ones look easy in the same metropolis where this record was waxed, and in the same period. The sweet saxes follow, but really as an interlude, setting the table for Shaw to return a second time against nothing but the rhythm section, and this time throwing out gorgeous, unusual chords, a superbly poignant effort, but also topflight jazz.

Auld takes the short tenor solo on "Deep...," as he now almost invariably would, and Helen, with the last stanza of the song reprised, concludes the piece. This version of "Deep Purple" is quite simply a romantic stand-out, with the vocal and Shaw's own solo work drawing out and reflecting the quiet, lyrical aspects of the melody. No more distinctive version of that tune would follow till the early '60s. In a very different period, now marked by the primacy of rock 'n' roll, Nino Tempo—himself a reed player and Goodman acolyte—and his sister, April Stevens (real name Carol LoTempio), then produced an also unusual version of "Deep Purple," so unusual for the period (thanks to Tempo's vocal improv) that it nearly fell by the wayside before becoming an AM hit. The fact that it was even released was due in great part to support from a heavy-hitting producer, Ahmet Ertegun. In my view, it would be both educational and enjoyable for listeners to play Shaw's 1939 "Deep Purple," then this wonderful Tempo-Stevens version of the early '60s, in order to savor both. Because each is a kind of masterpiece—in terms of Tempo's contribution, partly because he was so immersed in swing along with the rock of his own era. That of course is the way of such unique recordings: they are refreshingly original, much as the monster hit of the '30s, "Beguine," was, and equally, one of the biggest successes of the '50s, which could also be cited as a one-off, the Diamonds' improbable but still marvelous "Little Darlin'."

Shaw adds more fine fare in the same session, including an upbeat "I'm Coming Virginia" (from the revue *Africana*), and still seems at pains never to get stuck in one particular musical groove. And all the while his band remained super-accepted by the American public, which continued to gobble up whatever he had to offer; while he himself felt ever more tension from their expectations and those of so many business-legal types who were nothing but necessary evils to him.

The pressures, the great demand for more, more, more, were reflected in his many gigs, his movie appearances, his radio work, and yes, in recording sessions whose numbers grew like Topsy. How on earth could Shaw get band and arrangements in shape for yet another studio session of six sides less than a week after that of March 12? It seems almost superhuman! Vladimir Simosko has noted that after much rehearsing, Shaw's band would play carefully near the close in these sessions, often getting things done with a minimal number of takes.[4] Again, all that sounds improbable, but Artie was always one to demand a huge amount of himself and of those working for him, especially in terms of preparation.

So from six sides made on March 12, 1939, he and his orchestra were back for six more on March 17. It's astounding, but maybe one reason this isn't our favorite of his batches, though with everything here more than listenable, and still done with typically high standards. There were four songs that featured vocal interludes (three by Forrest and one by Pastor). And this delivered by a bandleader who didn't particularly like singers and would later reproach TD for so frequently featuring that languid young phenom, Sinatra, along with Jo Stafford and the other Pied Pipers.[5]

The remaining two of this 3/17/39 group of recordings aren't standards, show tunes, or even pop offerings of the period. Instead, they are both Shaw originals (he would later say that in his more carefree moments on location, less available now in the face of overwhelming celebrity, he enjoyed hatching ditties, sometimes along with his sidemen). As a change of pace he obviously wanted, both of these March '39 waxings become showcases for the band to play real jazz, and that they do here, and more than creditably.

"One Night Stand" was entirely by Artie, along with the arrangement. As an aside: Artie was apparently not much for one-night stands in his romantic life, being much more of a serial monogamist of sorts. So that how he hatched this title is probably open to debate and conjecture. Some might argue that "one night stand" also means a sole theatrical or musical performance. In any event, it's a perky tune, with Buddy's snappy, unbridled drumming evident from the top—this being the type of vehicle where Rich could let go more fully than in those numerous ballads the band recorded. The ensemble on "Stand" works well, too, but plenty of room is given the soloists—Privin on trumpet, in something of a Louis Armstrong style, and then Auld getting a chance to show his jazz chops, which in Rich's view bracketed him with the best Black tenor players of the era, including Auld's role model, Coleman Hawkins. "Booting" is a good word, "freebooting" even, for Georgie's tenor sax, which along with Shaw's solos, could inspire the entire band, again according to Buddy.

Then on "One Night Stand" comes Jenkins' trombone, also very right for this jazzy piece, and in a way that as noted, stirred even TD to a certain envy. Bob Kitsis, a polished Harvard man, follows on piano in a beautiful, elegant, understated way that's really apt for this tune as well, and for the Shaw orchestra (if maybe not flamboyant enough for another type of swing organization). But Kitsis is definitely classy as the band's keyboard man. And his restrained quality, following the earlier soloists, sets the table for the king himself—a modest king, but one who would long marvel at his own amazing standards of the era, if always trying to dodge the lure of egomania. And indeed, Artie was and is a wonderful jazz player on this "One Night Stand," descending beautifully, repeating notes with liquid verve, then offering light-hearted chirps on his clarinet against Buddy alone. The band returns, but with Shaw riffing constantly in the background (which was unusual), fully liberated, it seems. And the rendering stays fun to the end. One can really see this bluesy jazz original as a happily different kind of outlet for the band and for its mercurial leader, on what was originally a rather simple chart. But it's well worth listening to today as a more off-the-cuff AS product of the time, compared with other types of recordings he made back then.

He added to the same genre of sorts on this 3/17/39 group of waxings with "One Foot in the Groove" (co-authored by Shaw and Wen D'Aury, who together provided the arrangement as well). The band starts with a draggy intro in a wah-wah style that was unusual, and lets Artie in to provide a happy-sounding, compact solo, in which he again seems emancipated on his own piece, and in his own house, so to speak. Perhaps it brought him back to a paradoxically freer era for him, when he'd played as a much poorer, lesser-known artist with different groups on the way up, and of course jammed with some of the seasoned greats. And without any celebrity expectations to rein him in.

The rather simple band sound returns on "Groove," giving way to a muted trumpet solo not from the usual Privin, but Chuck Peterson, who'd matured with the "Beguine" band but wouldn't last the entire way with this edition. However, Peterson's marvelous here, and given plenty of space to use the primping Cootie Williams style to advantage in his first solo effort. He's followed by more Kitsis with his elegant piano touches, which serve as a kind of table-setter for Peterson to return and give more of his muted trumpet riffs that work so well here. Then comes Auld, and where on some ballads he's more perfunctory, here his tenor shows to very different advantage compared to Pastor's. It has an adventurous jazz feel for his initial solo; then the careful, crisp, yet beautiful band ensemble prepares for Auld's second chorus in that freebooting style of his that became such a mainstay of the 1939 Shaw band. Trombones nicely welded together take over, then Artie comes back a second time, and not in his usual legato manner; but rather, tonguing emphatically and aggressively in a high, insistent staccato passage. He shows his usual beautiful flexibility in the demanding altissimo range here. A sweet little ending ensues, and Buddy's bang-bang drumming ends things appropriately. And pros in the field may notice a number of interesting touches in this piece, such as an Ab opening which is chromatic and deliberately unpredictable. This record is easy to underestimate if one listens to it once only, and not a number of times over the months or years. But "One Foot in the Groove" along with "One Night Stand" from the same session show this 1939 band to be an authentic and compelling jazz organization, not one simply pandering to commercial tastes and the mainstream. Both are well worth checking out on the internet.

In terms of soloists, I've sometimes thought that Rich exaggerated the jazz impact on that Shaw aggregation of Georgie's tenor, though never of Artie's superb clarinet work, which was undeniably central to the band's success. But at this point listeners might conveniently go to YouTube to punch up that unbelievable version of "At Sundown" mentioned above, which really showcases the band's unhinged jazz possibilities (taped live on the Old Gold radio show, it became a "transcription" that was thankfully preserved). I still wonder why Shaw never recorded this one in a studio back then, and whether in any event he could have recaptured that free, spontaneous, yet disciplined quality on a 78. Most probably this version of "At Sundown" ran too long for recordings of that era. But Shaw is absolutely remarkable on the number as a jazz virtuoso, and I've never heard Auld as an improviser quite so marvelous and ebullient either, along with Rich shouting and thumping incredibly in the background. It's hard to describe Shaw's solo work flying over the base provided by the band on "Sundown"; but it comes off rather like a sailing piece of string, a kite, a parabolic rainbow, or even a hawk, soaring all over the compliant orchestral background far beneath it! Ditto for Auld, almost making this version of "At Sundown" another song entirely. "Sailing" is the best word to describe both solo masters dominating and driving the orchestra, and creating thereby, an absolute, if lesser-known masterpiece. Listeners should be as astonished as we remain by this live tour de force, mentioned here to show that it goes very well, and in exactly the same period, with the two Shaw jazz originals analyzed above. This might have been a side of his work that Artie would have liked to foreground more often, but of course he had so many pushing him to do what was popular and wanted, a dilemma he never quite resolved. He also had a real interest in making recordings a little easier when possible.

L.A. (a.k.a. La La Land) now beckoned via Goodman's old stomping grounds, the Palomar, where after migrating West, the Shaw band was to debut on April 19. But Artie became seriously ill at that time, partly from sheer exhaustion, leading to a bout of pneumonia, a high fever, and a case of strep throat. Too much sulfa was administered, and engagements were cancelled en route to the West. Once at the Palomar, the still weakened bandleader dropped to the ground his very first night there. And then came the diagnosis of a serious blood disease related to leukemia, agranulocytosis, which can bring death and for Shaw, almost did.

Under the veteran Tony Pastor's leadership, the band continued playing the Palomar and Old Gold shows, honoring its commitments. But a laid-up Shaw only started climbing back toward decent health near the end of April, a truly cruel month for him even in sunny California. His recovery came partly due to using medicine that wasn't widely available. By this time and through that summer he was really wondering, and seriously, about simply ditching this popular band that was bringing in such gargantuan amounts of cash. The many band dates, the business problems, nights spent carefully recording a flurry of discs in studios till the wee hours—all played a role in his thought process.

Shaw only went back to the band on May 23, coinciding with his birthday, and to the weekly Old Gold broadcast, which had now moved to NBC. The band stayed at the Palomar through June, and then came summer work on a film Artie loathed and from which he tried to extricate himself, even though "Dancing Co-Ed" featured a young lady named Lana Turner. It was all getting over the top for this strong but also sensitive musician (and person).

After a fairly long recording hiatus for this still top-rated orchestra (due to Artie's sickness), his contingent had returned with a bevy of recordings made in Hollywood, starting with five on June 5, 1939. Simultaneously, its leader worried that his outfit (owing to its huge popularity and being impelled to take well-trodden routes) was becoming a little too careful and predictable. So what if they were still lionized most everywhere? Winning the *Downbeat* poll as number one swing band in the nation over the former top dog, Mr. Goodman's, never gave Shaw any real satisfaction. His competition was always mainly with himself. But Buddy Rich, in a short interview for Brigitte Berman's documentary, remembered the win with great pride, as he did when speaking to Burt Korall for the *Complete Artie Shaw* liner notes. That moment when Rich learned this stunning news remained inside him even several decades later. As for Goodman's reaction, we speak a lot here of rivalry between the two great clarinet-playing bandleaders of the time; but on the whole it seems that rivalry stemmed mostly from a now somewhat dethroned BG. Apparently after the *Downbeat* poll came out, he spoke to Artie about how close the count was, citing the exact and slim vote difference, if not, however, challenging the result! Shaw was flabbergasted by all this and essentially told Goodman there was plenty of room in the country for both bands to flourish. He then declared, using a simple, well-worn Yiddish phrase, that Benny should just stay healthy. The exact wording in the original is "bah mir gesund," but the connotation was apparently dismissive, as in "be my guest," constituting a way for Shaw to quickly part company with the King of Swing. This was far from the last time when Artie would be surprised by Goodman's bizarre behavior toward him, and downright cattiness.[6]

Speaking of staying healthy, such concerns for the overloaded Shaw weren't simply *pro forma*, as he kept wondering how long he could keep up such a frantic pace and whether it was all worth it. He did, however, like the relaxed California atmosphere (versus that of a more frenzied Manhattan), and acquired a home base on Summit Ridge Drive above Beverly Hills. And despite fears about his band's direction and giving in to a certain "safeness," the antithesis in his view of great jazz, musicality remained paramount for this AS orchestra, and still very evident.

In the 6/5/39 group of recordings, an Irving Berlin tune, "I Poured My Heart into a Song" (from the film *Second Fiddle*), gets an extended Forrest vocal from the outset, which again wasn't her norm, except on the odd record like "Deep Purple." Forrest claims a lot of space here, emotionally and romantically right for the song, with appropriate sax support behind her. She feels to a listener like the apparent centerpiece here, and when the ensemble takes over exclusively, more compact compared to the way it was even six months earlier, it seems deceptively like it's about to close out the tune. Instead it merely prepares for another move to the bridge, and Artie then claims the spotlight with a surprisingly driving, jazzy, but sweet solo that's wonderful to savor even now, and with Buddy almost alone giving him a percussive platform beneath. That solo will remain in the listener's mind, with its lilting ornamental "sentences," and Shaw's declamation of sorts growing more urgent and joyful. The record will also introduce people of a very different era to one of the many songs penned back then that have wrongly fallen into oblivion.

Some will know "Out of Nowhere" better, cut at the same June 5 session, and here Artie allows the band to shine sans vocal, with his own extended and sweeping initial passage on clarinet announcing things melodiously from the get-go. The trumpets, using plungers, prepare for Shaw's second series of riffs, with the highlight a kind of tumbling cadenza. Then the full band takes control on this fine rendering of yet another romantic ballad of the era, but one that lasted. And unusually by this time, Artie selects Pastor, not Auld, for the tenor solo, a simple, enjoyable passage that's entirely right for the mood here. Near the close the reeds finally become more forthright, all alone and talking again, it seems; and after Privin's cursory trumpet solo, Artie flies back in at the end. As if to say: "Yes, we're making lots of records now with Ms. Forrest singing, or Tony, but we can still rely on the band itself to produce a fine disc, too." All the way through the Swing Era, Shaw wouldn't be pigeonholed, remaining always the surprising performer in this field.

However, one understands why at the very pinnacle of popular success he was feeling at times a bit too hemmed-in with this organization, as the band seemed to sound ever more professional and together, but sometimes, in an almost terse or elliptical fashion. But with no needless, humdrum touches to vitiate recorded results. And still reliably producing emotions in its many followers. Even on supposedly forgettable numbers, Artie's music from that period is frequently warm, beautiful, stately, and wonderful even for today's listeners.

Given that band's relentless musicality, it still feels tragic and inexplicable to certain observers that in the second half of his life Shaw spurned that entire world cold turkey, diving into a cognitive realm via obsessive reading and intellectualizing. Why do such a thing? This is a subject to which one has to return ever and again here, and we will do so in fuller fashion below. But for now we can cite one key reason for this big change to come. Which is that as warm and often poignant as Shaw's great orchestral work (and solos) were, the end products took a great deal of care and attention to all sorts of details, including mundane commercial-business ones, which felt increasingly repugnant to this idealistic person and musician. Once he'd dumped that life, would he ever miss it all? No more, as he said in a number of interviews, than a person misses the arm he/she had lost to gangrene.

Returning to the musical period at hand, from his session of June 5, 1939, Shaw went to another only a week later (on the 12th) for another group of five! The first four of these records were broken up by vocals, two by Forrest, two by Pastor. "Comes Love" starts not with Privin on trumpet (the usual soloist by that time on this instrument), but a melodic Johnny Best, eventually to anchor Glenn Miller's brass session and be replaced in the Shaw band by Harry Geller. Best gives us two fine choruses, and the brass take over mostly on the bridge, with Buddy increasingly and unmistakably central here, too. Then comes Artie, moody, sweet, and quiet, as he was orally on that *Tonight Show* of 1972. Helen Forrest sings corny lyrics, but in a pretty manner. In today's world such songs would be more than welcome, and in fact, I was astounded to hear this "Comes Love" at an outdoor wedding reception circa 2000, played by aging New England jazzmen who knew that the younger generations wouldn't automatically know or value such a ditty. On this '39 "Comes Love" Auld's riffing tenor follows Forrest, one of his better efforts (sometimes he seems held down by these tunes giving such space to the singers); and then comes a crisp, tasteful ending to another song that would be worth rediscovering. And for those who know music well, they will note here how Artie takes advantage of the D minor key, but also of the D major bridge, before a return into minor, reflecting an almost "headachy-type" quality to the tune.

On "Go Fly a Kite" an aggressive Buddy contributes marvelous touches on drums, briskly whamming away, and the saxes also attack in more staccato fashion than usual. Brass mutes have the bridge, and on the whole, this is a happy trotter, and not "draggy" at all. Pastor provides the upbeat vocal about ditching one's trivial problems, sweetly naïve lyrics that fit well in America of that era. Artie and Georgie then riff off each other (Shaw "short-trading" eights with his sax star in a way that wasn't usual for them), followed by a tasteful Kitsis piano solo. A strong ensemble finish shows Rich amply joining in the fun.

On "A Man and His Dream" Artie starts out nicely on his clarinet with the full band behind him for two choruses. The saxes and brass in call-and-response grab the bridge, then the reeds regain the main melody as a lead-in for Forrest's vocal, on a romantic night setting so often featured in tunes of that era (think of the many other songs that spoke warmly of the moon and its effects). This again is very different and, in many ways, better song-writing than what we now have: not overtly sexy, nothing but pretty and positive (even on the edge of wartime), and in an America that could not yet be called decadent, if certainly full of inequities. After Forrest Privin expresses himself via a bluesy trumpet solo, and this is yet another tune worth learning (for the many in today's "archival U.S." who don't yet know it).

For the remaining cut of the June 12, '39 batch, Shaw decides, in effect, that enough is enough! Or seems to.... His "Traffic Jam" is another of his contrastive forays into pure, unmitigated jazz, as if to declare that he couldn't just record romantic ballads! And perhaps wishing thereby to prove something to those who would place him in a certain musical category. This "Traffic Jam" is indeed jazzy, but also impressionistic, not surprising given that Artie had long been influenced by composers like Debussy and Ravel. And he and the band do convey a clear impression of what a traffic jam (maybe on a crowded New York street) would feel like, via a tune Artie co-wrote with Teddy McRae, the latter also credited as arranger here.

Fully unshackled, the incomparable Buddy is really slamming away and even shouting on this one, with Artie's "gliss" and more generally, licorice stick wildness powering that traffic effect; while Georgie also whips along on his tenor solo, with the killer-diller pace maintained throughout. George Arus' trombone solo is jazzy, too, and Artie comes back when he feels like it, while Buddy's going a mile a minute, very strongly so, and sounding truly liberated here. Artie darts all over the full orchestra to increase the controlled-chaos effect and all in all, this "Traffic Jam" is a marvelous original of its time. Again, one almost hears the clarinet virtuoso emphatically asserting via this effort something like: "I don't owe everything to song-pluggers, to fans who pressure me to play pop tunes, etc. In this particular case, I don't give one fig at all about my popularity!" And it's true that while such a rendering would have been fine for dancing, it could never have become a Swing Era hit. However, it's still worth a listen today, not least due to Buddy's great drum work, Shaw's unfinished thoughts in his solos somehow being completed off the cuff, and the creation of an overall effect that resembles a multi-car pileup, rather than a small traffic jam! According to Samantha Wright, a well-known British jazz clarinetist living in Germany, Shaw's contributions right from the siren-like opening "gliss" would be technically baffling and a real challenge for anyone playing that instrument.

For all that, however, I still find—and am far from alone—a significant Shaw proclivity for his slower, more poignant, and melancholy work of this period done on the ballads, where his own clarinet is almost reluctant, and *à la fois* strong yet soft. Shaw certainly featured a lot of this quality in his huge, recorded output through 1939. Were there again paradoxes here? No question. As seen, Ms. Forrest declared how gentlemanly and caring Artie was with her, and she would emphasize how his warm clarinet work helped define her singing style, too.[7] And yet this is the same Shaw who unfortunately was aggressive and even bullying with a number of his wives! One cannot at all excuse that, and it is all well documented (too many memoirs from such as Gardner or Keyes saying more or less the same thing on the subject). However, Artie's remarkable music remains our central focus, and onward we go to more of his romantic fare in another cheek-by-jowl Hollywood session of five tunes recorded 6/22/39, i.e., only a week and a half after the last one. (This busyness was partly due to the fact that the Tinseltown filmmaking world Artie disdained would soon claim his time.)

Two sides from the batch of June 22 were co-written by Shaw himself: "Easy to Say" and "Moonray," both featuring Forrest in their middle reaches. "Easy…" has a sprightly but natural pace on a pretty melody, with the entire band initially laying it down, preparing for Shaw alone against percussion, "speaking" yet again, purposely slowing things down, and emotive as all get-out. Then comes Forrest caroling the stirring melody and lyrics, matching the mood of this most romantic of all American eras. Love is the centerpiece, and all is sweet and insouciant in her warbling (despite the lethal expansionism of Hitler, Stalin, and Japanese imperialists abroad). And then the band comes back to star again, a remarkable precision instrument of brass and reeds co-existing, and sweetly. The record does have a certain formulaic repetition enhancing its appeal, and Artie damns with faint praise on his instrument, via a short, high-register "twiddle" of a goodbye near the end.

On "Moonray," another brooding Shaw melody, Artie starts off with his sad, leisurely, purposive lingering on clarinet, somewhat the way Billie sang, presenting two such choruses against Rich and Sid Weiss' bass. (The latter could also play clarinet, tuba and violin!) Artie doesn't bother with cheap virtuosity here, using his lush tone simply to convey a certain delicacy of emotions, and to comment in a way on the song's coming words. Thence to Helen, and the theme is the rekindling of unrequited, even jilted love via the moon, again central to many songs of the era (think "Moonglow," "Moon over Miami," and "Moonlight in Vermont," not to mention "Stars Fell on Alabama"), and no longer as significant in our own hasty, "non-noticing" world. A strong, sweet trumpet solo by Best follows Forrest, and Auld on tenor in his own pretty but complex way remains quite different from what Pastor had contributed via his sax solos. The entire precision band comes back to finish things off, and one can definitely see this "Moonray" as a nice dance number of the time.

Two others in that batch are cut from similar cloth. One, "I'll Remember," features Shaw's clarinet at the outset with the same kind of introspective feel that's all him. You can really hear him almost singing the lyrics through his instrument, though Forrest's vocal is more the main event against familiar orchestration. The aptly titled "Melancholy Mood" features a vibrato-ish Forrest interlude. The sole side made on this date that departs from this romantic template is a jazz original by Joe Garland, which like "Traffic Jam," is impressionistic as well. It's called "Serenade to a Savage," which of course might not please the politically correct of our time. On this one Buddy's again almost unhinged, using his bass drum sans snare to repetitively tom-tom away, and pulsing the entire band throughout, his instincts fully displayed and freely expressed. Peterson contributes a wild, muted trumpet solo to convey some sort of jungle or otherwise untamed scene; then Auld zips around on tenor, and his little triplet figures are immediately picked up by Artie, himself flipping skittishly up and down scales and registers. The Bb minor tonality here helps give "Savage" a certain blues quality, too, and it really winds, slips, and flows all over the place! In the latter part one can imagine dancers of the time fiercely jitterbugging, as the band grows ever wilder, and Artie lets his high clarinet wail all over it.

Of course Mr. Shaw didn't much like those jitterbuggers, to put it mildly. But according to Rich and others, this was a great part of his band's appeal that year; i.e., both listeners and dancers got what they wanted, and Shaw could pretty well cover the entire waterfront with this great swing organization of his. "Serenade to a Savage" isn't, however, quite as chance-taking as "Traffic Jam," even if again, it represents a clear shift of gears from the other four songs, all tear-jerkers made in that session of 6/22/39. And it certainly shows off Shaw's versatility as the ultimate shaper, the "final cut" man for this group—a key reason standards are so high and the results so pleasing here. In the same way, and to analogize, Jerry Seinfeld would be the ultimate "final cut" man on his immensely popular sitcom of the '90s. Too many suits spoil the creative broth? So it too often seems in our own period, but thankfully, not in Shaw's heyday. And yes, if he was indeed unique in the swing pantheon, one must also salute more generally the decidedly authoritarian, but creative band leadership of the Dorseys, Goodmans, or Ellingtons of the time, when such strong types could set the entire tone and personality for their contingents. And of course while Shaw was recording in Hollywood during its own golden age, there were real autocrats of the film world also bringing veto power to whatever finally emerged in pictures still so frequently deemed watchable. For the players in these bands, and for actors and actresses, too, there were real downsides to that almost dictatorial mindset, no question; but for the public, pluses as well.

In sum, paradox seems a key word when it comes to such musical greats as Artie Shaw. His very contradictions, amply on display just in his clarinet solos alone, were what helped make his swing fare at this point so unique. If we return to "I Poured My Heart...," where Forrest first sings, and then the band taking over seems deceptively set to conclude, before Shaw's gorgeous bridge solo, we see this paradoxical element manifested. That solo, and so many others by him, combines both simplicity and complexity, aggressiveness and sensitivity, strength and fragility, among other such contrastive traits. Was Shaw a romantic player and shaper of bands, such as in his most popular 1939 aggregation? No question. But in his marriages were there too many reports of downright abominable behavior to be coincidental or simply "he said/she said?" No question of that either.

In a more biographical treatment of this great musician, that sort of material would be placed more prominently in the foreground. One can't excuse such behavior, but more paradoxes inhered even in the Shaw of his often-rocky relationships. One is that types like Ava Gardner or Evelyn Keyes, having both suffered repetitively from his "moods" (to put it charitably), also remained friends of sorts after the marriages were long over, and still cared deeply about Artie all the way through, including what we might call his soul. But for us again his music remains the focus here, and to put it pithily, the world would have been much poorer in that realm had Artie never made these records at all.

A long break from this recording whirlwind ensued, due to the aforementioned film being made, then an exhausting series of live appearances in August, moving the band back eastward to places like Kansas City, Chicago, Detroit, and finally the Ritz-Carlton debut in Boston and that catastrophic event at the Boston Commons, which we previously sketched in its terrifying effects. This was one of the times when Shaw was scratched up by hyper-eager, over-physical, boundary-breaking fans. And when he subsequently sounded off—not really as an ingrate or paranoiac—about what he perceived as their stupid, even moronic traits!

Shaw and band then came back to a base in Manhattan, before some other touring in states like Pennsylvania and Ohio. And he got back to recording in the Apple, too, thankfully so. In his band's studio session of 8/27/39, the batch of six sides cut included three with Forrest vocals, which again, shouldn't be demeaned, given the period. Songs like "The Last Two Weeks of July" gave her material that Shaw sometimes downplayed himself, but which holds up today. How so? Well, on that number, the lyrics tell another love story of sorts, with Forrest completely apt, along with Artie's own dark-chocolate clarinet that so influenced her. And the band sounds happy, forthright, and pretty here, too. Pastor's vocal on "Put That Down in Writing" (treating the desire for an enduring marriage) also tells a story, if more humorously. And Artie's solo there goes from rather simple triad outlines to leaps into the higher register with relaxed élan, yet remaining well within carefully thought-out limitations.

A better-known song cut at that session was "Day In, Day Out." It also features a Forrest vocal and more than competes with other versions of the ditty, not least due to Shaw's warm clarinet contribution here. Artie begins with small, elegantly phrased individual lines, bringing out the heartfelt quality in the tune. The little four-bar intro to the vocal is a treat, as is his sign-off lick at the end of the piece.

But the bandleader made sure to complement that group of sides with two that have no singing whatsoever, and which remain absolute marvels. His version of the Gershwins' "Oh Lady Be Good" is so original it becomes almost another song! It's a jazz tour de force, with saxes pulsing at a lively clip, and Buddy flying, too, on a very rapid "drive" interpretation of the tune. The give and take between brass and reeds seems at its swing summit here, with Shaw predicting in various interviews back then that the high and loud era of that type of popular music would soon pass. On "Oh Lady" Artie keeps darting in with forthright, insistent, and at times almost screaming clarinet work, determined to be a main part of the dialogue, so to speak. Auld on tenor also explores with real jazz feeling here, reflecting Buddy's view that he was a worthy peer of the greatest players in that period. But this "Oh Lady Be Good" really excels by virtue of the entire arrangement, exciting and even electrifying, and with a whole skein of surprises, including a Rich drum solo, then Artie and Buddy "speaking" to each other (clarinet to hides) in a back-and-forth manner. Finally, Shaw lets himself go basically alone, soaring to the alpine summits, but still in his sensual, warm way even on such thin-aired peaks, where other players would be starting back down toward base camp, utterly defeated. This was another of those jitterbug tunes extraordinaire in the Shaw version, and yet, the second standout made at this session constitutes its complete and utter opposite.

On this B-side "I Surrender Dear," Shaw cribs from an old arrangement which his pre–"Beguine" band had played in a somewhat more meager fashion. In the present version his ultra-sad, even morose, but pretty clarinet at the outset, taking a couple of leisurely choruses, to me seems the purest, most essential Artie of the time. One can readily use adjectives like poignant and even slightly diffident here, but listeners would do best just to play this "I Surrender," savoring the work of a whole-souled master on it. The saxes, too, are gorgeous here, due again to how Artie oriented and wrote for them; and Kitsis' piano solo is also appropriate for this melancholy masterpiece. Finally to the fore comes elegant, mature brass, and Artie climbing back and forth to bring things to a close in truly unique fashion. Many years later he remained astounded by his tour de force playing here, including a signature hang on the highest-register F, rollercoaster descents, and the like. But even while recording at the studio he had no idea quite where his concluding clarinet cadenza would go, and yet wind up about where he wanted it to be! Yet it somehow worked, and this "I Surrender Dear" has to be considered one of the foremost and most affecting records made by that great Shaw orchestra; even while its head man increasingly wanted to drop this polished outfit for good![8]

The anxieties and emotional tug-of-war inside had simply gotten too strong for Artie, and a larger and larger part of him wanted to leave the big money (never his primary concern) behind, along with an entire organization he'd brought to a kind of apogee, one still much appreciated by the public. Dealing with all the practical types in suits and with myriad, intrusive "civilians" had put him well over his head, and he knew it. Which is perhaps one reason that for the first time since "Beguine," Artie began moving to recording sessions of four, rather

**Artie Shaw's solo clarinet cadenza on "I Surrender Dear," 1939 (courtesy Samantha Wright).**

than five or six sides at a time. And he was choosing slower and easier fare, too, with *in medias res* vocals more frequent as well.

After the band hit the Strand Theatre September 22 for the beginning of a fortnight's stay there, Shaw survived yet another taste of pandemonium, when nitwits whacking into his clarinet and threatening his teeth seemed truly dangerous, making him unload again on jitterbuggers. Only when the band began an extended engagement at the Café Rouge of Manhattan's Hotel Pennsylvania did it seem to have a safer musical home of sorts. "Seem" being the operative word....

Meanwhile, a recording session of 9/28/39 had the same cohesive band basically intact (except for trumpeter Best migrating to Glenn Miller and replaced by Geller); but as it turned out, on an autumnal precipice of sorts, so redolent of that season. There is a stately quality in this work, as if the orchestra itself realizes both its utter maturity and its ephemeral nature as well. The four sides cut on that September 28 of early wartime included three Forrest vocals, all predictably romantic, and which certain cynics or ironizers might be tempted to write off as what used to be called "schmaltz." But in fact, Shaw's romantic inclination remained prominent in his work and in the Swing Era, too. It was a key ingredient in who he was musically, and those who value that quality will love this work, as they do when watching old, emotion-laden films of the time (think simply of "Gone with the Wind").

These waxings of 9/28/39 include a Shaw–Arthur Quenzer original, "Without a Dream to My Name," sung by Forrest, and sweetly. But the romantic standout is a little-known tune by Sam Coslow and Dana Suesse, "A Table in a Corner," which softer hearts among us will truly savor in the AS rendering. It's downright gorgeous, and the contrast here to so much contemporary work is a huge one, indeed.

"Table" treats a budding love in a fine supper club–type milieu, with the man and woman obviously dressed formally, as of course Shaw always was, too, while leading his band. By contrast, think of so many musical groups today featuring members aggressively dressed down, wearing ratty, worn T-shirts and purposely impoverished-looking, and with miens of a baleful, portentous taint. There is little romance extant in such contemporary work at all; rather, these are musicians purveying themselves as rebels, but without any real causes. And very often, featuring "product" that seems to have nothing to do with making a woman or man happy at all. And though it's not politically correct to note, widespread weed use both by today's band players and listeners has obviously helped dull that quality in American music, too, starting in a big way back in the '60s, and only intensified since. (As a side note: Artie did try marijuana himself with this '38-'39 band; and according to a well-known anecdote, he thought he was really rocking on the stand, till a sideman, himself a user, told him how badly he was doing, and that he should desist!)[9]

Regaining the thread, do try "A Table in a Corner," with its melody that may haunt certain contemporary listeners, and with this Shaw band as majestic here as a fine fall day in Central Park. That band sets the tone at the outset, and then comes Artie for two lovely choruses, establishing the melody in his own manner, his clarinet pretty and "clean," as he would later call it, and yes, *très romantique*. On the bridge plungered brass is discreet, too, but then grows stronger along with the reeds when regaining the main air, building toward Forrest's entry. There ensues her appropriately heartfelt vocal about a couple in the corner of this classy place, with the lyrics themselves bearing a linguistic classiness, too, which back then rivaled the "gold standard" Brits, to whom Americans still felt somewhat inferior culturally. This fictional couple is alone, very happy with each other, touching hands beneath their table, hearing a violin behind them; and yes, it's an innocent and sweet kind of love, with of course the pornography revolution and such far ahead in the American future. After Forrest's vocal, Auld gives his own sweeping statement on tenor, and the natural, disciplined, and beautiful band seems to be concluding, till Artie steps in once more with dramatic verve to draw the proceedings to a signature sign-off.

Elegance? This tune and this band so much in sync with the times provide that quality in spades. Try it!

"If What You Say Is True" from that late September session also has nice lyrics, and a band more and more reining in the power it has, and still implying something like: "There's more here if you want it, but we choose to breast our musical cards, making less emphatically more." Pastor sings here in a high-pitched voice, not so humorously as on some of his vocals, but not quite conveying a romantic love theme, either, as Forrest (and Shaw) do more readily. But Artie's clarinet sound and jazz work following the vocal remain characteristically unique, as unmistakable as Renoir's or Rubens' painting style.

A month later (10/26/39) came another clutch of four in studio, including a slow, sweet "Love Is Here" co-written by Shaw (Goodman, by contrast, was not at all known as a popular composer of tunes). As usual, the great preponderance of songs making up Shaw's *oeuvre* of the era—including this one—emanated from Jewish-American songwriters, one of the key reasons they were often romantic and so right for his interpretations. Many of these Jews were first- or second-generation, i.e., recently emergent from the Central and East European strictures and ghettoization that had persisted for well over a thousand years, and longing for and valuing romance, which again, we've so lost in current popular music. The synergy with someone like Shaw (and his band) was exactly right back then, and the public universally validated it, too, which became an ever less automatic phenomenon for Artie later in the '40s.

Of course the heritage of New England puritanism was still strong enough in America to make love in such tunes almost the entire ballgame, and a very welcome change for the usually prim. But again, love generally denuded of anything one could call prurient. All that would have to await the rock 'n' roll revolution, with an emphasis that only grew through the wild '60s, '70s and beyond. Sure, a Hollywood elite was into multiple divorces and such back in the Swing Era—not least, one Artie Shaw himself! But all that was not yet "Main Street," and divorces were still quite rare. And it needs to be emphasized that the romantic element in many of these recordings was not at all put on, either. Women (in lyrics of the time) were often out of reach, devastatingly beautiful, even celestial. Anything like mainstream feminism was also not central as yet. Have we therefore tossed out baby with the proverbial bathwater? To a degree, perhaps. Hence the deeply nostalgic value of what a bandleader like Shaw accomplished in this era with his emotion-provoking music that will still bring feelings to listeners of the 2000s.

## Two. Shaw at His Apex

Those emotions come sharply to the fore in that batch of songs recorded October 26, 1939, including in the Shaw original "Love Is Here," co-written with Quenzer. It's a beautiful, slow-paced melody, and starts with Artie's gentle, unadorned clarinet work backed discreetly by the rhythm section, but with a nice lilt and real finesse. The result is clear and beautiful, if somewhat sad-sounding, too. The saxes are sumptuous here, and like no other reeds section of the period. And Helen sings the lyrics regarding the outset of another budding love emotionally, too. Always a good judge of talent, Shaw simply let her be in the way she wanted to interpret such songs. As he did with Auld, who was now taking pretty well all the tenor solos, and warm and draggy himself in his stint after the vocal on this "Love...."

Auld's heard again on "All in Fun," as is Forrest (treating yet another love affair that blooms where it didn't seem initially possible). However, the absolute romantic standout in this group, even though a B-side to "All in Fun," is a Kern-Hammerstein song that became a standard after Shaw recorded it so memorably during this autumn of '39. We're referring to his version of "All the Things You Are," and everything noted above about what went into such songs, including on the celestial quality of woman back then, holds absolutely true here. Artie's band interprets this one with sweeping authority, starting with a brief Kitsis piano intro, then Shaw's magnificent, sweet, but complex clarinet work unrolling the carpet of Kern's melody, his first chorus more or less sticking to the tune; the second using marvelous chords that will simply stir any heart that's ready to be stirred! Shaw isn't just a virtuoso here, though that he was; but also part of a greater whole, and in his lovely solo also paving the way for Forrest's entry. No wonder his future father-in-law loved this rendering of his song. It's definitive! The saxes on the bridge, *Shaw's* saxes (as his sidemen concurred), point beautifully upward, the stately brass regains the song's main melody, and the whole product reeks not only of taste, but of melancholy, partly because we now know that this AS band, arguably his best, was soon to be history. Yes, no more Buddy Rich, set to become a featured player with TD; no more Pastor, who would move on to front his own band; and no more Forrest, who would writhe under Goodman's leadership, then migrate to more stardom with Harry James during wartime. But Forrest's vocal on "All the Things You Are" should not at all be discounted or damned with faint praise. It's natural and right for such a pretty tune, with Hammerstein's poetic lyrics full of longing and awe, and again, about womanhood super-idealized. Question-and-answer brass and reed work follows her stint, but all done with suitable restraint, enhancing the overall effect.

The most contrastive offering in this batch of October 26 becomes a real foil for "All the Things..." and the other two romantic tunes mentioned. But "You're a Lucky Guy" is also one worth knowing, featuring an uplifting, emphatically less relaxed pace, and Buddy propelling the snappy band work with his forthright drumming. The saxes here are more staccato than on the slower, moodier pieces, and Pastor sings with full happiness about a Depression-era fella who ought to be happy with the lady who loves him, despite their lack of cash. A fine Shaw solo follows, swinging, short, and inventive, mimicking Pastor's demi-scat work, then sliding back into recognizable AS licks. The record ends with that sprightliness which made it apt for the era's jitterbuggers, the ones who so frequently disturbed Artie on the stand.

Two weeks later, as it turned out, came the last session of four recordings made by this great swing outfit, and one can already feel premonitions here of Shaw's grand, courageous escape later that November. How so? One reason: the perfunctory quality of his band's versions of two Cole Porter tunes included here. These are the A-side "Do I Love You" and B-side "When Love Beckoned (on 52nd Street)," which are among my least favorite in the entire canon of that great '38-'39 Shaw contingent. It seems as if Artie himself knew inside that it finally *was* time to bolt, even at the peak of his popular success. (And not due to the outbreak of a new world war in Europe, which hadn't yet touched America, but which had already toppled countries like Poland and was threatening a number of others in Europe.)

Of the other two discs in this last batch cut by the '39 band, one is a marvelous, sad, impressionistic version of Frankie Carle's "Shadows," far and away our top choice here. But as original as it is, the AS "Shadows" also seems to portend that surprising close-down of this important band. There is an almost reluctant, held-in tone on display here, with the saxes in an unfamiliar, linear mode at the outset and the trumpets also tamped down. Against that almost hazy quality, painting a picture of, well, "shadows," Shaw's clarinet solo eventually ensues, and it's simply remarkable and beautiful, even unbelievable. As he could do on certain records, he almost rewrites the song, his dramatic, rhythmic slurring, his "talking" and searching quality all revealed here. Professional musicians will note some odd chord changes throughout the piece, and in Shaw's bewitching solo work, too, providing unusual ideas and colors here. At the end the band becomes unexpectedly but briefly strong again. It's hard to believe that this fabulous arrangement of "Shadows" would soon become among the last in a Shaw edition that would never in later start-ups sound nearly the same (for both good and ill).

By contrast, the B-side, "I Didn't Know What Time It Was" (by Rodgers and Hart), starts with Artie putting forth the melody in a sprightly, joyous manner through two pretty but fairly expectable choruses, sounding, however, via quick vibrato rather like a high-register cello. And then come those Shavian saxes with their own quick, almost nervous vibrato, giving the listener so much. Forrest sings about another love appearing out of nowhere and making things suddenly add up. Auld follows with his tenor solo, and then the band finishes things off, at its seemingly effortless apogee.

How then did the end come for this topflight orchestra of the Swing Era? The story has been told and retold, so a certain brevity seems in order here, though it remains typically Artie, interesting and revealing about his fundamental character mix. One of his besetting tendencies at this or any craft he embraced was his obsessive perfectionism, and there is inevitably a great price to be paid for that. His interest back then, as he would later say so often in interviews, was only in making fine music; but he felt the business demands were getting ever more deleterious, the travel, too, and of course the fans who gave him "celebrity" treatment he never wanted, which increasingly interfered with what this cerebral man wished to produce musically. Another part of the problem was that as fine-tuning and downright fussy as he was, once committed to a project or band (and that meant *emotionally* committed, too), Shaw was also a true jazz player and person. That is, he was someone who loved to go off at unforeseen tangents and be spontaneous. Most bluntly put, he had gotten into a real rut as the year progressed, compounded by the fact that all the pressures on him had contributed to that severe illness he'd been fortunate to overcome, and at the least, to continuing bad headaches and other neurotic symptoms of a deep-seated malaise. And Artie, as his extensive marital resumé certainly shows, was not one for ruts!

Additionally, he felt that conventional swing bands of that era were on the way out (much as Bobby Darin would feel about rock when he moved from records like "Splish Splash" toward crooning circa 1960). Shaw had always had a wish to add more philharmonic-type instruments to the swing mix, particularly a string section, which hadn't worked out for him the first time around back in 1936. But most fundamentally, he was plain exhausted. As in the later Glen Campbell hit "Wichita Lineman," Shaw, too, desired a vacation, and badly. So that when such a person got off a treadmill, he got off! And into the bargain, he'd also escape what he often called the celebrity fishbowl. That was his way: either one was fully committed, and when it came to music, emotionally, too; or one completely pulled the plug.

Beyond all that was a person here who kept wondering whether the field of popular music, any of it, was really for him at all. Part of Shaw wanted badly to complete his education, perhaps to become a professor, and certainly a writer (when there was time, Artie loved seeking out and befriending literary luminaries like Theodore Dreiser or Sinclair Lewis). Part of him wanted more; maybe all of him always wanted more! Thankfully (for us) that "more" had remained well within his chosen discipline, the one he'd negotiated so wonderfully. He once told me that a person does the most good in life by being selfish. Well, he'd certainly been so absorbed with his work and that of his fellow players that today's YouTubers have a treasure trove of his fine, polished swing records to savor, ones that no one could replicate in our time. For certain this was an immense and wonderful gift that Shaw left from that heady period of '38-'39. By contrast none of his post–1950 literary and intellectual work compels so much, nor in a larger sense would his eventual assumption of the primacy of language and cognition over music, which is so very different. Why again would he eventually move so far from this one base, so to speak, to one at the opposite end of the diamond that was totally different? All this perplexed many, and not least, Shaw himself for a large swath of his long life; but thankfully, all that was far ahead, and there was more superb, eminently listenable recorded music to come, only of a very different sort from that of the AS brigade of 1939. But the sound of that most popular band of his was now to be stilled for good, never to be recovered.[10] At this point in his career, Shaw and Heraclitus were at one; i.e., you couldn't go back into the same river twice.

Near to its demise, the Shaw orchestra had been featured on a regular basis at that seemingly sedate Café Rouge of New York's Hotel Pennsylvania; but even in such rarefied circumstances, bigmouths, some of them drunks, who hassled the band and its leader still went with the territory.[11] And on the evening of November 14, 1939, one such self-server got to Artie big time, as a heckler of sorts trying to be grandiose for his date. In response the already frayed bandleader completely lost it, striding off the stand at 11 p.m., handing the orchestra over to Tony Pastor, and regaining his room, deciding he would soon pack! When the band was done playing, he summoned his sidemen and Ms. Forrest up to his room to explain his need to split, though they—and soon his agent, Tommy Rockwell, and lawyer Andrew Weinberger, rushing over from their homes—tried hard to dissuade him from this impulsive idea. Weinberger especially pushed hard, explaining that Shaw still had a contract for a few more weeks to honor. A young songwriter, Sammy Cahn, then Artie's friend, went up to his room, too, and tried to make the bandleader feel guilty about hurting all his players and their families, along with his singer, Forrest. He wanted to make Shaw feel that he couldn't break up this great contingent because it would adversely affect so many in his orbit. But Artie simply didn't want the band anymore, ill effects on any humans around him notwithstanding. Money concerns and commitments now seemed negligible to him.

After wrangling most of the night, the incredulous "suits" and everyone else still there finally gave in; and several days later (November 18) a liberated Shaw got into his red Packard, driving all the way to Arkansas, where he called his pal Judy Garland from Little Rock about his idea of roosting and recuperating in L.A. for a while. Ever protective, she flatly warned Artie that media hounds would be all over him there, and that he would find no peace at all in Southern California. This helped him decide to keep going southward and westward to Mexico, where he located a peaceful, out-of-the-way fishing village called Acapulco. For an exhausted Shaw it was blessedly no tourist trap back then, and in the cliché, just what the doctor ordered.[12]

There he stayed through the late fall and into early winter, while back home Georgie Auld tried to run the AS organization as a "ghost band," one that made little money and predictably, broke up in short order (early in 1940). Its players all scattered—Pastor to lead his own band and never again to play with his old buddy, Auld along with Robinson and Forrest to Goodman, etc. Even Artie's fine arranger Jerry Gray, whom he'd once nurtured at that craft, became a key contributor to the popular sound of Glen Miller's orchestra, where he also wrote songs that became hits like "A String of Pearls."[13]

Meanwhile, Shaw savored an extended and truly pleasant break in the action. He fished, one of his later passions, swam, and checked out the local music scene at night. He also broke a leg in the ocean, saving an American girl who seemed to be drowning there. Finally, in mid–January 1940 he flew to L.A., regaining his Hollywood home there, while thinking now of scoring for movies, but absolutely *not* of mounting another orchestra, with all the problems he knew that would entail.

However, he still owed Victor six contracted sides, needed income, and was finally getting tired of leisure. But what he came back with musically in a Hollywood recording session cum studio players constituted for any listener immersed in the previous Shaw band's work a huge shock! Yes, an utter, astonishing, and super-contrastive *shock*!

# Three

# The Second Great Shaw Orchestra
## 1940-41

No question that Artie Shaw was protean and also unpredictable. He himself would say he was afflicted with a real curiosity bump. An artist who never liked to stand pat, he sought to evolve, more so than most other swing band leaders. And yet the new Shaw orientation was so utterly different from the previous stringless one that it's hard to listen to them cheek by jowl, due to the aforementioned shock factor. However, he again came up with something that was musically major, important, and truly listenable.

To which some might say: Well look at Beatles fare pre-drugs and what followed in the *Rubber Soul*, then *Sgt. Pepper* era. Weren't they protean, too? Didn't they (with George Martin's exemplary guidance and production values) add more instrumentation and other original touches that took them well beyond their earlier and simpler brand of rock 'n' roll? Absolutely. But despite such comparisons, one is still jolted by how greatly Shaw had changed, and again, much more radically and adventurously than his swing confreres, who stayed more reliably in the same kinds of musical grooves.

Did Artie ever regret losing his '38-'39 band's feel and sound, and for the long haul? Intermittently throughout his post-music life (from the fall of '54) he would indeed express regrets on that score. Mainly, he argued that at the height of celebrity he hadn't been able to talk out his problems with anyone and stay put—yes, he expressed this quite iteratively. Here was a man who always knew how to adapt in life and move forward in interesting, fruitful ways; but one who was also clawed all the way through by these nagging regrets.

Excuse a tangential aside, but I've often been puzzled at Artie's answer to a question someone posed him during his elderly years, well after he'd left the world of professional music, and to this effect: "Was there anything you would have changed in your life to date?" Shaw answered bluntly that he would have started out with a different set of parents! This was an arresting response, indeed. On one hand, I suppose, this is the dramatic Shaw always desiring attention, as he did (and got) with the many musical surprises that are found in one recording of his after another. But I think there was also sincerity and, again, a certain regret in this answer. Some might think it pertains only to the music, i.e., the way Shaw wished audiences could have simply followed him through all his twists and turns in that realm. But I think it applies as well to his life trajectory "domestically." We know that Artie often felt after the early departure of his father that his mother lived through her celebrated son, acting almost as a wife to him; and all this aroused in him real incestuous concerns and fears. To him she increasingly became a tent personality (my term), one he wanted to keep away from but could never completely abandon. And this is a key reason that despite getting more than a few beautiful women to fall in love with him and care deeply, he could not perpetuate anything like a durable marriage or relationship with any of them. And in terms of his two sons, he was also nothing approaching a good father, either. This regret might have been equal to that regarding his musical evolution and how people responded to his work or didn't; but of course there was a big and crucial paradox here—that without all the angst and pain stemming from his only-child upbringing, and his bumptious father simply taking off in his early teens, and yes, his mother's personality, too, we would never have had such emotionally satisfying music from one Arthur Shaw! (Analogously, how much do we owe re the quality of Beethoven's great musical *oeuvre* to his abusive, drunken, exploitative father? Without such suffering, would his Seventh Symphony and so much else that he composed have had such soul and depth? Doubtful.)

Returning to Shaw's own substantial musical contributions, "Frenesi" (cut March 3, 1940) constituted a great surprise not only to critics and listeners, but to Artie himself! And this pertains to how it succeeded so hugely with the buying public. As they develop, great artists never quite know what will "hit," and in this case Shaw certainly didn't at all.

Using a large ensemble in Hollywood filled with studio players and featuring numerous—and for that time, adventurous—strings (violins, viola, celli), plus instruments like oboe, flute, bass clarinet, and French horn, as well as the usual Swing Era brass and reeds, Shaw's sound here was revolutionary. Of course he did have some big names for the solo work, such as Manny Klein on trumpet and in the background, honchos like Bobby Sherwood on guitar. Another surprise from that landslide reception for this new offering came from Artie using this tune he'd heard in Mexico and which he felt (to his great financial cost) was just a folk song; and unfortunately failing to make a proper deal with its author. The reverse side of the record also came from his stay in Acapulco and his immersion in things Latino—"Adios Marquita." Shaw hoped the latter might give him some modest sales on the record, and thus made it the A-side; but "Frenesi"? Though RCA did put this record on its better, pricier Victor label (after Bluebird), Artie never saw "Frenesi" coming like a runaway freight train, resonating so pervasively with the 1940 American populace that it became a gold record and number one hit, matching "Beguine" in that regard. This was the Shaw who had been thinking he'd completely give up bandleading and simply contribute music for movie soundtracks. Now he was coming back onto what he considered a treadmill, and still of course as a handsome and famous celebrity. Which helped him lure one Lana Turner to marriage at that time, a mixed blessing for both of them!

Artie Shaw and Lana Turner. Their 1940 marriage didn't last long (Alamy/Masheter Movie Archive).

He had met Turner while making that film with the previous band—a film, as noted, that he'd found inane. Back then he hadn't fixated on this pretty actress, but in February 1940 his buddy Phil Silvers took him to a movie set where she was working, and this time Artie was smitten. He apparently talked to her about home and family, but later mentioned Hollywood's codes and more generally, American mores in that period, and the need to marry in order to have what one wanted. On impulse Shaw proposed immediately, flying a compliant Turner on a charter plane to Vegas to get hitched, and then, within days, both discovered they were really strangers. She couldn't fathom his increasing fits of anger, including throwing the spaghetti she'd prepared for him and two friends onto the floor, then ordering her into the bargain to scour that floor clean, given what a lousy meal she'd had the temerity to offer them! Wanting to meet her mother-in-law when in New York, she had to do so on the sly, and that also enraged him. After divorce proceedings began within a mere four months or so, Lana's pregnancy elicited Artie's snide questions re her fidelity, neurotic doubts that seem right out of Strindberg's *The Father*, and which along with the abortion she then had in sordid circumstances, basically ended her love of this celebrated musician.[1]

Again, we are trying to avoid a purely biographical treatment here, and would love it if only the sweet, innovative music Shaw made was all there was in and to this man. But genius is often quirky, to say the least, one of the reasons "Frenesi" constituted the musical tsunami emphasized here, due to that revolutionary mixture (for the era) of a decidedly symphonic sound with swing, plus mariachi effects, too. It was a concoction that came together far better than even Shaw himself thought it would.

"Frenesi" starts out with ponderous, eddying strings leading the way, but setting the table for Artie's clarinet, which had miraculously adapted and sounds even more lush than in the '38-'39 aggregation, as he spins out the tune's melody. Yes, there is some jazz feeling here, but an incongruous French horn in the middle provides unique solo work, Morton Ruderman's perky flute has its moment, too, and Artie, back in after the bridge with another unlacing beauty of a solo, adds to the atmosphere, as does the large ensemble, presenting a brief swath with a swing-like feeling. However, the strings return and so does that decidedly philharmonic sound, which was so new for big band lovers. Even the piano solo by Stan Wrightsman has a stately, almost eighteenth-century quality, and indeed, in a number of spots, "Frenesi" sounds almost like it comes out of that era of men in powdered wigs clomping around and taking snuff, ladies tightly corseted and in extravagant gowns, and amiable fires blazing in the grates! It sounds like something at one with the French plays of Marivaux, or the atmosphere of German castles and British country estates back then; and there is a general "chamber music" feel here in parts of the number, where Shaw, along with co-arranger William Grant Still, obviously tried to inflict large and novel contrasts on what turned out to be (at least in this case) many willing listeners.[2]

Both classical and jazz musicians will appreciate touches in "Frenesi," such as Shaw's first solo dancing (for an eventual 16 bars), as if with leaps on one foot, then the other, and finally fluttering to the figurative floor in delight. Additionally, there is midway through the piece a solo cymbal "announcement" of sorts (unusual for this era of pop music), and a brief part that resembles a swath of the Shostakovich *oeuvre*; plus a two-bar group turned on its head with threes and twos, the confusion of a waltz with foxtrot pace, and the humor, too, that Still, in particular, tossed in from his high-culture background mixed with the liberating "low." Even Shaw's last teasing solo brings to mind a candy shop of taffy-pulling delight that doesn't really mirror what he'd done in the "Beguine" band. In sum, there was more than enough originality here, along with melodious warmth to interest both pros and average listeners of that era, and well beyond that period, too.

Was Shaw unusual in trying to assimilate aspects of European classical music into America's swing genre? Most definitely, and especially when compared to other bandleaders like the Dorseys, Count Basie, and so forth, though of course Goodman was immersed in "longhair" music, too (his recorded version of Mozart's Concerto for Clarinet still a standout). More generally, composers like Kern, Romberg, Arlen and the rest were saturated in that European, "high-culture" musical past. A positive point in such American artists back then was how they still felt their work was somewhat inferior to what came from more seasoned countries across the pond, ones that had produced Scarlattis and Beethovens, Strausses and Stravinskys; and in trying to base themselves on all that, but do original things, too, they gave us all so much that was unexpectedly distinctive, accessible, and enduringly classy. In this sense Shaw was a part of an at least somewhat highbrow American strand back then. But to reiterate our main point, his musical originality seen in "Frenesi" was far ahead of and beyond the entire Swing Era pack of bandleaders. (If still part of the swing canon.)

At that recording session of 3/3/40 and a subsequent one in Hollywood (May 13), Artie continued with a slew of studio mainstays, including those classically-trained string players, and with his own lush, legato clarinet remaining a key virtuosic feature—and still somewhat different and evolved from what it had been in his previous band. Just as Shaw seemed to have a taste for discovering new kinds of women on the horizon, so he also moved along musically, and that was definitely seen in the timbre and general quality of his always remarkable clarinet contributions. Of course other pros—including the man from Brockton, Mass., Dick Johnson, who took the often-demanding clarinet parts in a reformed 1980s Shaw band—could play these notes, too, or most of them; but never sounding at all like Shaw, or shall we say (given that surprising evolution on the instrument that Artie displayed), "Shaws."

In the recorded bunch of 5/13/40, Artie's work seems at one with a growingly more romantic and reflective mood in the States, well seen in its movies of the era. Wartime abroad, searing and serious wartime, was obviously part of the reason, and the fact that the U.S. was on the brink of its own entry into that terrible conflict. Perhaps Shaw was prescient in leaving a more jumping band behind and in the present session, emphatically laying on more schmaltz, such as on "Now We Know," including a vocal from Martha Tilton with typical lyrics for the time. Tilton was a Goodman alumna who had glittered on the Ziggy Elman vehicle "And the Angels Sing," one of those rare BG biggies without any clarinet work featured at all. Before she comes in on this Shaw offering, the eddying strings take the melody against suitably hushed brass (which otherwise would have overwhelmed those less dynamically powerful instruments). Artie's warm clarinet is even more romantic than in the '38-'39 era, and of course the lyrics sung by Tilton are so much a part of that rather naïve American *geist* of the time; but still listenable. Gorgeous ensemble work and Artie's equally lovely clarinet conclude the number following the vocal.

This "Now We Know" was never one of my favorites, but co-author Read senses the healthy effect here of Artie's Mexican respite. He finds the combination of strings and Tilton deeply nostalgic, and considers the clarinet intro sweet and inviting, with the strings amply continuing the mood in a long interlude. He does find Artie rather inward and even tentative here, but argues that his chromatic chord changes work, with the resultant effect of a casual, offhand melancholy so redolent of films from that period.

A better-known tune, Vernon Duke's "April in Paris," gets a more remarkable Shaw treatment in the same session. The arrangement by Bobby Sherwood has AS fingerprints all over both the initial sketches and final product; and it's masterly and again, downright lovely and evocative. Violins, etc., introduce the number in their sweet or what more cynical types might call saccharine manner (one keeps thinking again of movie scores from that period); then those whirlpool-like strings vie with suitably stoppered brass, and a French horn jazz solo ensues, which was again, unusual back then. Brass comes along in a stronger big band manner, but the saxes are tinkling and thinner than they'd been in '39, and all that prepares the way for the great Artie. And his jazz work on this "April" is utterly pretty and full of honey, or so it seems. A piano solo by Skitch Henderson follows, more stately than jazzy, and almost grave. Then Artie's back with that darkly warm licorice stick, making his jazz licks sound characteristically easy, as was often the case; and this becomes a marvelous interpretation of one of the best American songs of the era, a more than worthy take that must surely have pleased its celebrated composer (of "Autumn in New York," "I Can't Get Started," etc.). On this version seasoned musicians will notice a quirky intro with a violin solo, dissonant minor-second interjections (E-Eb), and the trumpets playing a modal version of the melody and creating thereby, a kind of mosaic effect. In addition, Shaw's fine solo work starts on an audacious Ab, then moves to F major. The band resumes with chromatic modulation back to Eb, but Artie concludes simply on his instrument—that simplicity always a key ingredient to go with the complexities denoted here.

These were certainly fine recording sessions, but agents and other business types were now urging Shaw to start up a regular new orchestra of his own. Financial problems also played a role (including in how much "Frenesi" royalty money he lost due to that legal snafu involving its composer). And so he used this large studio-player ensemble as a kind of launching pad. Reluctantly, Artie was now en route to his second major organization of the Swing Era, a great contrast to the first, but just as valuable to today's listeners. This time around it was an orchestra of over 20 pieces, including nine strings, and to fill out the brass and reeds sections Shaw lucked out when Goodman decided to disband his latest contingent off the Southern California coast. Benny was suffering, and quite stoically, from excruciating sciatica pain that was eventually identified as a slipped disc, and he was slated for an impending operation. In June of '40 Shaw came over to Catalina Island and hired a bunch of top men who'd been working with the King of Swing there. These included Bus Bassey and Jerry Jerome on tenor sax, Vernon Brown to go with the great Jack Jenney (and later Ray Conniff) as Shaw trombones; and on alto, Neely Plumb and Artie's ex-stalwart in the reeds section, Les Robinson, who always preferred Artie to Benny. Also from BG's ranks came Billy Butterfield, one of the great lead trumpets of the era, and critical in helping create the sound of this new orchestra. The rotund Charles William Butterfield had originally embraced medical studies, but music won out, and his sumptuous and full trumpet became a central facet in Shaw's present orientation. In the rhythm section, Johnny Guarnieri, a card who liked to dress up like Sherlock Holmes but who also had classical music chops, departed from Benny to become Artie's pianist. Like others Guarnieri was relieved to be away from Goodman and his regular put-downs, including his imitations of other great jazz piano players. Nick Fatool signed on as the new orchestra's drummer, and Jud DeNaut, another sideman who loved working with Artie, as its bass player. Al

Hendrickson provided the buttressing on electric guitar. And the whole cumbrous group soon went into rehearsals, which for Shaw remained very important. The novel orchestral sound was one that depended on delicate blending, a challenge especially when it came to recording in studios that were far less technically advanced than today's. And as usual, pretty well all these players interviewed in older age concurred that they had a superb and fair bandleader here.

Starting July 1, 1940, the new contingent appeared weekly on the *Burns and Allen* radio show, and in August went to work on the film *Second Chorus*, a wan effort featuring Fred Astaire and much music contributed by Artie. Astaire and Burgess Meredith played rival trumpet players in the flick, and Bobby Hackett took the latter's parts, while Butterfield played Astaire's. One scene involving Paulette Goddard shows her soothing an embattled Shaw as a surging crowd tries to engulf him, a theme seemingly drawn from his own turbulent past at the center of popular music.

No question, however: this orchestra was the second to feature a truly distinctive and still enjoyable Shaw brogue of the Swing Era, after that '38-'39 breakout group which had reached the top. The new one was marvelous, too, and right for the times, and by September 1940 was set to make recordings; but as if mounting a large musical organization that quickly developed a distinctive "singing" sound[3] wasn't challenge enough, Shaw decided also to spawn a smaller "band-within-the-band," too. Perhaps he was in part aping Goodman (with his trio, quartet, and then sextet); but in fact, Shaw also felt somewhat handicapped jazz-wise within such a complex contingent as he now helmed. For the smaller group he decided that five players plus himself on clarinet would provide what he desired. The name? "Artie Shaw and His Gramercy Five." (He had taken it from one of New York's telephone exchanges.)

This small group was a liberating departure for Shaw after all the strains and stresses of running a big band in the "Beguine" and post–"Beguine" era. And—would one doubt it?—his Gramercy Five became absolutely unique, and like no other small combo of the time. Shaw was that much the relentless artiste, invariably pushing the envelope.

In this small bunch he had the new instrument of the day, an electric guitar strummed by Hendrickson and given rapid prominence in the hands of Goodman's meteoric and innovative Black player in his sextet, Charlie Christian. Hendrickson's guitar sounds good in the "Five," but obviously primitive and plodding compared to what later emanated from such as a Hendrix or Clapton. To be fair, that instrument was mainly designated for rhythm in the swing period. Along with Hendrickson, there was trumpeter Billy Butterfield here, whom Shaw greatly admired; DeNaut on bass, also grateful for this jazz outlet; Fatool on drums; and Guarnieri, who at Artie's suggestion played harpsichord with the combo, which so helped create its singular quality. The six players rehearsed at Artie's home on Summit Ridge Drive, and then without using any written music, entered a Hollywood studio to record an initial batch of four songs, September 3, 1940. And while gossips preferred to hear about Shaw and his fraught marital life, musical aficionados found this bunch unexpectedly pleasing to the ears.

Its two standouts from this first session include "Summit Ridge Drive," named for Artie's street, and his original composition. It starts out quite provocative and sexy for that era, almost a striptease-type song (akin to Buddy Morrow's later "Night Train"); but then it becomes a more serious jazz vehicle with Shaw and Butterfield leading the way. The latter's trumpet cum plunger sets the pace for Artie to enter with a long, wailing C, persisting till the very last moment in a listener's rhythm expectation, before he then lets it drop. Guarnieri's compact harpsichord work is special, too, deceptive in its apparent simplicity, as he solos against DeNaut's walking-type bass. Johnny's instrument also contributes significantly to the ensemble blend, making this a kind of loose, wild animal to the end, yet also a successful blues piece with an entirely new sound. Basically the arrangement had simply been put together on the fly at Shaw's home, a synergistic effort showing these players having plain fun and enjoying their "vive la différence." (Not least Artie himself.) Nonetheless, "Summit..." made little initial money till re-released later in wartime, when for some reason, it surprisingly racked up sales in major fashion, becoming one of Shaw's gold records, and astonishing him yet again.[4]

One point needs to be underlined concerning Artie's hits: most of them were, indeed, unusual and innovative for their time, or maybe would have been in any period. "Beguine" was certainly a major, idiosyncratic departure from all else in the Swing Era to that point (1938). "Frenesi," with its strings, French horn, oboe, etc., and classical music-cum-swing feel was also, as stressed, something of a shock for that period; but it went through the roof, too. That mix was then somewhat imitated (as the sincerest form of flattery) but never remotely matched when Harry James, Tommy Dorsey and a number of other bandleaders eventually added "fiddles" to their ensembles during wartime. Finally, Shaw's "Summit Ridge Drive" featuring Guarnieri's novel harpsichord became a hit on re-release, and somehow seemed "progressive" for that wartime and even *après-guerre* period, and like nothing else around. True, Shaw did not always go the unusual, off-the-beaten-path way in his music, but in the Swing Era alone, he certainly did so more than his share. And at times it paid off royally (as in royalties!), which is as it ideally should be in this big world of ours; but to Artie's intermittent chagrin, sometimes wasn't (and isn't).

The Gramercy Five's "Keepin' Myself for You," recorded on the same date as "Summit Ridge Drive," features a little-known but fine tune that deserves to be heard today, and it's the other top offering here. "Keepin'..." has a gorgeous melody, and again showcases that compact, wonderful Guarnieri harpsichord, Artie's still lush clarinet (as with the bigger band), and Butterfield on muted trumpet. Shaw keeps taking the spotlight here, truly lovely and moving in his several solos, playing much like a sensual saxophonist. His typical figured, "weaving" style is unmistakable, as much again as a Renoir or Picasso painting. This record is super-tasteful right from the intro of parallel sixths, giving one the feeling that this Gramercy group had been together a long time (which it hadn't). Its 1940 "Keepin'..." is romantic and pretty, and again, worth sampling today. And Artie does seem a bit happier and certainly freer here than in the big band context, where there were more variables to deal with, and problems to overcome.

À propos of this, the novelist and *echt* intellectual Bellow once wrote of low-ceiling and high-ceiling literary masterpieces (as an example of the former he cited Dostoyevsky's *Crime and Punishment*, and for the latter, Proust's multi-volume *Remembrance of Things Past*). That manner of putting it almost encapsulates Shaw's musical direction of late '40, then into '41. Via his Gramercy Five he was making "low-ceiling" records of great quality; but in the much larger orchestral setting would also provide what might be called his "high-ceiling" work, some of it (as will be seen) magisterial, and ultimately, more "re-listenable."

Working regularly on the *Burns and Allen* show, and with extended engagements starting that September at the Palace Hotel in San Francisco and then from Christmastime, L.A.'s Palladium, Shaw didn't seem as frantically overloaded as he'd been when doing a slew of one-nighters and much else at the zenith of his popularity in 1938-39. Still it was quite a Herculean endeavor to make this new orchestra (as much a symphonic ensemble as a big band) ripe for recording, starting with an initial session of four sides on September 7, 1940, only a few days after the previous Gramercy Five waxings. Two of these full-orchestra records feature vocals by Anita Boyer, who passed muster with Shaw but never matched his former "canary," Helen Forrest, both in quantity and quality.

The record that stands out most in this first session for the large aggregation is "Temptation." There is a big nightclub sound here, a quick, skittish tempo to it, but also incongruous slowdowns, engineered especially by those calm and settling, but at other times suitably nervous strings. Artie starts things off with his clarinet also irritably gorgeous, as if being chased by "temptation" itself; but simple/not simple, that dichotomy that was so usual in his work, and still one of the reasons for its appeal. The band's reeds and brass claim the bridge, but then Artie returns in characteristically dramatic fashion; however, the strings bring things back to earth with that sobering and foreboding wartime feel heard in so many pictures back then. Jerry Jerome gets some long freebooting space on tenor, and Artie's capping glissando (not much used since his earlier days on Bluebird) and his almost beseeching high G conclude a rendering that's soft and strong, sensitive and tough, the whole paradoxical mix that made Shaw's work stand out so much. Even key changes here from G minor to G major, then C major contribute to that aesthetic quality.

A month later, on 10/7/40, Shaw and his orchestra were back in a Hollywood studio to cut another batch, this time of five songs. Two were comparatively forgettable (though nothing he did could be called bad), "Danza Lucumi" and "Marinella," the latter co-written by Shaw. But another co-authored tune he put together for the film *Second Chorus* became a record on this date, too, and for some reason, via playing (and replaying) it, can stick in a person's mind as a good romantic offering of the time.

On this song, "Love of My Life," Johnny Mercer contributed the lyrics, which are American-offhand and natural, if a bit hokey; and Shaw the music, which came quickly to him and was again, earmarked for the Astaire flick. But Mercer suggested a wait of several extra weeks before presenting it to the studio biggies, in order to show that the requisite amount of effort had been expended.[5] It's a fine song both for the era and even today, with Artie presenting his now more buttery clarinet work (compared to what it had been in '38-'39) from the top, and with a sprightly meter. The romantic strings are vital here, too, along with emphatic brass and the saxes asserting themselves as a unified section against the fiddles. Artie has a second short stint with his almost saccharine clarinet (I use the adjective positively); then comes Boyer's vocal, with those words that Mercer did so well in an informal style, still quite innocent given what was occurring in besieged Europe, where of course France, Holland and Belgium had fallen in rapid fashion to Nazi panzers and aircraft the previous spring. And where Great Britain was basically alone under Churchill's vital and intrepid leadership. Meanwhile, America was still blessedly exempt, just going ever more romantic and even square, it feels, in its films, and in this Shaw-Mercer tune,

### Three. The Second Great Shaw Orchestra

Fred Astaire (right) and Burgess Meredith (with trumpet) in the movie *Second Chorus*. Artie Shaw and his orchestra of 1940 made significant musical contributions to the film (Alamy/Photo 12).

too, hatched for one of those pictures of the time. (And receiving an Academy Award nomination for best original film song, as Shaw also did for the music score.) In her heartfelt warbling, Boyer reflects that blithe and relatively unperturbed American mood of the era. The band in its "singing" ensemble of strings, brass and reeds sweetly and strongly ushers things out, including via Artie's short bending of his last note as a suitable wave goodbye. This is an arrangement that's easy to underestimate, crafted as many were for this aggregation by Lennie Hayton, but with Artie's input.[6]

Boyer contributes a vocal on another film tune, "A Handful of Stars," and this one, too, is not only romantic, but what some could plausibly call schlocky, and not as memorable as "Love of My Life." "Handful..." seems to bring one a vision of small-town America of that period, and a guy and gal looking up at a fine moon and stars—the same naïveté, in other words, only more so, than in "Love...."

But Shaw always knew when to say, in essence, "enough is enough," and to shift gears in startling fashion. As another side he made that October 7, 1940, far and away the session's best, he picked a great American standard, and this time there was no vocal, though the tune has been much sung over the years. We are talking of his orchestra's magisterial interpretation of "Star Dust," a song Artie had the previous band play with a different arrangement at hotels and such, but which was never recorded in a studio; and in fact, never quite came together as a jazz original, either.

On this occasion Artie cut a decidedly different "Star Dust" with his new contingent, and knew on the day he made it that in his view, it was nothing less than a classic. And he wasn't being immodest. Of course there were other sensational "Star Dusts" already extant. In terms of the Henderson-arranged version for Goodman's band, I've valued it most as an air check from the great '37-'38 era and put on a '50s LP, with vociferous applause heard at the end. That one's another standout, and done at an unexpectedly rapid pace. *Pace* some possible put-downs of BG in our treatment, it's remarkable to this day, and shows off the King of Swing at his absolute peak. More well known was the dulcet effort in the era now under discussion presented by TD and his Pied Pipers, featuring Jo Stafford and a skinny young gent named Sinatra.

But the AS "Star Dust" of 1940 remains unique and really, an American jewel. Hoagy Carmichael apparently wrote it at the University of Indiana after being jilted by a young gal there, and this Shaw version amply honors the tune's stately quality of romantic longing. But it is plain great music, and yet in some ways not really typical of this fine new symphonic swing organization he was now helming. And that's because there isn't much ensemble work here at all, though backgrounds provided by the orchestra are certainly tasteful. Instead, this is a solo-driven masterpiece, starting from the outset with Butterfield's full, gorgeous trumpet giving us a long skein of jazz licks (but not too many) on the famed melody. It's something one has to hear and hear, which of course many have already done. Billy's horn is lovely and forthright on this number through to a short break by the careful, sweet strings. Then he's back to finish the main air once through, as the virtuoso he was, along with the band's suave and accomplished leader.[7]

The saxes then briefly set the table for Artie's clarinet now to take the spotlight, and his solo on this 1940 "Star Dust" is without a doubt, one of his greatest and most moving ever. Here he doesn't just lay on legato emotion, but instead climbs up to the empyrean, and yet his tone remains lovely, clear, and seemingly at ease a good octave above where most clarinet players would feel at all comfortable.[8] It's a remarkably beautiful offering, a kind of culmination or virtuosic harvest, if you will, after decades of hard work on the instrument. Again, Shaw makes what is enormously difficult sound deceptively facile, and certainly unique in the annals of American jazz—a hefty contribution, indeed. And he was playing on a plastic reed at the time![9]

Shaw's great contribution on this "Star Dust" is followed by yet another solo, provided by the underrated Jack Jenney's trombone, whose swing work can also be described as "eddying," and is often more compelling jazz-wise than what a TD produced on that instrument. Jenney's seamless octave leap here, via an "unprepared F" was unique for the time. On this great version of a celebrated ditty, the entire Shaw orchestra then takes us toward a stirring denouement, with Artie providing a few last "words" on clarinet; and yes, he was right: this version of an old tear-jerker, once one of the best-known of American songs, was and remains a classic, one that needs to be heard and heard again. And learned from.

À propos, Artie often liked to say (with variations) that teachers can only teach one where to put one's fingers on an instrument, and that one progresses best from imbibing the work of actual masters at the trade. In that regard his "Star Dust" will certainly teach any aspiring clarinetist a great deal, not to mention trumpeters (given the Butterfield tour de force, too), providing high musical mountains to climb, veritable Jungfraus on each instrument!

The next recording session of this large orchestra, following more painstaking rehearsals, came a couple months later in Tinseltown (12/3/40). Shaw and band made a batch of five sides on this date, none of which are among my favorites, followed the next day by three more in studio. The latter gaggle includes Artie's own composition "Who's Excited?" and "Prelude in C Major" (by Artie and Ray Conniff, soon getting a trombone chair in the band); plus an extended "Blues" (Part I and II), taking up some six and a quarter minutes on record.

One can never call anything Shaw and his bands recorded during the entire Swing Era unworthy, especially compared to so many of today's musical products. But his 12/3/40 recordings and those of 12/4, some of rather offbeat tunes, generally don't get through my personal turnstiles for extended analysis or recommendation, though more open, eclectic listeners might not only give them one or more tries, but also find them more compelling and memorable than I do. It's possible, too, that Shaw was doing some end-of-the-year rushing, by going from one group of recordings with the large orchestra on December 3 to another on the morrow, before his move to the Palladium. This was indeed a hectic month for the celebrated bandleader and his players in bewitching La La Land, so much the foil of grim, Hitlerian Europe. But maybe a sense of impending wartime for the U.S. was part of this Shavian alacrity as well.

In any event, one sometimes has to revise one's long-held points of view and try out old Shaw work that one formerly downgraded. So it was that I gave his "Prelude in C Major" of December 1940 another chance, and was pleasantly surprised by the intense musicality there, as I think many others would be, too. It's actually quite remarkable and deserves some analysis.

The record, really an exercise in impressionism or expressionism, or both, starts with grave strings against muted brass, sounding deceptively slow and simple, and a bit ponderous. The listener prepares to hear a tune that will remain on the somber side. But the "prelude" is set here for Artie to gorgeously pour on some strength and fire with his silken clarinet, ever the virtuoso. The band oscillates on this number between tough and gentle, swingy and European-classical. There ensues an emphatic Guarnieri solo on piano, starting cleanly and simply, but then whipping along the keys. Artie comes back with even more assertive jazz work himself, never to be denied. He would repetitively make himself a pest by calling Goodman, including to his face, only a clarinetist, while considering himself by contrast, a musician. But in fact, he was at least somewhat on the money in this oft-iterated comparison. The musicality here, both via Shaw's fine clarinet and this entire orchestra, is remarkable. Then comes Jerome soloing on tenor, though he would sometimes complain that such a sober setting constrained the pure jazz player in him (his own favorite on that instrument being the legendary Lester Young). On "Prelude" the Hollywood film–type backgrounds of the time produce many different effects here. In fact, my impression is that this composition would really belong best in some movie score of that epoch.

I talked to a dear friend about it, one with good taste, and played the number for her. After listening, she, too, immediately thought of Tinseltown flicks back then. This "Prelude" gave her an impression of one such movie scene, where several men are talking at a nightclub and the Shaw strings, brass, clarinet, etc. play in the background. When the men finish talking, the music blares more loudly, and when they get back to talking, it grows more discreet again. Then the fellows shake hands, leave, and "Prelude" comes to an end. It was interesting at least that she derived roughly the same feeling from Shaw's musically innovative effort here as I did. Of course "innovative" does not always mean popular, and that, too (along with critiques of Goodman), remained an intermittent trope of Shaw's for the rest of his life. He felt that taking artistic chances was something he had to do in his work; but apart from "Frenesi" and a few other gold records, including "Star Dust," this creative and great orchestra of his didn't "hit" so pervasively and profitably with the public as had the previous aggregation. And of course now increasingly in the foreground were crooners like Sinatra, so prominently featured in the Dorsey band that he could offer big competition for the public dollar. Soon enough a great roar at the Paramount for that skinny fellow from Hoboken would astonish BG, also playing there on the same program. Additionally, there was the burgeoning popularity of one Glenn Miller, outstripping that of both the former King of Swing and Artie, too.[10]

Still Artie kept going his own way, and so the next day after making that complex, unusual "Prelude" and the other two in the batch, he took his slimmer Gramercy Five into the studio to make four more records on December 5! One, Walter Donaldson's "My Blue Heaven," was a big favorite back then, and would later be a hit in Fats Domino's version of the '50s. This is the side I always recall best from the Gramercy's 12/5/40 session. And it's the one I'd most readily choose to rehear on the internet. With his five confreres around him, Shaw unrolls the melody of a fine, jazzy but melodious "Blue Heaven," indeed, backed by the solid Fatool on drums, DeNaut on bass, and Guarnieri's effective harpsichord, never hyperbolic or jarring.

The bridge features an even simpler Guarnieri, basically alone and thumping economically on his Old Regime–type instrument; then Artie comes back in his legato way, but zigzagging more on his licorice stick, remarkably so. He's followed by an electric guitar solo that's fairly complex jazz improv for the era, backed by Johnny's neat harpsichord touches. Butterfield picks up the pace with the plugged trumpet he liked to use for his own contributions to the group, and then comes an unexpectedly combined, small-band riffing segment, which again somewhat rewrites the well-known tune. It's a nice interlude, easy for the players and enjoyable for listeners, till Artie in his often surprising manner takes another flight on the main melody, before that repetitive "riff-riff" of sorts returns. This is still effective, if somewhat tight ensemble work, sticking well within the chord layout. All in all, the Five present a wonderful, unique "Blue Heaven" here, complementing so many other recorded versions of that American standby. By contrast, though pretty, the Gramercy take on "Smoke Gets in Your Eyes," while it might have pleased its composer and Shaw's future father-in-law, Kern, will make no one forget the Platters' hit recording of the tune about a decade and a half later.

However, one should not ignore a highly artistic offering in this clutch of Gramercy discs made at that session, one bearing the unusual title "Dr. Livingstone, I Presume," with Artie given as its composer. The listener is treated to a beginning here that quickly provides a sense of the African jungle via Fatool's drum-banging, and "impressionism" remains the handiest word for what follows. Artie's committed clarinet leads the group and listeners through the figurative jungle, along with a quite comical, repetitive ensemble theme. The pounding drums, electric guitar, simple bass, and Guarnieri's piano interventions keep that jungle feeling intact. My dear friend's impressions seemed similar to mine here, too—of a wild African milieu where she could see monkeys swinging through the trees, snakes hanging down, everything very green and humid, big bright flowers punctuating the landscape with riotous color; and of course Tarzan (hugely popular back then) coming to her mind as well. However, Artie concludes this unusual piece with a warm *frailach* of sorts on his clarinet, giving us a klezmerish feeling to go with the pervasive jungle element, and it works well.

That hereditary Jewish element in Shaw (kept alive by his encounters with loneliness, anti–Semitism, and parental problems in childhood, and obviously, too, by what was going on in Europe) was certainly important, and one can hear that clearly near the end of his "Livingstone." But it's also important to add how he himself felt on this score. In *The Trouble with Cinderella* he talks about being part of an "out" group when growing up, but basically says he ditched "Jewishness" as he grew into adulthood—i.e., that it was never central in his thoughts or self-conception. He was an American of that time, period; and of course many other second-generation immigrant offspring (think simply of Yogi or DiMaggio) felt similarly, before the ethnic revolution of the mid-'60s became mainstream. And yet Shaw did tell me that he had had a bar mitzvah. And there is no question that after the existence of the Nazi death factories became known at the end of World War II, he was bedeviled by the persistence of anti–Semitism occurring on such a lethal, gargantuan scale, citing Victor Frankel's book *Man's Search for Meaning* in that regard. In other words all this truly bothered him, even if on the outside he stayed a true American all the way. Was Shaw a synagogue or temple-goer after that bar mitzvah and through adult life? No way. But he did have a certain Jewish melancholy and put it into work like that "Livingstone" *frailach*, as well as many other records, and in a way that Goodman (growing up in a happier childhood milieu) never did so much or so well.[11]

A second offbeat offering from this Gramercy batch does not work as well impressionistically (or expressionistically). It's called "When the Quail Come Back to San Quentin," and has problems, though Butterfield is wonderful on his non-muted trumpet here, with that same marvelous sound he contributed so well to the big band, and with the small group ensemble sounding nearer to the orchestra on this number, too. However, there isn't much Artie on it, as if he wanted to give himself a real break after his previous major and onerous contributions on his instrument. There is a bass solo by DeNaut, but against the entire group background, not just the plinking harpsichord. Re this tune, my friend kept trying to see the quail walking around but couldn't (of course others know there's a metaphor here for young women of the human species!).[12] This was certainly not one of her favorites in the Shaw *oeuvre*. But given Artie's commitment to pushing the envelope both on his own instrument and in how he sedulously shaped ensembles, she did offer an interesting insight related to why he could never keep any of his many marriages going! She summed it up cogently re this compulsive perfectionist, to the effect that in life "one can't have two masters." And that seems an apt observation regarding this unusual musician and person.

Less than two weeks after the previous session, on December 17, 1940, the large orchestra was back in studio to cut four more sides. Two of them can easily be skipped over and will be here. They are "The Calypso" cum an Anita Boyer vocal, and "Beau Night in Hotchkiss Corners," also sung by Boyer, both written by Herb Magidson and Ben Oakland for the film *George White's Scandals*; but which again, other listeners, perhaps more ecumenical than I am, may want to discover them for themselves. The two remaining records made at this session were, in fact, composed of one long one chopped into two sides and highly unusual in the full, untruncated version! In later recopies (on LP, CD, etc.) one can hear Artie's "Concerto for Clarinet" (Parts I and II) without the break. Shaw would generally play down the significance of this long, one-off piece, averring that he simply cooked it up quickly for the movie *Second Chorus*. After sketching out what he wanted the band to do in this or that spot, and even while at the studio, he still wasn't sure quite what he himself would play in the many clarinet virtuoso runs that make up the bulk of the record. And yet it all worked amazingly well. Artie did find it somewhat risible that while "Concerto" didn't rack up big sales, it was later taught in university music schools and considered by many, and decades later, to be "important." Was he being disingenuous on the fate of this unique, home-cooked composition? Or simply modest? I think the latter is more correct. Might we even call it the modesty of genius? There was plenty of that in Shaw, however arrogant he could also seem to many.

"Concerto" starts with a slow, chamber music–style intro on clarinet supported by the strings; and then against a lean orchestral background, the master shows his stuff (somewhat as in "Nightmare," only more so). Guarnieri's boogie-woogie piano sets a quicker pace and keeps going for a while in his own jazzy manner. Then Artie returns and with his gorgeous tone on display, just flies all over the map, up and down, and with more *frailich*-like touches again very evident. And this becomes a real musical stunner, indeed. There are also solos contributed by the tenor saxist Jerome and Goodman's old trombonist from his band's golden era, Vernon Brown, with the strings behind, and then trombones together for a bit, too. But Artie is the utter star here, the centerpiece, and having fun, too, it seems, while being the committed master on his instrument at one of his definite musical peaks.

There ensues another slowdown in the piece, a real shift of gears tempo-wise, and Artie then offers his complex explorations with almost nothing beneath or behind him. Then against tom-toms from Fatool, he's back again with a different tune of sorts, much more emphatic and sprightly now. This is the real Artie, or one of them, on a clarinet tour de force, where he keeps on going, apparently having a ball, and culling from a long past of simply taking endless licks by the side of Willie "The Lion" Smith et al. The ensemble returns near to the end, but Artie dances all over it; and the last part is Shaw back alone in the spotlight, climbing up and down the figurative staircase, and ending on a vertiginous high C, but still as clear as a bell, and in thick timbre. My friend's take? She called all this "busy," and something that could also benefit from the visual element. She said it would almost inspire one to hurry and finish one's own job of the moment!

But to show how unique Artie was in his execution of this composition, I did have the pleasure of hearing his anointed player, Dick Johnson, play "Concerto," too (sans strings) with that reformed Shaw orchestra early in 2006. Johnson was roughly an octogenarian then, and as he reached for the heavens with his clarinet, a lady playing sax in the band almost maternally looked over at him, worried, it seemed, by the dramatic pressures of that instrument. But the main point is that however wonderful a player this Johnson was, he could never duplicate—nor could anyone—Artie's slurring, almost syrupy timbre in every register, including the very highest and most challenging. Why again did Shaw abandon this instrument on which he so shone, and at a mere 44 years old? One key reason (among a slew) needs to be emphasized—that he'd always given 190 percent at this pursuit and was plain tired of doing so. You can certainly see those lofty standards in this truly remarkable "Concerto for Clarinet."[13]

Of course there was a pattern in the man, and that was his reluctance to get stuck in any one mode for too long. So as if he'd had quite enough with pop-type tunes graced by anodyne vocals, and enough, too, with zany, interesting explorations by his Gramercy Five; and also with the formless but gorgeous clarinet explorations on such virtuosic display in the big band's "Concerto," where along with some basic 12-bar blues, his instrument was pretty well the whole show, Artie decided in his next studio session (January 23, 1941) to give us in four discs the absolute *crème de la crème* of his second great musical organization! Both I and Professor Read vigorously recommend listening and relistening to all four, and with no grade inflation or qualms whatsoever. All four are masterly, marvelous, accessible, emotion-provoking, and downright beautiful recordings, using originally romantic songs that were wonderful in and of themselves. And poignant, too, given the war that was worsening by the day in Europe and the Far East, and portending an ever more certain (and huge) American involvement. And also poignant because this second topflight Shaw orchestra had really come together as a unit and was at an apogee, before another sad and rather imminent breakup. It would be prompted by a needed move to New York and the loss of some key band personnel, rather than simply by Artie's usual need to move on to something different.

Bear in mind, too, that as 1941 began, Glenn Miller was very popular competition, and so was plenty of schlock provided not only by Guy Lombardo, Larry Clinton, or Kay Kyser, but even to a degree by both Dorseys, leaning heavily on female and male singers who warbled without much jazz feeling at all, but made hits that still linger for us (think a young Sinatra on "I'll Never Smile Again," etc.). Shaw would much later say that he (and others like Goodman and Ellington) "did more" than the Beatles, which I've considered comparing apples to oranges. But even in his own era, Shaw gave more than most swing leaders in terms of innovative sophistication and plain high standards.

In any event these four records his orchestra made on 1/23/41 are truly memorable, and still wonderful listening today. One is of a fine old song, "Dancing in the Dark," and gone here is Shaw going off in any and all directions. This disc, which along with "Star Dust," went gold, selling a million-plus copies, is pretty from start to finish, august and marvelous, with strings weaving the melody against muted brass in quintessentially romantic, early '41 fashion; but also preparing for Artie's gorgeous, authoritative solo to follow. His is a rather simple, legato, and beautiful jazz contribution, but quite simply, heart-tugging. In our era one hardly dares say this, but one understands very well why women aplenty back then went for this handsome, serious, and yes, sensitive bandleader and soloist. In any case the AS "Dancing..." is a lovely offering and definitely of the time. Butterfield contributes to its lovely ensemble sound with that fine lead trumpet of his. Saxes and strings vie in pretty fashion, before the reeds themselves blend gorgeously on their own; and again, Billy and the brass drive things to a forthright conclusion, with Artie's clarinet suitably topping it all off at the end. Romantics will love this one unreservedly. And pro musicians will dig the almost mysterious effects wrought by those tremolo strings, especially at the outset, and how Artie enters so seamlessly with a surprise squeeze overlapping the last measure of the intro, then continues the solo under a buttressing sax section. They will also note a coming modulation to Bb major, and Shaw using some Stravinsky-like chords (as in *The Firebird*), sliding to the high F for effect, as listeners are left with an unresolved dominant chord in mind. Was this record a masterpiece of the era and still today? No question.

But Shaw stayed in the same groove at that session with another gorgeous song, "I Cover the Waterfront," by John W. Green, who also wrote "Out of Nowhere," and one of the finest of all jazz standards, "Body and Soul." Green obviously had Weltschmerz aplenty (and brains, too, gaining entry to Harvard at age 15), and Shaw more than honors all that here. This "I Cover..." starts with those gorgeous violins and violas so redolent of the movie era, but only as preparation for Artie to take the melody, suddenly and surprisingly, melting his sensuous clarinet into the pillowy strings, and never more sumptuous. Yes, this was unquestionably another AS peak with that marvelous orchestra. There is so much emotion in his "I Cover..." (which for lyrics is best heard by Billie Holiday), and great taste manifested throughout. Jerry Jerome provides an understated tenor solo against those settling strings, but Artie's dramatic return for a second time is much more of a jazz standout, and quite simply superb. Butterfield and Shaw then trade a couple of short commentaries, driving toward a stirring denouement, and with Artie's final flourish moving up to a held C#. Most important, does the listener feel the lovelorn sadness on that desolate waterfront? In what is again a true masterpiece, he/she does so easily. It's a beautiful song done in ultra-classy and pretty fashion by this second great Shaw contingent.

Still sans vocals, Shaw includes at the same session another romantic tune of the era (and also known by others, especially singers), "Moonglow." This, too, is a classic song that was obviously inspired by the gauzy vanilla sheen enrobing the moon on some summer or autumn night. And the AS version of 1941 is a classic, too! My first Shaw LP, as noted, was called *Moonglow,* and one can see why the execs putting together such potpourris later on would highlight this recording. Artie again lays out the melody cum improv in memorable fashion, and you will want to hear this one over and over. The man who stressed that one does the most good being selfish put so much emotional commitment into his versions of tunes like this one, and yes, he did end up giving a great deal to a great many (shades of Jeremy Bentham) via that musical tunnel vision of his, and his amazingly high standards. In "Moonglow" he simply gets things moving from the top with his heavy-syrup, dramatic clarinet against the warm orchestral background, and keeps going right through the bridge in a lovely tour de force. Artie then cedes to fine sax work (back to his writing roots there), which is anything but schmaltz. This is—excuse the oft-repeated words—stately and classic, too. But it's also fine jazz and well anchored within the Swing Era. A simple Guarnieri piano solo, very basic with DeNaut's bass and Fatool's drums supporting him, leads into Jenney's languid trombone solo, reminiscent of the one he contributed on "Star Dust." Then Butterfield's first trumpet leads the band out in a stronger, firmer way, preparing for Artie finally to soar emphatically above that background as the star he remained. Seasoned musicians will note the almost architectural design patterns in Shaw's early solo work, then at the end of the arrangement how he drives the original Bb key to Eb major, with stunning modulation, before letting us down gently via chromatic slides. And you may even cry by the close of this great rendering! Despite all the technical details, the main point is that Artie and band keep one's attention fully, and all the way through. This "Moonglow" is yet another classic by that unique, philharmonic-tinged AS orchestra of the period.

A last cut at the 1/23/41 session is another "Alone Together" (Shaw had already recorded the song with his earlier, more popular aggregation) and yet this one's a marvel, too, and sadly, the last of Artie's *crème de la crème* with his second great aggregation. Shaw was of course intensely, deeply musical, and as emphasized, on the melancholy side too, and those traits show to great advantage on this '41 "Alone...," enhancing the tune's primary traits. The arrangement (by Hayton-Shaw, like all in this batch) brings out the orchestra's "singing" quality (to again cite Les Robinson). It uses all the colors provided by pretty strings, strong, Butterfield-propelled brass, and reeds, somehow giving the impression of a haunted house of sorts, where on a foggy night a Bogie or even Peter Lorre may suddenly appear. There is much technique here, too, but the listener really only absorbs the emotional beauty of the song and arrangement. Unlike on "I Cover..." and especially "Moonglow," Artie waits in the wings for a relatively long time on this "Alone...," while the orchestra keeps shooting out different hues, making the entire contingent more central here, and again, bringing sad or haunting films of the period to mind as well. When Artie does come in, he offers a pretty, playable solo on his clarinet (still thicker and more licorice-like, due to the strings and his need to fit in, than with the previous band). The gorgeous ensemble sound wins out, with some truly muscular, weighty band work, including in the strings, which were more frequently subdued. Near the end Artie provides some appropriate clarinet "words," in a way fighting off a kaleidoscope of orchestral hues and shadings to remain the center of attention. In sum, this "Alone Together" simply compels for those who want to regain a pre-oldies world of deep, ponderous, melodic music, yet well within the swing genre, if unlike anything else around back then.

One has to wonder how long Artie might have kept this second fine orchestra of his going had it not been for Burns and Allen relocating to New York, where Shaw and an altered bunch hung on only till late March. Probably to Pearl Harbor and a bit beyond? Perhaps. But life happens with all its vicissitudes, and George and Gracie did take their popular show from L.A. to Manhattan, and given that Shaw's orchestra was featured on it every week, he and some of his key players (Butterfield, Robinson, Jerome, Conniff, Guarnieri, Jenney, and Fatool), but unfortunately not all, migrated there, too. In terms of strings, he still had the usual complement (but with new names) when he took his restocked battalion into a Manhattan studio to record on 3/20/41, another gaggle of four. Sadly, those were the last discs he made with that remarkable orchestra. Great as it was, it hadn't lasted for even a year.

Its final recordings are certainly good ones, with some recognizable songs, workable arrangements, and no vocals; but not up with the four in the previous clutch of Hollywood (and Hollywood-sounding) waxings, the stellar and sumptuous "Dancing in the Dark," "I Cover the Waterfront," "Moonglow," and "Alone Together." Those genre-crossing standouts constitute the absolute acme in terms of this unusual band's output—the summit, as it turned out. From the last New York session of March 20, 1941, "If I Had You" is the best one, though the brass is tamped down, the saxes are good but not arresting, and there is a more dialed-in quality than previously. Partly that was due to the need for rapid and careful orientation of new players; partly to the fact that Artie had taken up digs in the Algonquin Hotel and was enjoying the literary surroundings and other such distractions from this new base, and something of a singles life, too! This "If I Had You" is a good tune, however, and the Shaw version of '41 could certainly stick with certain listeners. Billy takes the bridge with a discreet mute, and for good or ill, or both, that somewhat discreet quality follows all the way through. Experienced musicians will note a flurry of key changes here from C major to Artie taking off in E minor, having his say, so to speak; then to G, and to B minor, before returning to C major and E minor (enhancing the dance feeling), and Shaw almost stamping his final approval back in C major at the close, a satisfying series of changes for the listener.

Paying careful heed to this offering near the end of the line for such a marvelous swing organization, one has to conclude that this band (and Artie's own focus) had tilted more to those listeners and their needs rather than to dancers. In "If I Had You" there are two choruses in a row by eminently danceable, prancing saxes, but the brooding, almost swamping strings keep slowing things to more of a crawl, which would have made matters difficult for jitterbug enthusiasts. For listeners, however, this orchestra really stood out and still does.

In that group of sides there was also Hoagy Carmichael's "Georgia on My Mind," made more famous later on by the Ray Charles hit; and again, Artie is himself restrained here, with a slightly thinner clarinet sound, and the ensemble a bit more meager, too, if still pretty. Artie's nonetheless able to negotiate the risky upper register with confidence and security, and the emotional lacquer he always made a central part of his playing. There's an off-the-map high Ab here that almost electrifies like a flashbulb. Jerry Jerome takes a generous dollop on tenor, and Butterfield also contributes on trumpet; but this is anything but a classic, despite how recognizable the tune will be to many. Artie's thumbprint is still on it from the beginning solo, but there is no real attempt to hand listeners the tune, so to speak, via significant ensemble work.

"Why Shouldn't I?" is also a bit on the careful, simpler side in every sense (blend of the saxes, use of the strings, Jerome's solo that is almost not jazz, etc.). The arrangement is pure pop, and Artie himself offers conventional solos with easy-to-follow melodic adherence and little ornamentation. Part of that tentative, restrained quality would again have emanated from his getting habituated to new people in his orchestra, to a new home, and to different recording personnel in a Manhattan studio. For certain, Shaw would also have sensed the band's impending breakup on the near horizon. Maybe he was already intuiting the need in his early thirties for the "picket fence" life of a married man and father. This, too, remained one of his intermittent hopes, or demi-hopes.

That final stint of the full orchestra in the recording studio included a standard many will know, "It Had to Be You," which is sprightly in this AS rendering, but again, a "not quite" piece of work compared to the standouts cut at the previous session in Hollywood. Here we find security, discipline and focus in Artie's solos, well-completed ideas, but not much chance-taking. Maybe one is being something of a Monday morning quarterback, but again, all this feels like a last hurrah, and Artie saying once again that he's had enough. In any event Burns and Allen stopped broadcasting that late March of '41, and the bandleader now had his excuse to break up this fine organization by the end of the month. Among other sidemen, Butterfield was sad to see it go, finding Artie a good boss, one who had provided good pay and interesting assignments. As for Les Robinson, he went on within a couple years to play with a number of fine studio orchestras, and for a truly long haul; but he remained amazed in older age by the distinctive sound of this particular Shaw band, one that had worked incredibly well in those rather primitive recording circumstances of the time, and which was also remarkable in live engagements. He certainly wished younger generations could have savored its performances in actual ballrooms.[14]

After a hiatus of a couple months, Artie started moving toward something even more expansive along the same rough lines, including via more "longhair" homework he took on with an experienced tutor of sorts. Shaw long felt that this might have become his finest contingent if only Pearl Harbor hadn't intervened to kill it after little more than a half year. In fact, this one is not at *all* our favorite Shaw aggregation of the Swing Era, or even of the post-swing period from 1946 to 1954, when he intermittently recorded as well. To this point Artie had formed two unambiguously great orchestras, night-and-day different from each other, but both marvelous, unique, and copious contributors to American popular music. The orchestra he would now put together was no hit producer, but well beyond that, anything but close to great or well-realized compared to what had preceded. There was fortunately one more highly innovative band to come near the end of the swing epoch, making three that were very discrete and idiosyncratic, but each undeniably superb; however, we're both emphatic in declaring that this band of '41-'42 (persisting a bit after Pearl Harbor) was never going to be one of them, despite Shaw's high hopes there, and his later regrets.

## Four

# More (and Less) of the Same
## 1941-42

For his newest formation, Artie got his feet wet with the idea of bringing together some fine Black players of the era as soloists along with himself, but not in a Gramercy Five–type group; rather, with a large bevy of studio strings and such, in order to see how jazz (in arrangements crafted totally by Shaw) would do melded with a concert-style, European classical–type background. The best of these initial offerings, recorded June 26, 1941, is an arresting "Confessin' (That I Love You)" featuring Artie's clarinet, still thicker than in the previous decade, beautiful and liquid, playing his parts almost in slow motion and savoring each phrase and nuance. It also includes J.C. Higginbotham on trombone, alternating melodic jazz licks with Benny Carter's sprightly and pretty alto sax, and Red Allen taking one of the bridges on muted trumpet. It's truly a lovely rendering of this pretty tune, but unfortunately, not at all typical of what would follow for Shaw. Instead, this is a one-off of sorts, because the other two recordings with these three players feature vocals by Lena Horne, one of them, "Love Me a Little," worth recalling for the melody and Horne's contribution, along with Carter establishing the melody on alto and leading the strings. Lena is certainly romantic, but none of this will make a listener forget the previous, great Shaw bands. Artie himself said he was being a bit "careful" at the time,[1] and too much so, it feels. The perfunctory arrangement here constitutes the first swallow of a long summer and beyond.

That problem grew worse with the new AS orchestra of over 30 pieces (and sidemen like Guarnieri, Auld, and Robinson back, along with famed drummer Dave Tough) that began serious, long rehearsals in August '41. (Shaw alumni would sometimes complain about bathroom breaks being too few and far between during those!) After a few gigs, this large new orchestra made its first clutch of six recordings in Manhattan, September 2, 1941. There were now four trumpets here, including Oran "Hot Lips" Page (Shaw following Goodman's lead in integrating Black players), and three trombones, both larger sections than the early Swing Era complement; plus a baritone sax, quite new as well, and 15 strings, along with the usual rhythm section.

To repeat, nothing Shaw ever recorded could be called remotely bad. But this orchestra was simply no rival for the previous ones. And that included in terms of money-making popularity back then, where Shaw took a dip, especially on recording sales. Artie would blame the public's lack of taste (why they ever went so heavily for Glenn Miller always eluded him), and the fact that many weren't ready for his innovative efforts here. The great expatiator he became in later life expressed unrelenting "what-ifs" on this score. And to be fair, Shaw's appearances with this heterogeneous bunch at live engagements could at times—if far from all—whip up crowds, which were often overflowing. His jazz players would really go crazy and become unleashed in some of their one-nighters and in longer engagements too, especially later in the evenings, after the regular program was done. They could then elude the "careful" quality for those on hand to see that organization up close. Interviews of ex-sidemen who were there (trumpeter Max Kaminsky, Guarnieri, and so forth), along with Shaw himself make that clear. Some nights at certain venues with that orchestra could be special, indeed, especially due to the marvelous jazz work of Hot Lips Page on trumpet, whom Kaminsky gave himself credit for bringing to Shaw.[2] But for us Shaw's recordings of the time remain the focus, rather than those live explorations in more improvised jazz; and these recorded offerings simply don't compare with the plentiful best made by the two previous AS edi-

Artie was always searching for something new and different (Getty Images/Michael Ochs Archive).

tions. They don't remain inside near as readily, and in general, don't provoke numerous relistenings. And again, none were lasting hits, and for good reason. (Some also had alternative and/or then unissued recorded versions, which became available later.)

In listening to the group of six sides made on 9/2/41, one is hard put to place any alongside the many Shaw masterpieces (emotionally-centered ones) made with his previous aggregations. Johnny Mercer and Harold Arlen's "Blues in the Night," obviously familiar to many and featuring a long vocal by Page, might have worked well, but really doesn't seem very "Artie" at all. The blues aspect is more than acceptable, but it's presented against a lean orchestral background, despite all the players on hand, and there's little to the ensemble work following the vocal. You just don't feel that commitment here, which was so palpable in the previous Shaw orchestras. Page solos on trumpet against that rather skimpy, concert-like buttressing, but in sum, this one won't stay with many listeners at all. And there's a Shaw solo, too, one that isn't really an AS solo at all, it's that forgettable. This is good Hot Lips Page, basically well-arranged for him, but not much else.

We've highlighted how Shaw wanted to be different, very different from the Swing Era pantheon, and this is certainly reflected in that "Blues in the Night." It's seen even more in a work he thought cutting-edge for its time, but which again, does little for these auditors. We are speaking of Thomas Griselle's impressionistic "Nocturne," written by that composer in the '20s and brought to Shaw as a Jerry Sears arrangement, then forming part of this first group of recordings made with the large orchestra. It's purported to be jazz and symphonic music combined, and even better than in the "Star Dust" contingent; but again, it doesn't stick with one at all. It's just a mood, not a melody, and no one but an academic would give it more than a couple hearings. This, too, does not sound like memorable Artie, or even Artie *tout court*! No wonder many fans back then were confounded by such fare. There are a series of contrasts presented in this "Nocturne," but of course with no dancing possible or again, even an air to recall. This one, in sum, was not really what Artie thought then and in retrospect that it was. We keep stressing the point that like any great artist he did not always know what would really click. And again, his clarinet is negligible here, too. In a really rare response to his recorded output by this point, one wants this waxing on a sunset scene simply to end! It's that boringly restrained, though again, it could certainly have been worthwhile and apt for a film score of the period.

The last of the three we'll highlight from this gaggle of 9/2/41 is a rendering of Hoagy Carmichael's "Rockin' Chair," but unfortunately, this Shaw version will make no one forget others like Louis Armstrong giving it much more appeal. Shaw's "Rockin' Chair" has a sort of faraway quality to it which also won't stay with most listeners, as so many of his recordings with the previous organizations did and still do. Artie starts the main melody here on his clarinet, but not adventurously, and still with a kind of unseemly restraint, and too much of an apparent dearth of emotional sincerity, which had always made his work so distinctive. The strings and saxes come together on "Rockin'..." in a rather schlocky manner, and Georgie Auld's solo on tenor has none of the booting one heard ever and again in the first great Shaw band; instead, it sounds like he's in the rocking chair himself! When they take over, the strings are almost not there either, it feels. Artie comes back a second time, but still feels dialed-in and into other, distractive things (like literature, given where he now lived, whom he knew, and what he was omnivorously reading). This, too, is not one of our favorites, far from it; but we won't bother being equally critical of the other three in that orchestra's first batch. Nor can one call any of this bad music, either. None of it was. To be fair Harry James also became far more tame and anodyne with his popular band of the era than he'd been as the great trumpet star for Goodman back in '37-'38. But in terms of Shaw alone, this initial group of orchestral recordings elicits the analogy of a great pitcher winning 20-odd games several years in a row, then bringing fans a decent one of 14–10 or so. One can't demand greatness in every bite, and there is obviously a tremendous cost involved in producing marvelous things musically; but despite Artie's own hype about how pathbreaking he felt at the time, there is, flatly put, going to be little or no greatness, or even near-greatness in recordings made by this entire Shaw contingent.

Maybe he was rushing, too, i.e., to get out contracted recordings. Some have said that Shaw formed bands primarily to make a large number of records, before moving to something different. And money needs were a part of all this, not least due to a large monthly nut he needed to get in order to sustain such a large organization. Shaw's rehearsals were still long and onerous, but perhaps at this point he and those in his employ were simply in the recording studio too often and too hastily. For instance, the very next day after the session of six cuts we've discussed here, he brought in the 15 strings and a small group consisting of himself, Lee Castle on trumpet, Auld on tenor, Conniff on trombone, Robinson on alto, and the four rhythm players (Guarnieri on piano, Ed McKimmey on bass, Mike Bryan with a rather rudimentary but solid electric guitar, and the incomparable Tough caressing the hides).

Artie arranged these offerings himself (one could never reproach him with laziness), and the first discussed here, "Is It Taboo? (to Fall in Love with You)" starts with an interesting sound, bringing a grave movie scene again to mind. The ensemble minus the strings but with piano tinkling away promises the listener some auditory enjoyment; but again, there's not much of a melody here. The strings are almost hesitant when showcased, and Tough's tom-tomming is anything but Rich-like; instead, it's subdued, too, and Artie's solo work, while decent, has a slightly less thick and forthright timbre than previously. Auld also slurs his tenor solo in a tamped-down way against the strings. Near the end the strings vie with the small group of Swing Era instruments, and on balance, this is another mood more than a song, seemingly coming over a libation when the sun sets after a long, hard workday. To put it bluntly, "Taboo..." simply doesn't convince, even if Artie later rated it highly among other offerings in his *oeuvre*.

His composition and arrangement of "I Ask the Stars (and They Agree)" gets a similarly restrained treatment. Robinson's alto solo is faintly Hodgesesque but nice, Georgie on tenor remains subdued, and Artie on his famed clarinet doesn't rouse the listener, either—it's still as if all these players are in rocking chairs of sorts. Midway through, as the strings seem to be speaking discreetly, listeners may well want this piece to start going somewhere, or even to begin! Conniff's trombone sound is a nice one, too, but also restrained, the guitar solo by Bryan is simple stuff, and one hates again to say it, but this one doesn't move a listener, either. It's so quiet you almost feel the players need a shot of strong coffee to rouse them from their torpor! I don't like the fact that I scribbled "what forgettable junk" while relistening, because one really can't tax Artie with ever recording "junk"; and yet that's what came to me, notwithstanding Shaw's own estimate about that group's great potential, expressed in later interviews. To my co-author this "Stars..." is merely a safe, slow dance number primarily there to fill out Shaw's contractual disc-making assignment.

"Beyond the Blue Horizon" is the last Artie arrangement and record made with this unusual group, one that was never to hit the studio again and no rival at all for his Gramercy Five. We'd call this the best of the three cut on this date of 9/2/41, due to the melody, at least some snappiness, Artie's clarinet work with nice colors displayed against the sax section, and the fuller ensemble sounds. Things are happily more alive here than in those discussed above. In his rudimentary piano solo Guarnieri still comes off as sophisticated (as of course Count Basie often did with what he described as his own simple "plunka-plunka"). Unfortunately, the strings arrive to slow down proceedings and give the latter part of "Beyond..." a kind of waddling quality that doesn't enhance it.

The problem with such small group work cum a large orchestral ensemble was the lack of forthright beauty when players like Robinson led away with his beautiful alto against a wall of studio-type players, and Artie followed suit. One could almost call all the records made in this batch movie-scoring (what Artie first wanted to do on returning from Mexico), but with no movie, story, or characters to care about, and for that reason, too careful and too fundamentally aimless. Again, all convey the sense to some degree of mere contract fulfillment.

This AS orchestra then hit the road that September and through October, playing in a variety of states like New York, Connecticut, Pennsylvania, and Ohio, and eventually farther away to Iowa, Missouri, Oklahoma, and so forth, finally to end up at a Chicago theater by the end of October. Here in that toddlin' town there was another recording session, rather than in the usual Manhattan or Hollywood.

The large Shaw orchestra (all there was henceforth on records) went into that Chicago studio on October 30, 1941 to make another clutch of four tunes, three of them forgettable—"Take Your Shoes Off Baby (and Start Runnin' Through My Mind)," "Solid Sam," and Ray Conniff's "Just Kiddin' Around," plus one vocal number. As one who has listened to Shaw records super-repetitively, even obsessively, and for many decades, I still couldn't recall the melodies of the three mentioned here before playing them again. The fourth one, featuring Paula Kelly's vocal (more on this fine warbler in a bit), does, however, stick more with a contemporary listener.

From a New York studio session of November 12, '41, Conniff's "To a Broadway Rose" is also forgettable, as is the Shaw version of "Deuces Wild." The two-sided recording of "St. James Infirmary Blues" (but of course only one extended cut on LP or CD) is again, good Page both in his growly vocal and fine trumpet solo. But it isn't really good or typical Shaw. Meanwhile, the band accepted more live, extended gigs at theaters, including the Earle in Philly (site of that former mob scene for the first great, overwhelmingly-loved Shaw band) and the State in Hartford. The group finally ended up at a theater in Providence, Rhode Island. Sometimes Shaw would spice things up at such venues with updated versions of former hits like "Beguine" and "Star Dust." And then came...

Pearl Harbor! On Sunday afternoon, December 7, 1941, Shaw and his orchestra were playing that Metropolitan Theatre in Providence; and suddenly Artie received word of the surprising and almost incredible Japanese attack coming from across the Pacific, and the need for all U.S. military personnel immediately to reach their bases. The news came as the same massive shock to him as it did to millions around the nation.

The hall was rapidly vacated by most in attendance, and Artie (always impulsive) abruptly decided to give two weeks' notice to his band members, though he would bring them back for three last recording sessions near Christmas and in late January, and also for a few live appearances, in order to bring in needed cash. But basically, this was it for that orchestral edition, and from the present point of view, there was no big loss here at all. Infinitely more was being lost all over the world and soon in America, too, its Depression troubles vanishing in the face of human casualties that would spiral vertiginously abroad.

That last Shaw orchestra had already become prey to a kind of pastiche quality, and also to experimentation that wasn't quite experimental enough (while also not being sufficiently mainstream, either). Instead, these musical results ended up mostly middling and unmemorable. In the session of 12/23/41 there were two Paul Jordan contributions (both arranged by him as well), "Evensong" and "Suite No. 8," that make our point. "Evensong" is impressionistic and faintly Stravinskyish, along with nods to Debussy and Ravel, but nothing much more than a mood again. Artie's clarinet playing is simple here, too, utterly lacking in any dramatic feeling. This disc would surely have confounded James, Miller or Ellington fans! Terms like "Third Stream" may be apposite here, but the jazz part in "Evensong" gets simultaneously overwhelmed and underwhelmed by the symphonic effects, provided particularly by the foreboding strings. Again, this one simply won't stay with most listeners at all. In fact, it's even slightly ludicrous and/or pretentious. Professor Read also found a rather diffuse and out-of-focus mood here, and Artie trying too overtly for depth and a kind of escape from the conventional edifice he'd cemented himself into through his previous successes. However, we do differ somewhat, in that Read—and probably more legitimately—deems this on balance a quite fascinating piece for its time.

Jordan's "Suite No. 8" is another movie score–type piece, but again, with no story there. The listener can't wait for something to happen, and the Buckinghams' later hit of the '60s, "Kind of a Drag," came unfortunately to my mind on relistening! Because this "Suite" becomes at once rather turgid and kind of irritating, moving to a dainty, Old Regime pace for a bit, then bringing in an all too brief dollop of demi-hot swing. But that jazz part only feels like an epigone of an earlier, wilder period, and a figurative tip of the cap to the real thing. Artie's clarinet here is comparatively distant and thin, Georgie tries to pick things up on tenor and Page on his trumpet cum plunger; but neither do. And the use of tremolo strings, particularly near the beginning, has them wandering aimlessly, almost trying to find a melody and instead, portending a formless, eventless atmosphere throughout. Here both Read and I truly agreed.[3]

The other two recorded on this first post–Pearl Harbor date (America now firmly in wartime) feature singer Paula Kelly against Shaw backgrounds that are fairly linear but pleasing enough. On "Someone's Rocking My Dreamboat" the saxes aren't beautifully blended, just simple, as many such sections in other bands were then, too. Meanwhile, Shaw is simply OK but no more on his clarinet. However, this is a pretty good song, and forthright Paula, an Irish-Catholic of the era with a certain moxie, does well by it. You get a suggestion here of her own potential and come-on nerve. I remember looking at a photo of the pretty young singer with Shaw (before her later fame with the Modernaires), wearing a flower in her hair; and how I'd asked Artie in a tentative way on the phone what he'd "thought" of her back then. I rarely said anything about his women, but he knew what I was getting at here, and snapped back (in pre–women's liberation style) that Ms. Kelly was simply his "vassal" in that particular orchestra!

To me, however, she was among the best of his female vocalists, and on her other side here she takes on a biggie of that time, Frank Loesser and Jule Styne's "I Don't Want to Walk Without You," which became a big hit for the Harry James Orchestra and his singer, Forrest, partly due to all the young men who would be apart from their ladies for war service, and too often for good. It was at one with now sadder times, the Swing Era having turned decidedly less "swingy" and raucous. On this Artie version, however, his clarinet still feels dialed-in and not nearly as thick and compelling as in the "Star Dust" contingent. He seemed to be implying that he had little more to offer at this juncture, and that others could claim the spotlight and he'd be fine with that. The brass section seems hardly there either on this cookie-cutter arrangement, but at least Paula K. has that sweet, forthright way about her on "Don't Want to Walk" that was growingly right for American wartime. That conflict certainly had a major effect on the film world (think only of the iconic *Casablanca*); so why not—being charitable to this AS contingent—a similar effect on the music of one Arthur Shaw!

On January 20, 1942 Artie recorded four more sides in Manhattan with this doomed orchestra, which truly needs (and has gotten in this treatment) sharp distinguishing from its predecessor, however similar they might superficially seem to be. He used another good female singer here, Fredda Gibson (later known as Georgia Gibbs), on three of the four records cut on that date. "Somebody Nobody Loves" features anodyne, unblended Shaw saxes, much simpler again than had once been the case, but at least there's a melody here. Wartime schlock? No question that that's a factor in such work, but Gibson does have some oomph on this piece. The band, however, doesn't. Auld's solo on tenor almost isn't one again, and Artie's clarinet remains subdued, as if to admit that a part of his mind was really onto other matters.

A better pop tune from Tinseltown's *The Fleet's In*, "Not Mine," features nice Shaw clarinet work—"nice" being the operative word, but lacking in any innovation or development. I do like Gibson (or Gibbs) on this one, waiting under an unresponsive moon for love, such a big theme of the era. Her deep voice conveys a good kind of sadness on this "Not Mine," and in fact, it's the best of her three here. In "Absent Minded Moon" (that orb still central to so many Swing Era ditties) Les Robinson leads on alto, and the fine section player is again faintly Johnny Hodges– like in what he offers. Those clambering, almost cloying strings slow things down on this number co-penned by Johnny Mercer, and from it in the AS version you get another sense of small-town, still comparatively innocent America of the time. But it's a negligible piece of work, compared to so much fine material that Artie and his players had given the world to this point. Shaw playing along with the sax section near the close proffers but a small nod to his past glory days.

The one side in this batch with no vocal, "Hindustan," is entirely unmemorable, too, with again, unblended, one-dimensional saxes, Artie alone against faint tom-tomming (and/or Persian drumming), all of it middling and forgettable, as if to declare emphatically, "Let's just get it done!" This "Hindustan" doesn't manage to give off an exotic spell, and instead, provides a muddied impression of hopelessly lost and forlorn explorers *manqués*.

Speaking of "getting it done," Artie rushed the band into a studio the next day to make his final clutch of four, probably too adjacent to the ones done the day before. And yet again there's none here that will stay with the average listener, either. They are Paul Jordan's "Carnival," a Ray Conniff tune, "Needlenose," by the future fine arranger-leader of the '50s, Jordan's "Two in One Blues," and a Page vocal vehicle, "Sometimes I Feel Like a Motherless Child," arranged by Lennie Hayton, who had worked so well with Shaw in his previous orchestra. "Carnival" is again, swingy pastiche, the saxes simply on top of each other and monochromatic, and with another "let's get it done" feel palpable here, too. The brass section comes alive only for a bit, trombones in ensemble set down a melody of sorts, Artie's far from arresting on his instrument, and this "Carnival" just doesn't work well at all. Rush, rush, rush, deadlines, deadlines, deadlines: this is what one intuits re this point in Shaw's musical career.

No more compelling is the AS rendering of Jordan's "Two in One Blues," again with saxes too uni-dimensional, Artie almost an automaton in his initial solo, Page on trumpet merely acceptable with and sans plunger, Guarnieri's piano a bit Jess Stacyish, Tough overly discreet on drums with bass underpinning, and Auld aimless and unused in his tenor solo as well. Shaw's ensuing glissando is adept but well-nigh worthless here. Again, such an offering just doesn't feel like swing or good material at all. Enough negatives: this Shaw orchestra was soon to be history, and from our point of view, anything but tragically so. One can scarcely demand constant lofty standards that produce superb results, but there is comparatively little worth saluting in what Artie nonetheless hoped could have become the greatest orchestra he ever fronted!

To be fair, if the suave bandleader was taking a kind of downward turn, or so it feels to us, so was Goodman with his own rather simple arrangements of early wartime, featuring a young singer named Norma Egstrom, who was making it big as Peggy Lee.[4] That kind of work couldn't compare (as swing) with the marvelous Fletcher Henderson or Jimmy Mundy kickers back when Benny was the genre's monarch. But a part of BG in this period did try as well for significant innovation, seen in forward-looking charts contributed by Eddie Sauter and Mel Powell and the hiring of important players like Ellington alum Cootie Williams and the drummer Big Sid Catlett, who had influenced the work of Buddy Rich. As noted, Harry James, Goodman's former trumpet virtuoso, was in a more lacquered wartime mode, too, now as a popular bandleader and soloist. Tommy Dorsey still leaned more on popular vocalists as well, compared to when he'd burst to the top in the '30s via rompers like "Boogie Woogie" and other orchestral masterpieces (think, for instance, of his "Song of India," featuring Berigan and doing superbly by the Rimsky-Korsakov original). Of course Shaw always tried his best to be different from what these bandleaders were producing; but still, his comparative slide from the heights is undeniable for this period.

Additionally, Artie had long had those intellectual-literary ambitions roiling inside (fervently reading high-minded fare, meeting and talking with notables like Dreiser, Budd Schulberg, etc.). In the part of Manhattan where he then roosted, all that beckoned as an enticing kind of competition for him. He once told an academic he'd like to try working in a college environment, too (first he had to have undergraduate and graduate degrees!); but the professor told him to stay put in the musical field. Finally, the Shaw who'd worked himself silly at his trade since his early teens, and who suffered from exhausting self-demands, not least on his own instrument, and a need to be relentlessly artistic, yet pleasurable in his work, could certainly plead a certain burn-out by the time the present orchestra was set to disband. And last but far from least, the war was now grabbing center stage, over-trumping pretty well all else.[5]

## Five

# Bringing Music to the Troops

That January of '42 Artie's draft status became 1-A, so he knew service was impending, and he consequently aimed himself toward the Navy branch. As was often the case, Shaw had to be firm and single-minded in this decision to eventually join up. The same lawyer, Andrew Weinberger, who had tried to dissuade him from quitting his 1939 band in November of that year also tried to talk him out of any big move away from his current professional responsibilities. Another complication was that for a short time before putting on a uniform, Shaw was in L.A. again, where he saw the possibility of a "picket fence" life of sorts, via a whirlwind romance with Elizabeth "Betty" Kern (the composer's daughter and not one of Artie's usual starlets), followed by a marriage on March 3. At least she would henceforth live in style; when they returned to New York, Artie brought her to a gorgeous apartment he had on Central Park South. A snazzy Lincoln convertible he owned would become Betty's as well, along with plentiful cash. But the world conflict and its needs rapidly closed in on Shaw, who was certainly patriotic during "the Good War." Definitively entering the U.S. Navy on April 28, 1942, he rose to chief petty officer, but was initially treated much less well than Glenn Miller in the Air Force. Shaw found the duties, drills, and routines to which he sullenly submitted to be mind-numbing and a waste, given what he wanted to contribute. He was soon saddled with a poor, inappropriate bunch of musicians to make up a potential band; but if that was to be what the "brass" wanted, it had to be done the right way, or so he felt. Finally Shaw decided to abscond without permission to D.C., in order to persuade someone he knew, a person with real clout, that he would do best leading a truly good band for the troops. As Under Secretary of the Navy, this James Forrestal gave an affirmative to Shaw's idea, and that did the trick. (Never one to miss a chance to meet notables at their trades, Shaw would also get close later on to other maritime honchos like Admiral Nimitz.) Given this requisite green light, Shaw put together a band during the fall of '42 which he called the "Rangers," consisting of fine players he knew like John Best and Max Kaminsky on trumpet, Sam Donahue on sax, the pianist Claude Thornhill, an old friend; and again on drums, Dave Tough, whose fragility and epileptic condition, and especially his pervasive alcoholic bent would be a constant challenge for Shaw.[1]

That, however, was to be far from the main one. Bureaucracy was another problem for him. For Shaw really wanted to go into danger zones with his band members, who first played patriotic fare for recruits at New York's Pier 92, then took a train to San Francisco for a stint there, before embarking on a refitted cruise ship to Honolulu, arriving at Christmas of '42. There they remained for several months, playing at the Breakers Club for servicemen on Waikiki Beach and for officers in the evenings, along with other gigs around Hawaii. Finally Artie got his wish, and the band departed on the battleship *North Carolina* for Pacific war zones in April of '43, minus Thornhill, whom Nimitz loved hearing on piano and kept in Hawaii to form his own band.

Things now began to change significantly for Shaw and the Rangers. French Nouméa in New Caledonia, the band's first stop, lacked decent refrigeration, so that food poisoning was always possible, and the plentiful, gluttonous mosquitoes brought enervating bouts of dengue fever and/or malaria, too. Kaminsky was very moved at the time by the many white crosses for American servicemen who had been killed in the Battle of the Coral Sea, and also how the wounded in hospitals whom the band visited came at least briefly alive by hearing fine jazz. The Rangers were transported to various designated venues by ship or plane, or hitchhiked (Shaw's term) to ever more dicey destinations, somewhat mirroring what MacArthur called his "island-hopping" strategy.

These peregrinations certainly brought musical cheer to troops spread out in the huge, demanding Pacific theater. Even when the band played the national anthem straight up and with no jazz riffs, they could move men on aircraft carriers or elsewhere to tears. But some of the Rangers' concerts took place in grim circumstances, indeed. The band members went in and out of foxholes on different islands of the New Hebrides, and by late spring and then summer of '43 were ever more challenged by malarial fever and the plentiful critters who spread such things, not to mention bad drinking water. Jungle conditions were far different from the Paramount or the Strand! In July the Rangers were on Guadalcanal, now past its nadir; but where enemy bombs were still so loud and insistent that Artie, himself taking refuge in a foxhole, had the hearing in one of his ears damaged for life by one such pounding from above. From then on, he'd play with the only one still functioning well aimed at or near a piano (and this partly explains, too, that

Artie Shaw and his wartime band, the Rangers, March 5, 1943 (San Diego Air & Space Museum).

bellowing "hell-o!" I'd sometimes get on the phone during my calls to his homes in California).

Shaw's sidemen and their equipment got badly worn down by such environs, due in part to temperatures that could consistently hit 110 degrees. The Japanese bombs came down from the air several times a night, sirens wailed, and band members like Kaminsky even had to dodge native headhunters, placating them with cigarettes. The band then did some backtracking for more gigs on islands they'd already passed. Finally in late August they were sent out (not without potential peril en route) to more peaceful, though flea-ridden New Zealand, the Solomons, and then Australia to play there. Shaw marveled at how quiet and deferential certain crowds were in these still British-oriented dominions. Finally his Rangers were considered spent as a functioning war instrument by the higher-ups, and on an unescorted Liberty merchant ship the tattered bunch made its way back across the vast, dangerous Pacific with its lethal Japanese subs in wait, sometimes taking their turns manning the guns; and fortunately, they made it all the way to America's West Coast.

Shaw himself was very happy to reach San Francisco November 11, 1943, and then get some much-needed R and R in an American hospital, before being allowed a short trip out to see his family at his father-in-law's home in Beverly Hills. That environment shocked him as another and overly pampered world, fully antithetical to what he and his men had been experiencing in the Pacific theater. French soldiers returning from service in Vietnam later in the decade and still demanding rice for dinner at tony Parisian restaurants would have felt similarly. But after his full discharge Shaw had to try and adapt quickly, including to a still new wife and a first son, Steven Kern Shaw.[2]

Unfortunately, his efforts at creating a stable home environment didn't root for long, leading to a rather precipitous separation and eventually, a messy divorce, another swallow of a long Shaw summer. Mainly, this musical icon came back from the war almost completely disoriented, and with no firm sense of what he henceforth wanted to do in life. Money needs were at first (and in an illusory way) no real concern to him. So in L.A. he started seeing an analyst each weekday morning at 9 a.m., which he found a liberating experience.[3] Finally Artie felt healed enough from delving into his troubled past, and impelled as well by cash needs (including to pay alimony) to make another try at the one thing he could think of doing. That was luckily still bandleading, but this time his idea was to do so sans strings, and in an era when Charlie Parker, Dizzy Gillespie et al. were changing the face of jazz. They were inventing—via phrases of varied measures, different kinds of chord use, atonal or dissonant qualities, and just a new, cooler bunch of sounds—what came to be called bebop, or more simply, bop. Count Basie certainly began adapting, and soon, other adventurous bandleaders like Woody Herman and Stan Kenton did so as well![4] In sum, Heraclitus Shaw knew that he, too, couldn't go back into the same old river; and with the whole wartime episode as perhaps a necessary prelude, one of suffering and uncertainty for him, he was now poised to make a new musical departure, producing what ultimately became (despite his comparative modesty about it) his third and last great band of the now fading Swing Era. And via an aggregation that would be very different, his clarinet included, from each of the previous fine ones discussed here, a wonderful blend of swing and these exciting new sounds of a jazz revolution!

# Six

# Swing Sunset and a Last Great Shaw Band

Auditions for Artie's new musical organization soon occurred at a brisk pace, though many players were still away in the service. Shaw was a good judge of potential talent, and when getting this new contingent together via vigorous vetting, he mainly went for young, unheralded musicians (often teens or circa 20), ones he could rapidly mold. There were no more Riches, Aulds, or Guarnieris here. By the end of October '44 Artie was rehearsing his new charges at full tilt, and as usual many later interviewed spoke highly of their musical teacher and shaper.[1]

Getting away from the tension of his splintered "picket fence" marriage, Shaw found a number of advantages in his personal life during this period—though he was perhaps not fully aware of them. One was having a home base in Greater L.A. That gave him more emotional stability and fewer distractions (even then Los Angelenos had to drive everywhere) than in his Algonquin Hotel or Central Park South days in New York. As seen, the orchestra he'd led back then wasn't and isn't among our favorites, partly because all sorts of literary-intellectual and other notables were so near at hand in the Apple for a susceptible Shaw. Now he could concentrate more fully on what mattered most: his American brand of music, and what surprising, wonderful music it would be!

A second source of stability came during that fall of '44 and into '45, enduring through this last heady period for the icon of swing. It was presented in the alluring form of one Ava Gardner, a young Hollywood actress who tumbled deeply into what was later called by Mr. Cash the "ring of fire," dating the master clarinetist constantly and recovering from her own marital wounds (provided by a self-centered gent named Mickey Rooney). When eventually Artie and Ava lived together, he would snap at her about him having to take care of the home, paying the electric and so forth, and ... what did *she* do for *him*? Well, she loved him was her pithy reply. That was, in fact, a great deal, because this lady certainly knew how to care for a man she loved; and even later in the '40s, after their Artie-impelled breakup, when she was with another heavy named Sinatra, Shaw (still a confidant) retained a certain pride of place inside her, his strength and even a bit of caveman brutality, plus his vivid intellect outdoing Frank's in those regards.

Artie's intellect was indeed a demanding creature of sorts, and he would make fun of Ava's country simplicity and foist weighty literary classics upon her, plus teach her chess and play with her, till she had the temerity (in a well-known anecdote) to beat him! But all that notwithstanding, Ava (or Avalah, as he'd sometimes call her in a Yiddish manner) really provided Shaw a bedrock of sorts during this important '44-'45 musical era, and through to their marriage (necessitated by Hollywood and other American standards of the time). Ms. Gardner truly dug the great sounds Shaw and his players produced in that period, allowing him simply to concentrate on what he really loved career-wise. Given those high standards of his and his need always to move forward into uncertain terrain, this was a large contribution, indeed.[2]

Of course the handsome Shaw had many other women hoping to get close, too; but by and large it's fair to say that he did best when monogamous and committed within his phases, however transitory—both workwise and personally. On balance Ava was a big plus for him during this last, poignant swath of the swing epoch, and a key reason Shaw made such unique music in what remained of it (given the vogue of crooners like Como, Sinatra, Peggy Lee et al. becoming ever more preponderant). This was swing's own fall now, and that autumnal quality is shot through Shaw's marvelous band work of the time. It's music that often feels painted by a strong, sensitive artist and his superb new collection of players.

These sidemen, whom Shaw obsessively melded into a boppish ensemble that ended up so different from its AS predecessors, included comparative oldsters like Conniff on trombone, though he was replaced within months by 17-year-old Ollie Wilson; but mainly, this was a young band, with some amazing talents Shaw used to advantage, such as Michael "Dodo" Marmarosa on piano and 21-year-old Barney Kessel on electric guitar, along with Herbie Steward playing tenor sax, among others one could name.

Marmarosa was a Pittsburgh eccentric who had been roughed up badly during the war after playing with Gene Krupa in Philadelphia. Sailors in the place ragged him about why he wasn't in the war, and gave him a beating that induced a coma, which remained with him as a

## Six. Swing Sunset and a Last Great Shaw Band

psychological trauma of sorts, perhaps making him even more unpredictable. His big head and unprepossessing looks got him the patronizing moniker "Dodo," and his later life was tragic, too, given that his wife eventually absconded with his two kids and offered him a deal absolving him from more child support payments, the quid pro quo being that he would be unable to see his kids at all. But for now this young phenom (only 19 when he began with Shaw) would make a large contribution to the current contingent via remarkable piano work, rooted as he was in both a strong classical background and more recently, a real immersion in bebop, learning from the greats playing the new stuff. Finally, Dodo practiced round the clock in an almost monomaniacal way, even skipping meals in the process.

Artie had one big star in this new band, the Black trumpet artist Roy Eldridge, who also made major contributions, though Shaw was never one to let any strong soloist stand above the ensemble. Eldridge found racial discrimination of the era (against which Artie sedulously fought) onerous and off-putting, and yet he fit well with Shaw's new bop-tending bunch. In fact, a number of other players later interviewed spoke about Artie's very strong work demands, but also the contented, harmonious chemistry in the band among its varied members.

It's always hard to describe the sound of music, and that certainly remains the case here. But suffice it to say that the AS orientation of '44-'45 was extremely different both from that of the '38-'39 breakthrough aggregation and the fine '40-'41 philharmonic-tinged one. In what follows we will put limits on our choices for analysis and discussion, and no longer tell the reader at any length which Shaw pieces we deem forgettable, as was easier to do with his pre–Pearl Harbor band. Here the problem is quite the reverse: there is a true plethora, an *embarras de choix* of novel, well-realized recordings put out by that '44-'45 edition, one Shaw somewhat underestimated himself. In this section we'll choose from only some of this modernist band's output, a pleasant enough task, and saving present authors the trouble, too, of dissertating positively on more than those chosen here, which one could easily do. Instead the reader (as at a wine and cheese gala) will hopefully get enough taste of the flavors here that he/she may want to sample more— i.e., embrace other AS offerings from that late wartime era, now handily available on the internet, and which we rather brutally or at least arbitrarily leave out here. Finally, we plead guilty to a certain partiality— for mostly recognizable, good songs by the great American composers, and done in a quintessentially poignant, but "with-it" manner by this remarkable organization of the late Swing Era.

After working his men hard in rehearsals and at one-nighters, teaching and orienting as he went, Shaw's first studio session with the new contingent came November 23, 1944, with France getting liberated, but still much hard fighting to come in Europe, and even more in the Pacific theater Shaw had gotten to know first-hand. Maybe a certain gratitude and humility (given what he and his country and much of the world had been enduring) helped make this such a pleasingly great and unique Shaw band. Another part of it is that while Artie recalled putting in the most labor of all on the '39 contingent in its varied functions and many assignments, he actually took the most time and care with recordings made by this present outfit, to the great profit of listeners. Without any question or hairsplitting in our minds, this is indeed the third and last great band he ever fronted.

However, we'll slide over the bunch of four cut in his first 11/23/44 recording stint, though it featured a well-known Mercer and Arlen tune, "Acc-Cent-Tchu-ate the Positive," which was perhaps too "sunny" for the way this Shaw group would more usually sound; and also Jimmy Mundy's arranged tribute to the great Billie Holiday, "Lady Day." Instead, we'll skip forward to the next group of AS recordings, made January 9, 1945. The band now included one of a number of player replacements to come (generally more youngsters entering the orchestra), in this case, the strong trumpeter Paul Cohen, whom I later saw and heard with Count Basie. Cohen was part of a powerful Shaw section of four trumpets (versus three in the earlier Swing Era), and besides the oomph heard there, one could also add the three trombones and Charles Gentry's effective baritone sax as complementing forces.

Re the four sides cut on 1/9/45, one could easily divagate on all of them. But the one that stands out most as typifying the end of an era in American music and even history is "I'll Never Be the Same," with that poignant, autumn-like quality heard throughout, and a painting kind of feel, too, which will be the case with quite a number of others. This "I'll Never Be..." is downright melancholy and fully grabs one, and somehow, it's perfectly redolent or reflective of the period. And it showcases a new Shaw sound on clarinet that's at once truly sad but also bop-oriented, and quite different from earlier ones. And that sound melds marvelously with a band that amply follows suit, an outfit that's much stronger and more forthright than the last one, and also benefiting from better recording equipment, where technical improvements kept being made.

So the Shaw listener should surely savor this "I'll Never Be the Same" from early '45, a gem that (excuse the inadvertent reference to a later Carpenters tune) can even make one cry. If one wishes to hear the lyrics and another emotion-grabbing version, do try Billie Holiday's much earlier recording of 1937, alongside the incomparable Teddy

## Six. Swing Sunset and a Last Great Shaw Band

Wilson. But this orchestral effort is much fuller, and replete with gorgeous, interesting colors, not least via Artie leading the way on his clarinet, now triply poignant and pure October! The brass is strong, simple, but marvelous, Jon Walton on tenor sax is more ample and modern than Auld had been with the previous bunch, and Artie returns here—clear, bold, but speaking sincerely on his instrument, not just creating the kind of uncommitted pastiche heard in the edition of '41-'42. Another great soloist here, deeply admired by his employer, is the vulnerable young Marmarosa on piano, truly part of an era featuring more and more far-out jazz piano. He, too, grabs the listener on "I'll Never Be...," along with Conniff providing an emotional trombone solo and, really, the entire aggregation, with Eldridge contributing a special kick to the brass in particular. Artie darts in at the end, searching and still figuratively painting a sunset era in song—melancholy as all get-out, but also showing off a sense of inner security and care more lacking in the pre–Rangers orchestra. That final Shaw solo on "I'll Never Be..." is a mosaic of twists, hesitations and moves forward, and like a great baseball hitter, gives one a sense of waiting (as on pitches) before providing the last definitive statement at record's end. His creative reluctance is back here, but a strong, *bop*-oriented reluctance that works beautifully. In sum, this "I'll Never Be the Same" of early '45 is nothing short of a masterpiece!

Artie was no longer much into featuring vocalists with his new band, but "Can't Help Lovin' Dat Man" (by Hammerstein and Kern, the latter passing away at 60 this very year from a cerebral hemorrhage) is arresting, too, if mostly sung by Imogene Lynn, and against that strong orchestral background. And here's a rendering, too, which can make one blubber if so inclined (by the loss of love, etc.). On "Can't Help..." Artie finally steps in after Lynn's long stint of warbling, and, disabled ear or not, he's gorgeous and talking again, and meaningfully, on his secure, novel-sounding licorice stick. Yes, the great composer Kern died that year and much else was dying, too; but a lot was being born (think just of "baby boomers," not to mention an improved version of the League of Nations in the U.N., plus the terrifying atom bomb, and Artie himself flirting with faintly Communist, pacifist groups, hoping to rid the world of any and all conflict for good!). Returning to Bobby Sherwood's arrangement of this "Can't Help...," it, too, moved with the times, and is also worth a contemporary listen. However, we'll skip through the other two made on this date—"'S Wonderful" and Buster Harding's "Bedford Drive"—more jumping sides and not as much our cup of tea from that Shaw contingent. But of course the melody and words on the former will be known to many, including from old movies; and Professor Read sees touches in this version of "'S Wonderful" that are worthy of classical composers like Brahms, with rhythms and dissonances that come at one when least expected.

The next AS studio session ensued April 5, 1945, with sideman replacements coming thick and fast, though a thronged schedule of live dates helped absorb them quickly within the band, bringing these new recruits up to speed. Those newbies included a young Ollie Wilson on trombone and another relative pup, Bernie Glow, taking over for Tony Faso on trumpet. Like many, Glow loved working for Artie, such a fine, dedicated teacher, as he always felt. Was the band becoming ever better? That would be hard to say, but from 4/5/45 you simply *have* to hear its version of Kurt Weill's well-known "September Song," utterly gorgeous in this rendering, *très* autumnal, and melodic all the way, and with Artie's clarinet work especially original and downright heart-tugging. For us this one's an absolute must! One also has to tip one's cap here to the fine Ray Conniff arrangement, where he really gets the essence of the song, starting right from the ostinato brass' pointillistic intro, used throughout the piece. I once had a Shaw LP (before the "Complete..." series came out) titled *"September Song" and Other Favorites*; on the cover was a picture of a clarinet festooned with autumn leaves, yes, bringing to mind an evanescent season indeed, though in the song that obviously extends to life itself.

And again, this Shaw contingent captures all that superbly here, with Artie's brief intro on clarinet suitably morose and more dedicated, it seems, than he himself would sometimes remember of this period of his career. The saxes are together, but stronger than in early wartime, and very full and modern establishing the melody. The trombones against Kessel's pricklings on guitar continue on, with autumn very much in the foreground. But all that is really a kind of prelude to Artie's full, dramatic, and extended solo that captivates the listener as jazz worth hearing, but even more, as beautiful, stirring music. Yes, he always seemed petty calling Goodman a clarinetist and himself a musician, but here that contrast really shows. So does the fact that Ellington's clarinetist Barney Bigard dubbed Shaw the greatest big band player there was on this instrument, even as the whole swing mode was en route to a kind of extinction; and it still remains a credible estimate. It's all highlighted in Artie's ultra-poignant solo work on "September...," and as the arrangement reprises its beginning chords near the end, you may want to cry here, too!

Experienced musicians will note different touches in this masterpiece, as for example when Artie weaves across and through the harmonies, melding swing and bop and yet departs from both before letting

## Six. Swing Sunset and a Last Great Shaw Band

a spring of sorts unwind. They will also notice (back to the speaking analogy) that his subtle, arresting solo work constitutes a kind of lucid conversation between himself and the band, providing listeners with a marvelously creamy wave of sound and texture.

We realize that in our treatment total objectivity (whatever that is) would be nice, and that we should therefore devote space, as others have done, to a very opposite-type waxing from the same session, "Little Jazz," featuring Eldridge's strong, contemporary trumpet work, if not Artie. But we'd prefer to stick with the powerfully moving, fall-ish aspect of that great band, drawing from what was left of the swing idiom, moving credibly toward bebop, and somehow stirring as all get-out. Thus we move rather precipitously to a studio session coming a week and a half later (4/17/45), where this AS April continued from the viewpoint of record prep and production as nothing like Eliot's "cruelest month."

"But Not for Me" (which the band cut April 17) is one of those great Gershwin tunes highlighting the unrequited or unfindable love theme. À propos, I remember tramping all over New York in February 2018 (pre–Covid), finally locating a patrician older piano guy with a glass for tips playing at a small restaurant; and just after entering, I went right into singing "But Not...," even getting a compliment from a couple there (sounds like "the Velvet Fog," the husband said). And of course that elderly pianist knew the tune, and did a fine job of accompaniment.

Naturally, Artie's '45 "But Not for Me" is in a vastly different league. Here he has another newbie, Ralph Rosenlund, on tenor in place of Steward, the latter only 18 when he came to Shaw but already armed with progressive jazz chops, and later, playing a key role in Herman's "Four Brothers" of the Second Herd. As usual, Shaw knew and prized young talent and was always ready to give it a chance. Why Monsieur B. Singer, this once comparatively young pup, never took him up on an invite to meet him in California during the '80s and perhaps help edit the sprawling autobiographical novel he'd been working on (*The Education of Albie Snow*) I'll never know! But Artie was certainly encouraging, patient and unpatronizing when it came to the callow (me included); which is one reason this particular band glittered so much and so contrastively from his previous aggregations.

The '45 "But Not..." is snappy and strong, Artie establishing the melody on clarinet in his almost diffident, but also clear, strong, and lovely way that seems so much a step forward. The saxes are marvelous, too, powerful and pretty when they do their "collective solo" talking of sorts. Brass goes from initially muted to downright full of itself (shades of Basie et al.). And Artie returns with his searching clarinet, yes, at another of his creative peaks, and emphatically much better here on the "stick" than he'd been in late '41. Rosenlund on tenor is clearly bop-tinged, the young Ollie Wilson gets one of his many fine trombone solos (and opportunities) on "But Not," Artie comes back yet again, with more painting of sorts; and this entire take on the great Gershwin standard works wonderfully for any musically aware listener. As for pros, they may note a kind of false ending at 1:24 into the piece, a form of musical brilliance, along with how Artie weaves his solo bits in and around section activity and orchestration, till a simple, surprising real ending concludes matters in a satisfying manner.

The other two from that same session are not among my favorites but still marvelous, and both are again, well-known standards. Artie had carte blanche with such recordings (though corporate RCA would eventually put its foot down), plus he got lucrative, guaranteed cash, and had another advantage: the band was playing live engagements a good deal of the time, then diving into the studio fully primed ("ask a busy person…"), as if he knew this contingent better record like mad for posterity, while he still had it together and it was working with such collective panache.

The April 17 "Tea for Two" features Artie on rapid-paced, boppish choruses from the outset, but the whole orchestral effect here wouldn't be near as popular as, say, Les Brown's "Sentimental Journey" (cum Doris Day) of roughly the same time. Not that that seems to matter, because Artie was really into showing off his band's jazz credentials here. On his "Tea for Two" both Cohen (before his imminent departure) and Eldridge solo on trumpet, and again, the palpable modernism (especially via Artie's clarinet and Dodo's piano) shows to advantage in this arrangement, crafted by Goodman's former killer-diller, Jimmy Mundy. Again, this isn't a favorite of mine, and Professor Read also notes some orchestration here with little life, and a nod to being dance music, rather than a pure jazz piece. Artie flirts with his favorite high F's, then F#, but in both our views, doesn't really save this one sufficiently, despite how well-known the song has remained.

And then in the same April session comes Shaw's remarkable "Summertime," which I don't usually replay much, but which is *sui generis*, thanks to Eddie Sauter's innovative arrangement. Trumpeter Bernie Glow recalled in '70s retrospect how much originality Sauter contributed to this idiosyncratic version of the Gershwin chestnut; and in Berman's documentary *Artie Shaw: Time Is All You've Got*, she has an aged Shaw listening reverentially to that record's chords, splaying out in what sounds anything like summertime at all!

Instead, Sauter, using Artie and Dodo for unusual contributions

## Six. Swing Sunset and a Last Great Shaw Band

on their instruments, makes this version of the piece sound not only fall-like, but full of foreboding, and almost reflecting how one tragic period has come to an end (or near it), and another is set to take hold. As many have noted, Sauter essentially recrafts the song, though Eldridge's wah-wah trumpet solo gives one a bit of its original flavor. But even there Artie had a struggle on his hands, an unexpected one. Eldridge sometimes wanted to go his own, "star billing" way, and after Shaw's painstaking rehearsal work for several weeks, Roy surprised him in studio by dropping the plunger on a first take of this "Summertime." He simply didn't want a growling effect that seemed in his view to duplicate that of another trumpet artist, Cootie Williams. He fought hard, but Artie held his ground, just as he did when another horn player in his band, Cohen, unexpectedly threw in a very high note on another tune during a rehearsal. Shaw was the ultimate welder, the final cut man, and he finally convinced a reluctant Eldridge to do things his and Sauter's way here. But others contribute to the general effect as well. Marmarosa flying about on piano demonstrates his own synthesis of classical music and bop; Artie, too, prickles you when he comes back on his anguished-sounding licorice stick; and melancholy band chords near the end reprise those heard at the outset.

This, in sum, is anything but a happy "Summertime" at all! Masterly? No question, as Tom Nolan in his own extended analysis of it (while skirting many other great AS products for lack of space) suggests in his fine Shaw biography. Nolan is marvelous on all the strange touches here, and quotes Cohen to the effect that Sauter was almost like a novelist who was going to make something very different out of a traditional story. This of course is part of what made Artie's work so wonderful. In his partially great novel *The Red and the Black* Stendhal rendered the first part memorable by going well beyond and around a true story that had initially inspired him. The later parts worked less well when he tried to adhere more to the original non-fictional base. Similarly, Artie's role was crucial here in allowing Sauter more or less to re-create in a modernist jazz manner a tune that was familiar to many. But Nolan also shows how demanding Shaw was in terms of final recorded results, citing Eldridge to the effect that Artie could keep trying over 30 times at some points for what he wanted in all-night studio sessions. Cohen was also amazed by how immaculate Shaw made his organization's final recorded products. But again, this "Summertime" is simply not my re-listening favorite from that great '44-'45 band.[3]

Nor was it a fave of my lay listener friend, who said she simply didn't care much for this unusual arrangement of the well-known ditty (she knows pretty well all of them from that period). Unlike me, she did feel some languidness here, and saw in her mind's eye something like a big, old weeping willow of summer; and yet, she wasn't taken by all the "extra stuff" in there (almost confetti-ish, she said), the bold flourishes and dissonant embroidery detracting in her view from the song's main theme. On the whole she found this highly experimental "Summertime" too busy.

For my co-author, however, the entire arrangement is a miniature masterpiece, starting right from an intro that in his estimation could have come right out of Ravel. He finds tremendous drama preceding the first trumpet solo, and digs the episode of Artie almost screaming above and within the orchestration, itself fantastically dark at some points. In Marmarosa's eerie piano work (himself of course tormented), Read finds suggestions and shades of Milhaud and/or Stravinsky. He considers the last band "episode" as purposely close to atonal, enhancing what Sauter wanted (and where again, Artie gave that arranger plenty of freedom to remake the piece as he wished, before rendering it AS-worthy). In sum, there are certainly different ways of evaluating this recording that many have found so important and unusual for its time. Perhaps had he still been alive, Gershwin himself would have appreciated such creativity on a well-known number he'd penned a decade earlier.[4]

Jump from there to Artie's studio work of June 7, 1945, and you have another great change of gears, or certainly from that highly unusual version of "Summertime." In fact, the listener now gets new *crème de la crème*, via two superb tunes, "Easy to Love," then "Time on My Hands," both marvelously done here. This evolution reminds one of how Shaw waxed super-romantic, wonderful versions of "I Cover the Waterfront" and "Moonglow" in 1941, following his spectacularly different "Concerto for Clarinet."

On this "Easy to Love" of 1945 Artie remains (partly due to the surprising changes in his inimitable jazz brogue) the greatest big band clarinetist around, as Bigard had it,[5] and this is quintessential listening for any Shaw aficionado. Put it on after "Summertime" and you get to the acme of his efforts within his last great swing organization—an "Easy to Love" (and to enjoy) that's melodic yet modern, and where Shaw's superbly liquid, moody, and clear clarinet sound seems perfectly at one with this contingent, and also like no other. But as usual, with Shaw's fingerprints all over that ensemble sound. Easy to love? No question, and we put asterisks and exclamation points after our estimate here! This lovely record is typical Artie with his last superb aggregation, and we can't recommend it highly enough as one of the most beautiful, realized offerings of that entire edition. Both Shaw on clarinet and the marvelous saxes (anything but weak or one-dimensional, as in the

## Six. Swing Sunset and a Last Great Shaw Band

**Artie Shaw and the glamorous Ava Gardner. She truly supported his last great band of 1944–45, but the couple had inevitable troubles, too (Getty Images/Keystone-France).**

previous orchestra) tug at one, making one again feel, well, autumnal, and yet ... would this be popular? Not nearly so much as some of what even a Vaughn Monroe produced back then. Which in the long run— and have we had the musical long run!—matters little. Shaw did somewhat underplay this band's work, again feeling that it remained en route to full fruition; but that contingent's "Easy to Love" is vital, wonderful listening, and enduringly gorgeous. Artie took chances relying on some of his youthful band members here, and as an example, the teenaged Ollie Wilson provides a trombone solo that's totally right for this grand Cole Porter song, with Shaw, however, the central contributor in his solo work. At the end his searching, quite contemporary licorice stick gives the listener full emotions and a dramatic denouement. The band's tight, refined, yet driving on this wonderful waxing, but Artie's instrument steals the show with its ineffable beauty, reflecting the star he still remained.

Was he playing so well and authoritatively in part for Ava? It does seem that that aspect of his personal life in L.A. was significant, including in the home the couple eventually occupied. The good thing about Ms. Gardner was that she certainly knew how to treat a man, particularly one who was so unusual, and how not to tread on his occupational or in this case, creative toes. She would simply groove at these sounds, as fully and sensuously as she much later did to languid Sinatra records, which she played repetitively even near to her death in London.

Artie couples "Easy" with a superb B-side "Time on My Hands" (check the lyrics as sung by the great Billie in her 1940 version); and again, he grabs the main melody from the get-go, so minor-ish and so "him." The pace is sprightly, but still fall-like and again, reflecting the end of an era; and it's another pleasurable masterpiece by this marvelous band, going through the paces on a truly strong, meaty chart. Artie's solo work here is simple, deceivingly so, yet assertive, and the brass is appropriate and despite its bop flavor, doesn't overwhelm the tune's romantic nature, which in this jazzy rendering is more than given its due. The saxes provide remarkable "collective soloing" against bass and drums, and in those passages seem somehow to embody both old (pre-strings) Shaw and new Shaw, too—a summing up, yet a real step forward. Both trumpet and tenor solos are apt here, too, simple but correctly forthright for the time. And then comes great ensemble work on "Time..." nearer its close. To wind things up on a fine arrangement, Artie's clarinet once more prances forward in a glancing, offhand, yet powerful manner, effectively topping off this recorded masterpiece. And yet: would this 1945 "Time on My Hands" have been right for, say, jitterbug dancing? More so for listening, we'd say, and that would be the case whether putting it on the record player back in the '40s, or procuring it online at the handy computerized point where we now find ourselves.

The next day, June 8, came two more masterly Shaw contributions, the Gershwins' "A Foggy Day," and a version of the standard "These Foolish Things Remind Me of You," which again, you *have* to hear! Contractual demands for quite a slew of recordings forced Shaw to keep this band very busy, indeed, but always in his and its own way. Autumn again on this "Foggy Day"? For certain it's palpable here, and this is another of my favorites in Shaw's end-of-the-war "book." Our frequent references to this band as almost "painting" in music seem apposite and exemplified here, too.

"Foggy Day" sprints out in an earnest, quite rapid meter and isn't as romantic as the piece could be when done by others in a more leisurely way. There's great lead trumpet here by Eldridge, and a fine band sound verging a bit on the Basie mode, but with Artie still the virtuosic star. Those with training in classical music will note incongruous "Old Regime" touches, such as a startling, yet effectively-ornamented baroque tribute, complete with terminal trill at about one minute into the recording. I reiterate my preference for the sad, romantic, and poignant by this AS edition, and thankfully, one gets that even more so in a superbly moving "These Foolish Things," cut on the same date.

Wilson's trombone leads in fully on this standard against muted brass (Artie ever and again giving this teenager his chance); then Shaw's brooding clarinet unfurls the melody cum unique flourishes, clear as a fine September day, truly major jazz work on parade, with solid percussion beneath him on this Conniff arrangement, and Artie still demonstrating that "painting" quality in his work. The leaves are definitely turning, then falling in this lovely rendering of "These Foolish...." Love is lost, but savored in retrospect, and in no way does Artie vitiate the tune's original flavor via his marvelous bop-flavored contributions.

Continuing our analysis of "These Foolish Things," which we highly recommend, the saxes on the bridge are bent rather like those of '38-'39, but different and definitely committed. Rosenlund on tenor is at one with modern players of his time, though Artie still wanted and stipulated a certain simplicity in such soloists. The trombone ensemble and Dodo's touches beneath on piano keep that super-autumnal tone intact, and Artie returns, still the greatest, most sensitive, emotion-producing swing clarinetist ever. Near the end of "Things" he engages in some of his characteristically poignant "searching," and thus concludes what is among the most affecting of recordings made by this superb band. To Read, the sound here seems burnt-caramel rich, and with a kind of opaque, dense, and warm core that feels truly unique (to his classical music–seasoned ears)!

The day following the recording of "These Foolish Things" and "A Foggy Day" Artie cut but one side, a fine, if then unissued "You Go to My Head," featuring Dorothy Allen's vocal. Again, singing wasn't central for the 1945 AS band, but why this particular effort wasn't released back then remains a bit of a mystery.

Several days later (6/12/45) came more quintessential, fall-ish band work, especially on another great Gershwin tune, "The Man I Love," also mysteriously unissued at the time, but thankfully easy to find later on. Of course Shaw had already made an entrancing version of that standard with his popular band of 1939; but this one is equally great and poignant, if embodying the old French "vive la différence" concept. I simply can't believe that in retrospect Artie knocked his comparative lack of "dedication" in this era or often considered the 1949 "progressive" band he later formed more ambitious and important. He'd unfortunately fail to add that it was far less emotionally satisfying than this one. And more confused in its orientation, and often too wan. Again,

I have to think that one positive in this particular Shaw era of late '44-'45, and which should be highlighted, was the anchoring he felt via the person who was maybe the most "quality" of his women, that sincere if fetching Ms. Gardner. For whatever congeries of reasons, we find Shaw's work of that time, including this "Man I Love," truly and completely committed.

The arrangement here is by Eddie Sauter, but this is emphatically no "Summertime." Sure it's marvelous jazz, but it also honors the melancholy, melodic timbre of Gershwin's great song in a way that the more experimental "Summertime" didn't. This recorded result is accessible, gorgeous, and definitely emotion-creating. But it's still somewhat "progressive" for the time, too. A strong big band intro gets proceedings moving quickly for Artie, whose boppy, complex, yet emotional clarinet captures the piece's essence, while also being idiosyncratic jazz (and of course that tone of his—much stronger and more compelling than in his last philharmonic-type brogue—is still central). Artie riffs superbly, before a bridge where tamped-down brass plus trombones joust against the reeds; but then he grabs the spotlight again on this lovely rendering—both wild and controlled, his usual complex self on display. This is masterful, moving jazz indeed. When the Bellows visited and I played the earlier 1939 Shaw "Man I Love" for them, I also wished I'd played them this one of '45, with its probing, stunning and sometimes unpredictable modernist lines.

Continuing on this later version of "Man...," Artie is the great melancholy star there, but the saxes eventually take the melody, mirroring his own searching quality with their fine blend. Eldridge provides a solid open-horn solo, an ebullient player, if suffering deeply from that hurtful discrimination of the era at various venues where this orchestra was playing. The full band drives to a close, and this is another recorded marvel mirroring that end-of-the-war ambiance we keep citing here. Above all, Artie's liquid poignancy and amazing jazz technique is at one of his true clarinet apogees, seen also in his lovely work on the Rodgers and Hart song, "I Could Write a Book," made at the same session.

Skipping through the next studio stint where he cut three little-known songs by Conniff—"Kasbah," "Lament," and "Lucky Number," none among my favorites—Shaw and band recorded "Love Walked In" and "Soon" on 7/3/45, both by the redoubtable Gershwins and both arranged with a similar flavor by George Siravo. Of the two, "Soon" stays more in mind. It canters quickly from the top, featuring that muscular but lean ensemble, with a big, lavish sound; but setting up for Artie's urgent, much lighter, yet thick clarinet, embracing and "massaging" the main melody. Trombones continue on it, until Artie reenters the fray in a rather simple way, not as chance-taking as on Sauter's "Man I Love" chart, but still lovely. Eldridge's muted trumpet solo is certainly acceptable, but he seems more himself on the louder, unplugged sorties on his horn. Reeds take over and are beautiful as well, Eldridge returns, and that powerful band prepares for Artie's reemergence via brief clarinet comments; but again, displaying that "searching" quality, as if his delicate but irrepressible clarinet is fleeing the powerful Herman- or Basie-type ensemble, his strong and soft, powerful yet sensitive sides apparent again here. Great contrasts on "Soon" of smooth saxes and hard brass, and just the whole ambiance here show clearly that swing's on the way out, and bop's now in the saddle!

A few days later came "Keepin' Myself for You" (7/6/45), a gorgeous song Artie obviously loved, as he didn't usually re-record one he'd already done (in this case with his first Gramercy Five, and beautifully so, in 1940). And yet the '45 version with the full band absolutely shines. The polished ensemble asserts itself on the intro, then Artie splays out melody cum jazz riffs—reluctant again, it seems, melodic, melancholy, yet also speaking in a sincere, non-cynical, beautiful way, which is romantic yet modern. The plugged-up brass takes over discreetly on the bridge, and saxes regain the main theme, more emphatic than in previous Shaw editions, and well-mixed. When it's their turn, the trombones also give us a fine nostalgic blend, their own kick at the melodic can. Tenor sax player Walton is "glancing" and boppy in his solo, then Artie again sails in, this time on the bridge, and is again beautiful in his licorice-stick work over suitable band fills. The powerful, full ensemble drives toward the close, with an AS arpeggio at the end, and this constitutes a second fine "Keepin' Myself..." for those who like the tune.

We've decided to skip a one-record 7/11/45 studio session featuring a vocal interlude, and jump to that of 7/14/45 several days later, and a lovely rendering of "They Can't Take That Away From Me." This is another Gershwin standard, arranged here by Siravo, who helped give this band its personality. Artie is wonderfully right for it in an understated, yet bop-oriented way, meaning that he's a bit "off" on the main melody, which he takes marvelously into the bridge. Again, he's not as adventurous here as on, say, "Man I Love," but still gorgeous and emotionally committed! (Which remains the handiest way of describing his work in this period.) His chamber music–like trill, a stately interjection, ends the first half or so of the record, a bit of baroque ornamentation that will surprise the listener. But the saxes stay modern and strong on the main melody, with more closed voicings than in '39, but still a great section. Muted trumpets also embrace the familiar melody, Eldridge's solo is more than acceptable, there's another chamber music–type comment by Artie near the close; and in sum, this is a wonderful rendering of a timeless American chestnut. On his version of "They Can't Take That Away," we hear Artie playing with musical phrases that admirably honor that song's lyrics, constituting a poetic enhancing of the composer's original intent.

As does (at the same session) the AS version of "Our Love Is Here to Stay," again by the formidable Gershwins (and written for a film—*The Goldwyn Follies*—as many of these songs were, if often crafted for Broadway, too). This may sound repetitive, but Artie's remarkably pretty and poetic again on this '45 "Our Love," taking the well-known air from the top and almost making one lachrymose in the process. No question: Ava must have adored such fare, and him, too. Shaw was absolutely the emotional best at his trade, or certainly at this point. Of course he had technical chops that astonished other clarinet players like Bigard or Woody Herman; but whatever the register (including the highest), the feelings he aroused remained crucial. For some reason this one strikes a poignantly portending chord in the listener, given the baby boom generation around the corner and much change to come, not least in popular music. On "Our Love..." Artie returns for another romp, trying consciously and quite successfully to be "with it," yet without sacrificing that trademark sweetness of his. Powerful lead trumpet work swings the band forward, and Shaw comes back again, clear in the extreme, and highly listenable. The great brass ensemble glitters, but an obviously more dulcet Shaw darts in for what feels a sixth time or so on "Our Love..."; and ever and again, one feels the tragedy of a great composer (including of this tune) dying, as George G. did, so very young. Again, Artie honors that remarkable man with orchestration that's both dramatic and simple here, and with his own contributions showcased, legitimately so. How he assimilated new aspects of bebop without sacrificing his romantic quality constituted a real tour de force.

In the same session he sticks with the Gershwins, this time on one of their lesser-known tunes, "I Was Doing All Right," arranged by Siravo and revealing the strength of this splendid band. Did Artie not have quite enough time really to get it together with that bunch, as he'd claim? Wrong, or let's say overly modest, self-estimation. In "Doing All Right" his "newish" clarinet speaks well against that more overwhelming ensemble, with Artie dynamically softer on his instrument, but authoritative in the riffs he sprinkles or peppers into the dish! Midway through, the fine trio of trombones takes the melody. Walton on his tenor solo is simple but right, Kessel gets a short break on guitar; and the ending has a melodic similarity to some of the other tunes here, thanks to Siravo, who provides an arranger's predictable "product," you

## Six. Swing Sunset and a Last Great Shaw Band

might say, but appropriately so, given Shaw's unmistakable editorial stamp on all such recordings.

Three days later the band was back for more recorded artistry, the '44-'45 "oeuvre" enhanced and expanded without any loss of depth or verve. In this session of July 17 we get yet another from the Gershwins, one of their greatest and most well-known tunes, "Someone to Watch Over Me." But Sauter's arrangement removes some of its usual yearning quality, giving a rapid pace to the Shaw version, and with the full orchestra, not Artie, taking first chorus, prancing forward with brio. Ollie Wilson, so competent on trombone and really wonderful given his age, grabs a second chorus of the melody; then Artie jumps in at the bridge, languidly energetic, but quicker than might at first be apparent. The big band powerhouse driven most by the brass takes over the melody, and this "Someone" remains anything but its usual melancholy number. The poignancy is more of the period, and also what this AS edition at least somewhat augurs of post-swing progressive jazz. But Artie never sacrifices his sense of beauty here. On his return in the song's second half or so, his clarinet's still gorgeous, and what a major musical organization you feel here! How he worked them (Silly Putty–style) into a cohesive unit of such high quality beggars the imagination. On this his ex-sidemen would pretty well all agree. Near the end of "Someone" Shaw's repeated intrusions on clarinet have him competing in his typically yearning, effective manner against that strong, united band, the resulting masculine-feminine interplay well displayed (a way of putting it that would perhaps have been less controversial back then). In sum, this 1945 "Someone to Watch Over Me" is another melding of bop and swing that works, bringing out the best, and brilliantly, in the Gershwins' familiar tune.

In terms of the masculine-feminine dialectic noted here, and just as I've perhaps "triggered" by such a view, I think it's also worth highlighting again the strange mix in one Arthur Shaw of sensitivity (which his band players knew up close, as did some of his femmes); and of something very forceful that could even reach a point of Putinesque brutality! That mix did not always work well in his personal life, far from it. But at his musical peaks (including in this period) it was a mélange that produced something truly wonderful and unique.

A couple days following the previous session, on 7/19/45, the Shaw band cut one record only, a tune called "The Maid with the Flaccid Air," written and arranged by Sauter as a tribute of sorts to Debussy's "The Maid with the Flaxen Hair" ("La Fille aux cheveux de lin"). And this one's remarkable, too, surpassing in my view Sauter's more lauded arrangement of the AS band's "Summertime." "The Maid..." has that painting quality we've been stressing so much here, and impressionistically (à la Debussy) makes us see the young lady perhaps sauntering along on a pretty spring or summer day. The Shaw orchestra has a marvelous feel here, using truly playful chords that are hard to describe. In fact, this is another masterpiece of popular music. There are such colors here, such a sweet tussle between reeds and muted trumpets, and even a Seurat-like pointillism in the layers and interweaving of instruments. Trombones on the bridge, Dodo's unusual piano work, and Wilson's sad solo full of longing feed right into Artie, sprinting around beautifully with that unbelievable tone of his, especially interesting against Gentry's baritone sax. "Maid..." is so pretty that Ava surely must have savored it, the sweetness, the sadness, the strangeness, the flavorings and flourishes provided by Sauter, and played by this topflight group to do his and Artie's bidding.

Why Shaw kept saying this contingent wasn't as "ambitious" as the '49 one he later mounted eludes me. This was a far better, more melodic, and emotion-inducing bunch of players and arrangements. It had a sound, an accent, a personality that unlike either the '41-'42 second-edition stringed group, or the short '49-'50 "progressive" effort we'll later sketch, really stays with you, adding significantly to Artie's previous best. There are echoes in this band of Shaw's first great swing organization, but this one's more complex, especially on Sauter products like "The Maid...," if less earnest, less sweetly romantic, less popular for sure than that earlier band had been. However, this one is still wonderful as a well-realized, finished step forward into aspects of post-war, post–Swing Era jazz. And yet this still *is* the Swing Era! If in its final phase.... Again, do punch on "The Maid with the Flaccid Air," both daring Shaw, but melodic, tender, and well worth hearing. It's a masterly piece that deserves its own place in the history of that period, every bit as much as does more accessible fare by this or that popular crooner of the time. And perhaps you'll end up for a day or two compulsively and repetitively whistling a tune you'd never heard before.

But back then Artie had a fight on his hands to get RCA's approval for this unwieldy (to them) but innovative "Maid...." Thankfully, it made it onto a 12-inch record (versus the usual 10-inch 78), and with Sauter's equally unusual "Summertime" finally released with it as well.[6] Tension with the execs, particularly a self-important Eli Oberstein, wouldn't subside and became ever more intolerable to Artie, who certainly knew his music far better than they did!

After "The Maid..." he got his players back in studio the next day (July 20) to record one more (versus the bigger batches of yore). This "No One But You" was co-written by Shaw and featured another good Siravo

## Six. Swing Sunset and a Last Great Shaw Band

arrangement. Artie's solo from the outset is lively and lovely, just skipping along, and one thinks again of Ava, Ava, Ava! And of how much she must have dug (and helped inspire) such fine work. The strong band grappling with Artie's darting, and yes, more feminine clarinet creates a fine contrapuntal effect. Eldridge provides a trumpet solo that's modern and strong, and on piano, Dodo solos as the bop master he'd become, giving us strange chords anticipatory of so much to come in the jazz world. Saxes and clarinets "speak" beautifully near the end, Artie flits warmly above them, and this is not at all '39 Shaw, yet marvelous. The orchestra unleashes its great ensemble power when it needs to—taste being the hallmark here, relentless, unremitting taste. As usual Artie not only heard an evolving sound on his own instrument, but an entire band flavor he wanted, too! And got.... There is such an *oeuvre* sort of quality here, where the further one goes in the AS recording history of '44-'45, the more each arrangement (with exceptions like "Maid..." or "Summertime") becomes an interestingly varied rubber stamp of the previous one, but still emphatically pleasing. You can feel that strong editorial hand (emanating primarily from Shaw and his arrangers) at least as much in this swing organization as was the case in his two previous top ones. And it works very well, indeed.

The next day (July 21) the band was back for another solo waxing of a good tune, "They Didn't Believe Me"—penned by Kern with Herbert Reynolds for the stage musical *The Girl from Utah* and arranged here by Sauter, whose work Artie so prized. How the Shaw band could busy itself in rehearsals and live events, then record such tunes so seamlessly, yes, after round-the-clock engagements and other warm-ups, boggles the mind. "They Didn't Believe Me" has a gorgeous intro, with collective clarinets giving off a kind of Western twang, and you just have a sense of youthfulness here (remember how young so many of these sidemen themselves were) and exhilaration. Rosenlund's tenor solo is followed by the great and grand Artie, playing for Ava, it still seems, and at a real peak. On "Believe..." he sounds downright regal, and already "après-guerre." Then Dodo gets unleashed for one of his own careful but free piano solos, offered by one of the band's real characters. Wilson again contributes on trombone with much feeling, so often absent in today's musical efforts. And the powerful band is Herman-strong near the close of the disc, one that again, you'll want to hear, with its complementing, contrastive, utterly tasteful flavorings; but overall adhering to the tune's fine melody, if showing off a unique band's chops very adroitly indeed.

Lest one think I've pushed my co-author into agreement, he, too, finds brilliant colors in the record's opening, and via the doubling of clarinets and saxes, a kind of statement, as if to say: "We're painting with a new brush here." Reared on and playing the classics (but also a veteran of L.A. studio work), Professor Read hears AS soloing with real intention on "They Didn't Believe Me," turning each phrase into something of great interest, and into conversations, too, with the orchestral ensemble—short, economical, yet virtuosic. At 1:14 into the record, Read finds a fountain of sorts splashing out with a figurative burst of sunshine. I've also kept foregrounding the "painting" quality of this end-of-an-era band, and am simply amazed that someone with a far greater sense of musical history echoes that same viewpoint here.

As this fine AS contingent pushed to its own close, soon to break up (partly for lack of popularity) and end a long Swing Era stint with RCA, two great records followed, cut July 24, 1945. Many of these sides will be welcome discoveries to the uninitiated and may (as Artie would have liked) help certain young people evolve musically in their own ways, too. The band's "Dancing on the Ceiling" (by Lorenz Hart and Richard Rodgers) starts with a forthright lead trumpet intro; then the trombones, marvelously knit together, take the main melody, followed by a Walton solo on tenor in his unmistakably boppish, yet almost terse manner. After the brass shows its cohesive oomph, Artie speaks, and again in almost feminine charge of his clarinet. The powerhouse brass returns, and if alto player Les Robinson said the Shaw orchestra cum strings of '40-'41 "sang," well, so does this one, and with unexpectedly marvelous chord work. Artie comes back for a fuller airing on his instrument, searching and searching, as if chased and not wanting to let up (the man was of course "in search" his entire life!). Then on this "Ceiling" rendition comes open trumpet work and that of a clutch of reeds stepping out on the town, it feels; and more solo work, including Dodo's wonderful piano stint on the bridge, and ... what riffs here! What a modernist sense! What gorgeous frills and touches near the end of this version of "Dancing...," with Artie ranging upward one more time on his licorice stick. This one's easy to love all the way, and again, Professor Read sees Artie having the kind of canvas here where he could really sketch a detailed landscape of sorts. On this one Shaw also gives himself more prominence than on certain other records he made in that period, and reaches real alpine terrain (including a high G) that feels natural for this distinguished clarinetist.

The B-side features the AS take on a great American song, Vernon Duke's "I Can't Get Started with You," known as a hit in the Berigan vocal cum trumpet rendering of 1937, and one of the top American standards ever created by the composer (real name Vladimir Dukelsky) of both "April in Paris" and "Autumn in New York." (And co-written in this case with Ira Gershwin.) As the AS band—in our view, the last of Artie's great swing contingents—approaches the end with Victor, and soon of its existence, I think of sad Dodo soon scattering, and yes, an always searching Artie, too. All that poignancy helped make such recordings so moving.

This "I Can't Get Started" (made on 7/24/45) features a fine intro from that great brass, and you know Shaw will then embrace things beautifully from the get-go; and indeed, a listener won't forget his unspinning of the main melody, which is sumptuous. Shaw takes two choruses, with his sense of musical beauty and his "painting" proclivity again paramount here; and then on the bridge, as if not to destroy what the listener just got, the brass is decently reined in, while discreetly jostling against the reeds. Then the full ensemble takes the melody again, and some great lead sax work follows, sprightly and delicious against Dodo's piano fills. All this is both arranged and phrased in masterly fashion, with fine trombone work following, and Eldridge on trumpet wonderful, too, but subordinated to the entire band's overall "feel." It does remind me of those books Artie recommended in conversation, particularly Halle's *Out of Chaos* and Thomas' *The Lives of a Cell*, both authors lauding the virtues of symbiotic or synergistic togetherness in civilizations and physiology, and they might have added, in music, too. (Think of the later, John Phillips–honed "Mamas and Papas" sound, or Brian Wilson's Four Freshmen–tinged "Beach Boys" blend.) On this particular number, what a self-assured, cohesive Shaw brogue one gets! The ensemble call-and-response between brass and reeds is emphatically '45, not '39. But it works. At the close of "Started..." Artie arcs upward on clarinet, and this is a far more than worthy version of the Duke number, and one of the last masterpieces cut by a doomed musical contingent, all the pieces of the puzzle about to fly away "come le foglie," as the Italians might say: yes, rather like light, blowable autumn leaves, a truly apt way to put it for this most autumnal-sounding of swing bands.

Weighing in with his refined sense of the classical music past (one Artie shared), Read calls this version of "Started..." AS chamber music at its best, the orchestration drawing listeners into a compact, intimate realm, but Artie in a figurative silk bathrobe still the star, moving in every direction, yet regaining the theme and finding the "entrances" again and again with security and balance. Read sees a simultaneously laid-back and intense quality here, a kind of sound that may have later influenced the Modern Jazz Quartet.

The next day in July there followed another sole waxing, "Just Floating Along" (composed by Siravo and Shaw), which we will skip past, though other listeners may not wish to do so. And three days later

(7/28/45) came the band's last recording of a standard for RCA, Dorothy Fields' and Jimmy McHugh's "Don't Blame Me," unissued at the time by spiteful company execs; and cut at the same session with a forgettable "Yolanda," which inexplicably was, the latter including a male vocal. All that was left for Shaw with this company was one more recording by the big band, then a few done by the latest edition of Artie's Gramercy Five. Why had the end now come into view? Well again, it *was* the end of the Swing Era, the crooners obviously set to take over and win out with the record-buying public. And Shaw had also had an acerbic war of words going with that know-nothing suit at RCA who wanted this and that musically, and wouldn't get it from this tenacious, highly qualified bandleader and player. In addition, Artie had tired of playing different venues in different places, wanting to put down marriage roots with Ava. That old "picket fence" idyll was something he kept intermittently seeking, but of course couldn't sustain.

But rather than accentuate the negative, we must once more credit Ms. Gardner for truly inspiring Artie during this last fabulous musical period of his. Did they quarrel? No question! Himself a voluminous, if interesting talker (as I can attest), he shut her up repetitively at parties. In a well-known anecdote he derided her as well for reading junk like Kathleen Winsor's novel *Forever Amber*, then, ironically, moved on to a subsequent marriage with ... Winsor! Additionally, he criticized Ava for not paying attention to home realities, ruing ever and again (through to his last wife, Evelyn Keyes) his repetitive penchant for marrying starlets who couldn't cook very well. (Although one of Shaw's sidemen remembered a fine Thanksgiving dinner at Shaw's home on Bedford Drive in L.A. during the fall of '44, one la Gardner prepared wonderfully for his band members, some of them badly missing families in the East.)[7] He was also good at overwhelming and marginalizing Ava's former friends and associates. À propos, he'd been similarly adept at ridding himself of Lana Turner's clingy mother, who had a habit of dropping in on the couple. When the bell rang yet again, and when finally he'd had enough, the impulsive Shaw decided to come to the door on that occasion in the altogether! Lana's mother, too, learned to keep her distance.[8]

Was there, however, real depth in this relationship of Artie and Ava, both similarly hurt by the "fishbowl" nature of what their fame had brought them? Certainly. Gardner did value Shaw's Jewishness and would use his full Hebrew name at times, while Artie would employ the diminutive "Avalah" for her, and with obvious affection as well.

Returning to the music made by this last great AS band, and again registering a certain astonishment at how all three of the top ones were so different, marvelously so, I also have to reemphasize both Shaw's overestimation and underestimation of things he did professionally (as with certain people he knew). How in subsequent interviews he could keep playing down this '44-'45 organization in favor of a more "ambitious" 1949 one (he loved repeating that adjective)[9] just confounds the present observer. Because this end-of-the war aggregation was far more realized and enjoyable for listeners, including now. It had more than sufficient emotional musicality, a wonderful blend of so many different elements, whereas the '49-'50 band (see below) would palpably lack emotive verve and sincerity in its recordings, and even Shaw tried to do there what he and Heraclitus never wanted to do: i.e., step back into the same body of water one more time.

In connection with moving forward creatively, Artie once told me on the phone that "you have to write what obsesses you"; and I suppose being fully and above all, emotionally obsessed in the musical world amounts to the same thing. And that he definitively showed with this '44-'45 band, as he didn't nearly enough with some of his later, post–Swing Era comeback or synthesizing attempts, before completely abandoning the métier in 1954. This element of real caring was again, a critical one in all three of his great swing contingents, the last one (despite his subtle auto-critiques and usual jibes at know-nothing audiences) a more than worthy part of that triumvirate.

Speaking of writing or playing musically what obsesses one, what (for you who'd like more "backstory") of the main author here? Has he been "obsessed" with producing this book on a great Swing Era icon? Absolutely not. In the period when I spoke to Shaw on the phone, from the summer of '78 through 1984 or so, I never thought of "cashing in" that way. Has the present "senior" author been obsessed with listening to (and relistening to) Artie's superb recorded work over many years? For certain, despite the fact that in one of our conversations Artie called that a form of laziness. In a well-known anecdote illustrating his mindset here, Shaw once responded to an admirer's praise of his work on the licorice stick by mailing the fellow a clarinet![10] What of those endless talks with the master? Was I "obsessed" with speaking over the phone approximately every month or so with this great, but somewhat gruff man? No, no, and no. Why assume the private person and artist are identical? Why keep trying to pierce that veil? Well, I did, and the "why" is open, I admit, to a variety of psychological interpretations, aimed not at Shaw but at yours truly, or at least who I was back then. Artie would sometimes speak in this regard of my search for a substitute father of sorts. But again, was it somewhat futile to try and pierce that artistic curtain? Of course it was. Shaw's imposing musical output was and is the main event, not what he expatiated on in his prolix, strong, and relentlessly intellectual manner. This I know and probably should have known back then. At least I eventually stopped calling!

Returning to the AS "Don't Blame Me," recorded in the summer of '45: one virtue here again, as we close out our assessments of this great contingent's work, is how Artie's old recordings can still introduce many new listeners to a slew of fine, romantic tunes hatched in the '20s, '30s, or '40s. His version of "Don't Blame Me," along with his different bands' takes on many other songs, presents a kind of "Great American Songbook" of yore, and in a very pleasant manner.

The following point also needs underlining: and that is how much Artie benefited by taking tunes from composing masters and then enhancing them. Many of the great composers back then were Jewish—Rodgers, Kern, the Gershwins, Romberg, Duke, and on it goes. Many had huge romantic longings that found their way into their work. Often their parents and certainly grandparents hailed from *shtetls* in Central or Eastern Europe, *Fiddler on the Roof*-type milieus, where getting to know pulchritudinous Gentile goddesses was an impossible no-no, and for the better part of 2,000 years! Music, of course, was central in Jewish religious services over all those centuries. So was plain suffering, which certainly helps create moving tunes, as many in those synagogues were. And finally came the happy, grateful embrace of "golden America" with all its incredible opportunities. You get that deep, parvenu-ish (if you will) love of a brassy, cacophonous, romantic U.S. in much of the songwriting produced by these masters, and just for openers, one could cite George Gershwin's masterful and unique composition *Rhapsody in Blue*. Naturally, too, one must add in all the gigs provided for these great tunesmiths by a thriving Broadway and Hollywood, run back then by no-nonsense types who wanted good, copious product, and by the proverbial two weeks yesterday! From all that inter-stimulation in a truly classy period, Artie certainly benefited, and so have his many listeners.

The AS "Don't Blame Me" waxed 7/28/45 is based on another Siravo arrangement and it's marvelous. It's got a pretty intro, and then Artie's dramatically soulful on this wonderful melody, simple but not simple yet again, as he takes top billing from the get-go, and justifiably. Here he amply reveals the swath inside him that was so sensitive, and which I rarely got from within his tough outer carapace in our conversations. (Though in his documentary interviews, i.e., his performances of sorts, one does.) On "Don't Blame Me" the strong band plays on the bridge, Artie dives back in, showcasing himself as a delicate foil of sorts, then the saxes grab the main melody; and Walton's ensuing tenor solo is oblique and bop-flavored, but not recondite or heavy-handed, rather like that entire band. Dodo, too, is fabulous in his novel piano work here. Eldridge's lead trumpet swings things through to the end, but Artie comes back a couple more times for pretty interjections of sorts. Read also considers this "Don't Blame Me" a kind of musical jewel, displaying a truly inward-looking mood, as if Artie were retreating and crying out simply to be left alone!

Two days later came the last recording on RCA by this full AS band, "I Can't Escape from You" (7/30/45); and it's going to be a real discovery for some, and seems highly apt as the "closer" of sorts. Artie spins it out, and his clarinet work here is sad, earnest, and appropriately repetitive (he keeps going back to the tune's main, haunting refrain), making for a plaintive, unusual, and nicely self-centered effect. That anguished, repetitive element in Shaw's "I Can't Escape..." will stay with a listener, too, just as much-repeated refrains in rock hits of the '50s and '60s did for many boomers. This is Artie both moving onward and giving up, it feels—hopeful but also regretful. The whole number is a polished masterpiece, with the '45 Shaw band now a near-extinct machine of redoubtable, unified intensity. The record—especially those stubbornly iterated, lachrymose clarinet variations—almost shows Artie talking back forcefully but sadly, expressing his anguish to the hidebound "suits" at RCA, a company he'd been with since the summer of '38, and which was finally dropping him.

I speak above of the repetitive refrains in quite a number of rock hits to come and would like to present a recent insight related to Shaw on that subject. I had long agreed with Artie's own view that he'd gone as far as he could in the jazz world before calling it completely quits in the fall of '54. I always understood his need as well to educate himself in a wide variety of other pursuits, hobbies, and work-related endeavors, versus immersing himself with such tunnel vision in the field of music (a wide tunnel, indeed!). I could also comprehend his oft-expressed regrets—saying, for example, that he didn't miss the clarinet any more than a person who had a gangrenous arm removed misses that limb! (How sad such an analogy becomes in light of all the recently paralyzed and maimed American vets.)

What I *didn't* think till recently, after decades of being enmeshed in things Shaw, was that had he somehow held on to his demanding instrumental and arranging chops he could have adapted to rock, too; and maybe even regained a certain popularity (despite growing baldness and wrinkles). Perhaps he might even have crafted an unexpected hit or several in that genre, why not? And not as simply another Acker Bilk or Pete Fountain!

This, however, was the man who pointedly said that he, Goodman,

Ellington et al. did more musically than the overwhelmingly popular Beatles (he might well have added Elvis or the Stones). Even worse, he felt that the Beatles ruined popular music itself!

All that notwithstanding, I do think that had he wanted to shelve all those other pursuits he later embraced, Shaw could possibly have adapted to the rock mode, even if only behind the scenes. And that he might have contributed significantly in that direction, and again, in a way that a player like Goodman, great as he was, could never have done. Artie's protean nature, his extreme curiosity, insatiability, and penchant for change—all these attributes (minuses as they could also be) might well have been worthwhile in this regard.

The Artie-Benny discussion or tussle (which no "Shavian" can ever seem to avoid) reminds me, again parenthetically, of what a perceptive "ex" of mine once said, examining swing album covers with an avuncular, bespectacled Goodman on this or that one, and a handsome, dashing, full-haired Artie on others. She blurted out something interesting, perhaps understanding Goodman's one-track, dogged nature (dying with his boots on while practicing like mad into his seventies); versus Shaw's constant need to change directions and be more spontaneous, ecumenical, and ultimately more interesting. She declared bluntly, "I would have married Benny [he of one stable marriage only and a family man]. But I would have had an affair with Artie!" Chris Griffin, Goodman's fine trumpet player in the '30s, painted something of a rather similar contrast between that single-tracked, quite predictable Benny and the more human, well-rounded Artie in a conversation we had.

There were two last Shaw studio sessions for RCA (August 2 and 8, 1945), but not with the full band; rather, with a reconstituted Gramercy Five, which was anything but a replica of the initial one. This Gramercy featured Shaw with Eldridge on trumpet, Kessel on electric guitar, Dodo on piano, Morris Rayman on bass, and Lou Fromm on drums. As if thumbing his nose at RCA, particularly the contentious Oberstein, Artie chose to cut five originals on these dates, one August 2, four on the 8th, all composed by Shaw himself with John Carleton.

The first of them, "Scuttlebutt" (8/2/45), used a recent slang term for its title and has an interesting collective sound, again quite different from that of the first Gramercy contingent. This one's a real swinger, and Dodo, albeit classically trained, is ultra-modern on piano here, though there isn't much of a melody about. What one gets is a novel "feel," particularly fine bass and drum work complementing Marmarosa's up-to-date work on keyboard. Artie contributes to the collective sound here, but doesn't solo till three-quarters of the way through, and then lets himself go jazz-wise. Kessel, too, is more unleashed than usual on his guitar solo. Those execs notwithstanding, lots of new fans these days might be drawn to such work.

On August 8—anything recorded in studios now heavily overshadowed by the lethal nuclear clouds over Japan, portending a dangerous world to come—came this combo's last offerings for RCA. "The Gentle Grifter" has a neat ensemble sound, and Dodo, such a sweet, beaten soul (literally and figuratively), again contributes sensationally on piano; while Artie makes this a species of swing, just as that musical mode was pretty well done. His clarinet work is fabulous on the number, Kessel again gets a chance to show his worth on guitar, Eldridge cum plunger prepares for Dodo to return marvelously on the ivories, and the group collectively regains the melody at the close. By contrast, something called "Mysterioso" is not one of my favorites, with a predictably eerie atmosphere presented, and featuring Artie, but only a bit "Nightmare"-ish in his solo work here. Let's face it, however: pretty well everything Shaw and his groups did had taste, even as he was now starting to leave the center of American music.

He and his sidemen had been recording at breakneck speed over that summer of 1945. The band rehearsed within an inch of its life, played many live dates, but kept going into the studio to make those records, too—many, as noted, superb. Finally, there was a blessed two weeks of respite in the second half of August, which for Artie meant Malibu beach time with Ava. The band was back to playing in September, but once Artie got a final divorce nailed down with Betty Kern in early October, then married Gardner a week later (on the 17th), this great band was now to be broken up for good. Shaw's two versions on that? One is that he just couldn't stay too long with this onerously prepared bunch, given all it required of him; and the other—that he wanted to make the Hollywood "picket fence" life work with Gardner, which predictably didn't take for very long.

Of course cynics not only about the mercurial Shaw but about such a place to make a marriage last might say something like: "Hollywood? Are you kidding?" But in fact, there was a big difference between today's L.A. and Artie's back then, where he'd already been leading a stable private life and a thronged, satisfying professional one, too; and yes, with Ava as a kind of human ballast. Paradoxically, New York, with its concentrated congeries of talents in varied fields, was much more distractive, one might say, for a type like Shaw; and soon it would also beckon him in the classical music department as well.

Artie had six more sides in the can from that great '44-'45 organization, but the band was gone for good by mid–November and he no longer had RCA to bring out these discs. So he moved to a jazz-oriented "indie," Musicraft, and, using his own cash, had that company release these recordings. However, such tunes as "The Hornet" and "Let's Walk" wouldn't make much of an impact. That band and its orientation were done, as was swing itself (with quite a number of other big bands broken up at the time). Was Artie set now to embrace the literary life, among other possible pursuits? Not quite yet (though it would have been an appropriate place to close a movie or novel on him). Still, it was thoroughly predictable that whatever he did musically in 1946 would be very different from what had preceded. This any intelligent observer should have seen coming.

Meanwhile, RCA got its pound of flesh by at first not issuing some of the fine records Artie's band had made with them. Certain ones only appeared on 78s after a year or so, and even then in stingy amounts. Some only became available later on LPs, and fortunately, are now easily found on YouTube, etc. All this corporate spite of course made Shaw sound off in the media, as he'd done previously re the music business and its war of sorts with true artists in the field.[11] Of which he was definitely one himself!

## Seven

# Toward Musical Retirement

All of the foregoing notwithstanding, Artie still had some good work in him, but not real swing anymore. Singers, many having first cut teeth by working with various dance bands, were now all the rage on their own—Sinatra, Como, Peggy Lee et al. In April '46 Shaw decided to go with various groups of studio players to make records, including the usual brass, reeds and percussion, but also plentiful strings, plus instruments like oboes, flutes, etc. These were massive affairs, sometimes including as many as 40 pieces, and persisting for recordings through the summer, finally ending in an L.A. studio in November. One album of 78s was called *Artie Shaw Plays Cole Porter*, and a later LP *Artie Shaw Plays Cole Porter and Irving Berlin*; but basically, all these discs for Musicraft, where Shaw was back to being his own man, became available in the public domain, and could then be found on a number of "budget labels" like Royale, Allegro, Viking, etc. And of course they are easily located on the internet today.[1]

In Hollywood Shaw got musicians together for these intermittent studio sessions, and many were familiar names. Within different, large complements, all called Art Shaw and His Orchestra, one could find trumpeters like Manny Klein, Zeke Zarchy (a fan of Shaw), and Ray Linn; sax players like Les Robinson, Skeets Herfurt, Chuck Gentry, and Babe Russin (who'd played with Goodman in the '30s); Milt Raskin, formerly with TD, on piano; guitarist Dave Barbour, also an alum of the BG band, where he met and then married Peggy Lee; and Nick Fatool on drums. There was also that big string section, again with certain familiar names, some added while playing here or migrating there; but this whole AS effort in one sense constituted something of a step backward. And yet a forward one, too, though in a different way for those into his swing *oeuvre*. Because this bandleader who'd always disdained singers, particularly "boy singers," brought in for certain sessions, and partly to make money, a young warbler from Chicago named Mel Tormé, along with his Mel-Tones, a group of four men and women. He also engaged

141

Kitty Kallen for some numbers. The Tormé group was quite heavily featured, and their contribution was all faintly be-boppy, scatty, and decidedly postwar. The later Hi-Lo's come to mind, and as Tom Nolan argues, the Four Freshmen, too; not to mention the Ray Conniff Singers and other such groups of the future. Artie's clarinet was still lush on these recordings, but in a decidedly pre–'44-'45 way, yet worth a listen, especially on numbers like "In the Still of the Night" (sans vocals). That's a lovely piece of work and clichéd as it sounds, easy on the ears. But the nod here toward a European classical heritage doesn't make it as well for Professor Read, who calls this Shaw version of "Still…" a rather hokey arrangement featuring the strings, harp, and a wan flute in the intro, and Artie staying carefully in mid-register to continue an overall syrupy effect. I also like Shaw's "I've Got You Under My Skin" from this period, where in a sweet arrangement the expansive, stately strings seem to complement Shaw's clarinet legato and thick jazz riffs. But again, Read sees some incoherence here, too, including a simple, dance-like solo on piano made for another time or place, giving somewhat of an effect to him of mustard thrown on spaghetti! He also finds the strings stereotypical and not quite fitting with this well-known song, either, and really part of an overall attempt here to pander to the period's listeners.

Another enjoyable one (to me) is a once racy tune that Shaw does well in this postwar era, "Love for Sale," in an arrangement cum clarinet work that stays with you. On this one Read lauds a tighter and more refined brand of orchestration than in the records noted above, with fine detail wrought by the saxes; but in his view, the strings on this number are more apt for a movie soundtrack than for this kind of work. Shaw's '46 "I Got the Sun in the Morning and the Moon at Night" at least did well money-wise, with Tormé and group contributing. The latter's young "velvet fog" verged on corn syrup in songs like "Guilty" (with his solos against the Mel-Tones more modern than Sinatra's with the Pied Pipers for TD, but not so different as to preclude some irony here, given how Artie had once derided Tommy for using singers so sedulously). However, a melodic "Get Out of Town" gives more space to Shaw's warm, expressive clarinet, which leans in comfortably against the billowy strings. There is also a solo effort here that Shaw specifically sought from Tormé (sans Mel-Tones), and which apparently helped launch the "Velvet Fog"'s crooning career. Musical pros may note an introduction on "Get Out of Town" that seems to come right out of Debussy's *La Mer*. On the whole, as good as many of these records are (including right now), they are again, basically AS après-swing, and won't remain as much in mind as his earlier masterful work of that era.

I do, however, feel catty in saying anything even mildly or obliquely derogatory about such a crooner as Tormé. However, I'm with Shaw on this: singing is the lower pursuit, so to speak; and in some sense, placing a great jazz player and arranger like Artie in a setting of equal top billing with Mel and confreres would be rather like Guy Lombardo appearing with the New York Philharmonic. Perhaps that's not the best way of putting it. Bluntly, I've always thought this AS mixture of 1946 was too much apples and oranges, and not something you would want to rehear on a regular basis. And not truly worthy of the great swing virtuoso and band shaper that Shaw had formerly been. Maybe a better analogy than the Lombardo-"longhair" one is, say, melding Artie, had he lasted that long, with Herb Alpert's Tijuana Brass! Perhaps via Mel and group Shaw was finally acquiescing to that old Sinatra–Pied Pipers orientation he'd formerly disdained; but in fact, TD's band and trombone work were so linear and plain romantic back then, as on hits like "I'll Never Smile Again," that such a mixture made more sense for that group, and lucrative sense, too. I wouldn't rate Artie cum Mel (and his group) quite as high or right in that regard.[2]

As he cut such records into the summer of '46, then fall, Shaw was now distracted by other matters, one being increasing arguments with Ava, whom he'd regularly disparaged in the company of others as a North Carolina hick who ought to "stifle," despite the fact that she was very bright. This starlet who had always valued Shaw's Jewish origins (and even his Hebrew name, Avraham Ben-Yitzhak Arshawsky) found definite prejudice on the other side. In addition, Shaw was to a degree obsessed in this period by the depredations of World War II, and by the Holocaust, and started taking a number of supposedly pacifistic groups seriously, including those near to or actually Communist in orientation, which would come back to haunt him.

He and Ms. Gardner separated during that summer of '46, and by October he'd also had it with his latest musical direction as well. He was now ironically moving toward Kathleen Winsor as a significant other (one recalls how he'd critiqued Ava for reading lowbrow material like Winsor's *Forever Amber*); and professionally, he was also aiming himself toward other possibilities, including movie production. Apparently Shaw was no longer able to muster a full, emotional musical focus, which he'd previously done so well. Divorce with Gardner came on October 24, 1946, and only a few days later he married Winsor just across the border in Mexico (October 28). As practical as he could be, Artie was always impulsive and impatient, too. Unfortunately, there were still problems pending from the Gardner divorce terms, along with the ending of Winsor's previous marriage as well.[3]

Off he zoomed with his new wife to Norwalk, Connecticut, leaving

**Artie was initially happy with yet another lady he married in 1946, the writer Kathleen Winsor (Getty Images/Bettmann).**

all those studio musicians behind and Tormé, too, and about to eschew any kind of jazz recording through 1947-48. Shaw acquired a huge house back East, where he could instead work, if fitfully, on literary labors, especially an autobiography, and where Winsor could do her work, too. Her *Forever Amber* surprisingly went through the roof and made big money, becoming a movie as well; and perhaps Artie was trying to match her when he hatched the idea of collaborating with his friend of sorts, William Saroyan, on a musical comedy. He was still searching, only this time not in his actual and best métier. What he found was that Saroyan and Shaw methods were entirely different, and the whole project came to nothing.

Back Artie went into analysis, this time with the scholarly Abram Kardiner, who would become an intellectual guru of sorts. Again, in all of 1947 the swing icon made no records at all. He took an apartment in New York, and it was probably this period when Bellow remembers Shaw dragging him off to hear jazz at Birdland. (Artie told me he couldn't remember that, but did say Bellow would later base his play *The Last Analysis* on the clarinetist's penchant for lying on the couch, and only belatedly stopping for good when Kardiner eventually declared that Artie now knew himself as thoroughly as did the therapist!) When I discussed Shaw with Bellow in 1982, the Chicago novelist was also a bit acerbically ironic on Artie's numerous marriages. Bellow said that this musician would get hitched at the drop of a handkerchief (reminding one somehow of Voltaire's *Candide*).

Professionally, Artie now got bitten (at least for a time) by the classical music bug, where Goodman had already led the way, playing commissioned pieces by Bartok, Copland, etc., and more standard fare by the older European greats in the field. Shaw seemed to have enough cash to indulge himself in different directions, but the money didn't stay put. Winsor turned out to be quite the piranha in that regard after their marriage devolved into the usual round of arguments and outbursts, mainly his; and things got even worse when she started slinging mud in the papers, leaking furiously about what Shaw had said (or yelled), how he could be violent, how he was a Communist sympathizer, and so forth. Any divorce with her would cost him the proverbial mint, partly due to their previous marriages being only demi-resolved legally, and messily so. Finally Artie agreed to an extra-court settlement with Winsor that cost him a huge amount of dollars. And which made his up-and-coming IRS problems even worse. He had stopped sticking to his knitting, and at a price, reflecting the old Spanish saw, which I paraphrase: Take whatever you want (and be whomever you want, too), but pay! (This is one he himself obviously liked, and much later used to characterize Harry James' life and career in a back-cover blurb for Peter Levinson's biography of the great trumpet player.)

Staying in an aphoristic vein, it strikes one that when a great falls off his perch, good is somehow no longer good enough. Because Shaw did put out a lot of good in the "longhair" mode during that late '40s "lay-off" of his. But he was far from popular at it. Which was fine by him, and probably would be fine with careful music or historical scholars even now; but not really with most of the listening public then or today. This was indeed Shaw attempting to cultivate other potential selves, financially viable or not. His period of searching and essaying one new pathway after another kept extending itself.

In 1948 Artie played compositions by Poulenc, Debussy, Shostakovich, and the like, and commissioned pieces by such as Nicolai Berezowsky. But he also took on Mozart with symphony orchestras (probably doing to that genius' work what no other clarinetist had ever done). Shaw did try throwing shafts of jazz into material that was mostly classical-oriented, but this was mainly what we might call his academic phase in music (where he was evidently trying to prove "legitimate" credentials). And it wasn't to last, either.

When Shaw played opening night at Manhattan's new Bop City, April 14, 1949, he confounded many in attendance, including a number of celebrities, by staying classically-oriented there, and confusing. A spate of publications including *Time Magazine* panned his effort as thoroughly out of place. During a subsequent week of appearances at the same venue, Shaw relented and started riffing more on his clarinet in a jazzy fashion, including for Ms. Gardner, who stayed a loyal admirer, and to the chagrin of her flame lit in this period, Frank Sinatra, with whom she had her differences.

Shaw made more of a splash at Carnegie Hall with Berezowsky's Concerto for Clarinet; but all this—had it persisted—would still have constituted Artie the musician trying on other selves, and still unsure where to go at this point in that craft, or in other potential ones. His classical mode remained fitful in '49 (mainly via concerts he'd committed to playing), and was basically done at the outset of the '50s.[4] Meanwhile, ever more people were looking back, and lucratively for him, to his great Swing Era output, which would give Artie plentiful royalties via album after album that came out as LPs in the '50s, '60s, and '70s, and then as CDs, too.

Given that nostalgia craze (seen also in films like *The Fabulous Dorseys* of 1947, and eventually in ones devoted to Glenn Miller and Benny Goodman), Shaw thought later in '49 that he'd give serious big band jazz one more try. His hair was thinning badly, and he would eventually try a radical shaved-head look; but he thought yet again that he could shape the young, and maybe go back into that old river another time, but hopefully with some different swim strokes. From our point of view none of it worked nearly as well as Shaw felt it would have, if *only* audiences had warmed more to his ideas. He thought he'd go even more "ambitiously" boppy than in '44-'45, buoyed up by players of quality like Zoot Sims and Al Cohn on reeds, Jimmy Raney on guitar, and others who were well acquainted with the "new stuff." In fact, we don't think this band was ever quite right or nearly as good as the boppish one that preceded it in '44-'45. What we *do* see (or hear) in this new group was that definite lack of emotional commitment, in contrast to Artie's previous and great end-of-the-war bunch, where all the Shavian techniques and those of his arrangers ended up delivering his very soul on a plate of sorts, and pleasingly.

This change in '49 to a less realized orientation had something to do with his private life as well, and his proclivities now going out in too many directions. One was the political scene, as Shaw's flirtation with

## Seven. Toward Musical Retirement

socialism and pacifism continued, and as he quickly and unguardedly signed more petitions and such than he probably should have. He moved to a 240-acre dairy farm in Pine Plains, New York, which also claimed a good deal of his time and energy. Back taxes owed were another problem, and one of the reasons he decided to form this new band, where some of his alums like Steward and the ever nuttier and still frail Marmarosa came back as well, though decamping early. But when this contingent toured from September '49 (starting at Boston's Symphony Hall) and through the fall, it met with cool, somewhat mystified responses from audiences, except for one rocking two-week engagement at Chicago's Blue Note. That audience problem became a Shaw refrain for years to come as the real reason this band didn't last long (recording only from early December '49 and into January 1950); but those records—and there are quite a few, including on MusicMasters, Thesaurus "transcriptions," and Decca—do provide us a better series of reasons for its comparative lack of popularity.

Bluntly, I've never put this '49-'50 AS band nearly up in the same league with the three great ones of the Swing Era analyzed above. As a "pretty good" effort at best, this aggregation that Shaw thought so full of potential suffered from a real dearth of emotional beauty, which had been front and center in the earlier triumvirate of topflight musical organizations. Another major problem was that the '49 band was trying to be several things at once. Some of the stuff in Shaw's "book" was really a retooling of well-known, earlier successes, using mildewed arrangements (sans strings) as a base. Other pieces were more adventurous contributions from young arrangers and/or songwriters like Tadd Dameron and Johnny Mandel. And then there were some attempts at injecting vocals into the mix as well, which we'll skirt here, given that Shaw himself didn't even play on a number of those and as a seasoned instrumentalist, was still condescending toward singers. But one understands why all this didn't really pull in audiences, including record-buyers of the era, in lucrative enough numbers.

Take Mandel's "Innuendo" of late December '49, which is just a pacer sans emotion, almost Christmassy, yet overly "cool" in tone. Of course Artie still reveals himself here as a jazz artist extraordinaire on his instrument, one who could move with the times, scatting around marvelously against the ensemble, challenging and almost demanding on his famed "axe." Al Cohn's sax solo is quite extended, too (he was such a bop virtuoso that Artie disliked following him on the stand), and Sonny Russo is thoroughly modern on trombone. But however interesting, one sees why such a recording wouldn't garner big sales back then or remain deeply in many musical minds.

"So Easy," recorded at the same time, was composed by Dameron and features a pretty Artie intro, where he still talks to the listener and is unmistakably in charge against a background ensemble splaying out cool chords; but really, it's all too wan and chilled-out for me, if not for Read. The saxes staying together and unharmonized at one point take a brief bow back toward the World War II era, and Artie dances back sideways, too, it feels, and yet in a modernist vein. This is one of the band's better efforts, no question, but again, not as memorable as much of what the AS contingents had produced in the swing period.

"Similau," a new song by Arden Clar and Harry Coleman, recorded by Krupa's orchestra in January '49 and also in that year by Peggy Lee, got its Shaw treatment at a session of early January 1950. His version gives one a cacophonous impression of a world in chaos, a jungle-like one perhaps, where all you get is an eerie, slightly comic mood but not much else. And yet Artie considered such an interpretation as groundbreaking, and of course thoroughly misunderstood! For certain it was an advanced score, but without enough melodious center or anchor to resonate well with the public.

Cut at the same time, something called "Fred's Delight" (composed and arranged by Dameron) features clarinets welded together and Artie playing along with the reeds, before he steps out, spreading his subtle phrasing over the top of the section patina and giving it an enhanced flavor, rather like chocolate syrup poured over ice cream (in my co-author's analogy). But other solos here are so constrained and short that we never get a chance to hear the jazz element there. In the full band's orchestration there is a rather loud, harsh, and forced quality, too. Only Artie himself brings back an inner, reflective quality here, as he so often did with other groups. There are also some strange pauses and tempo "goofery" in "Fred's...," which surely would have confused dancers in that period, and listeners as well. Too much here is simply a nod to the vanished swing epoch, and yet not all that modern either, falling unfortunately between stools. Most problematically, there is no real emotion and no sustaining melody in this recorded epigone of sorts. Aside from Shaw's solos, the only one that stands out is Raney's on electric guitar, but of course such work has been greatly surpassed for listeners aware of later trends, when that instrument hit the top and center in popular music.

As in all pastiche (think of Johan Huizinga's views in his seminal book *The Waning of the Middle Ages*), there is humor in some of these AS efforts, too, and in the very song titles themselves; and even a certain sarcasm mostly lacking in the romantic era of '38–'45, when Artie's various musical organizations moved so many with their emotion-tugging, polished contributions. That humorous and/or sarcastic quality is found, for instance, in the curiously titled "Aesop's Foibles," another that seems a wan look back as much as it's putatively supposed to be a move forward. Artie's burst of dazzle on his instrument midway through shows him still to be unique on his instrument, but it comes too late (and presents too little) to save this effort. This is another mood piece and not a real melody at all, only a congeries of effects and colors. And yet again, it lacks emotion, partly by forcing a "casual cool" tone to the fore, with the band there, but almost not there (because of course this is '49, not '39, with "progressive jazz" now so very central).

The Latin-style pieces for this somewhat boppy Shaw band were usually arranged by John Bartee. But his "Mucho de Nada" is another completely forgettable mood piece some may want to hear ended as soon as possible! "Orinoco" (or the version one gets most often on the internet) gives us a cha-cha or tango-like rhythm complete with suitable percussion work provided by Latin-oriented players brought into the session. There is a brooding, even mysterious mood here, but never brooding or mysterious enough. The attempt to remain "cool" was a kind of killer there, too. Artie stays out of this one for a rather long time, and meanwhile, tempos become mixed up and in a way that would again have confused dancers. Artie's eventual solo is brief and this "Orinoco," too, is anything but a lasting contribution to the weighty and imposing AS *oeuvre*. The Shaw who had once been derisive about rumbas and such when they were requested at hotels in his heyday had given in here to a vogue that wasn't really right for him. But maybe more of a problem was that he and his arrangers were again trying to do several things at once via such work. For Professor Read a rendering like this '49 "Orinoco," despite its interesting, promising, and unified intro, ends up a non-tune, which no one could go home singing! He, too, says we're starved for a melody here and finds Shaw's clarinet work on this piece nothing more than a tease of sorts.

In addition to such novelties, Artie really did ignore Heraclitus by basically redoing the old arrangements of great recordings like "I Cover the Waterfront" and "Star Dust" (sometimes spelled "Stardust" in this era); but this time without strings, and with his clarinet more modernist in its licks. And oddly enough, such efforts really work best with this band, in some ways anticipating what he would do with Dick Johnson and a nostalgic AS contingent later in the '80s, but without Artie playing. In fact, these "oldies" would still have been listenable right in '49-'50, no matter how often Shaw and sidemen got irked by requests for them at live events. And they'll still work for many of today's listeners surfing the internet, though you'd be best advised to try the great originals first.

To be sure, Artie's arrangers essentially pirated the old scores for these contributions, but somehow the process works on such former standouts as "I Cover...." Despite the hype, however, this stuff really isn't very boppish at all. After the brief intro bowing to that original "Waterfront" recording of 1941, Artie saunters in with his clarinet, which is, granted, different than it was a decade or so earlier; but not so different that it discards his characteristic sweetness and pretty timbre. Shaw remains his old dramatic self here, the melody goes forward undisturbed, and this basically works. Even Zoot Sims' tenor solo on this resurrected "I Cover..." complies, happily so. Being neither here nor there still remained one of this band's besetting and unfortunate tendencies, but not on such fine revival efforts.

As for "Star Dust," trumpeter Don Palladino pretty well follows the hallowed Butterfield solo that starts the earlier version, but with his own neat touches, too. It's again the same famed arrangement sans strings, and this cozy band ensemble somehow does it well, and quite seamlessly, even without the "longhair" elements in that earlier AS classic. Shaw riffs here on his own great and difficult solo, with some contemporary touches, but also over-the-top effects that bring back his more formless, unrecorded "Star Dust" scored for the breakout '38–'39 band. Fred Zito does creditably on this rerun of the Jenney trombone solo that remained a challenging one to cover. But Artie's quiet ending has a kind of "running away" element not nearly so evident in the original "Star Dust." Part of the reason was again the era, with big bands now clearly on the ropes, badly out-pummeled by the crooners; but also because Shaw had other potential career ideas inside, plus serious gallbladder troubles right when this band was touring, then recording.[5]

The "'S Wonderful" made by this bunch elegantly rips off Conniff's original arrangement of 1945, but with high clarinets more beseeching here, and Artie's solo work more contemporary and "slidey"; but as a whole not appreciably novel or different. Artie concludes with an old-time glissando, showing well that he could still "bring it," and then some.

Cut at the same time was another throwback, "I Get a Kick Out of You," which Artie lays out from the top against rather lean orchestration. He sails into the bridge, still the virtuosic star; but again, this one doesn't move a listener quite the way earlier Shaw work had done. Even Raney's guitar solo has that glancing, reluctant, and super-cool quality that hasn't worn well. And the entire orchestra sounds at times bored and conventional, too. Artie seems to regain a playful, even teasing mode at the close of the piece, but a short-lived one.

Giving in to financial reality, and simply not able to stick with this

## Seven. Toward Musical Retirement 151

new orientation, despite all the heavies he'd recruited, Shaw broke up the band after its last recording session of January 6, 1950. His gallbladder problems, including a stint in hospital for surgery, certainly didn't help, but neither did all of Artie's other interests importunately jostling for his attention.

It isn't worth listing all the brief band efforts that followed, including an eventual one that was so laughingly "stock" in its arrangements that Artie himself would double over at the compliments his least adventurous work could procure. In this period he delegated as best he could, letting Lee Castle put together one contingent for him in March 1950, which then went into Bop City, at the very moment when a still Shaw-admiring Ava was in New York with Frank Sinatra. A bit later came the well-known episode when Ms. Gardner went to complain about her latest involvement to her ex, and an irate Frank and his friend and business partner Hank Sanicola stomped over to Artie's hotel room to threaten him with a gun. Shaw talked both off the ledge, but Sinatra later used the rod at his own hotel to fake a suicide, shooting into a mattress, and terrifying Ava in the process.[6]

Meanwhile, Artie cut records for Decca, working with such arrangers as Gordon Jenkins (and his orchestra and chorus), and also with popular vocalists like Dick Haymes and Don Cherry. There are still interesting sides from all this, but nothing really stuck or lasted for long. By 1951 or so, Shaw felt that he was basically done with the big band mode, and there were no more groups of any size worth extended analysis until his very end period of 1953-54. That last hurrah was no longer with an orchestra, but another Gramercy Five sextet, and where Artie's playing took one final and remarkable jazz turn that made him more than the equal of anyone in that field, though he was from another era entirely. With the curtain set to go down for good, he at least proved he was still anything but a dinosaur at his trade.

Before arriving at that last surprising, worthwhile turn in the musical road (if not as compelling as his old work from the golden age of dance bands), Shaw drove to a close on his cerebral autobiography, *The Trouble with Cinderella*. It came out in May '52, just before his seventh marriage to Doris Dowling in mid–June of that year. The latter constituted yet another try at a conventional home life, complete with the birth of a second son, and a couple years of relative bliss. However, in 1953 the House Committee on Un-American Activities dragged Shaw on the carpet to pelt him with tough, probing questions, and Artie pleaded in almost teary fashion that he'd been a dupe, that he hadn't always known what he was signing, that he'd been above all, looking for a peaceful way in this broken world of ours; and that he was truly an

American patriot, and grateful to the country that had given him such opportunities in life.[7]

*The Trouble with Cinderella* was an apt title for a memoir concerning a man who'd kept producing and reaping marvelously, but found the prices far tougher to bear than he'd ever thought they would be. This is easily Shaw's best published book. His later volumes of short stories or novellas never really made it for this reader at all. *Cinderella* is arresting, but it says nothing about his women, which in a way is commendable, and it's good, sophisticated reading start to finish on how Artie embraced the jazz life, starting with that lonely, difficult childhood in New York and New Haven. It's a more than worthwhile autobiography, but a little portentous, too; and unlike some (even those co-written by baseball greats of yore), not a memoir to be read over and over. Once will do.

Some of the chapters are exceedingly short, and the philosophical "intellectualese" may get in the way for certain readers; but again, this is a fine memoir showing off Shaw's usual industrious and thorough standards. One sees how this lonely, only child put all that hurt into later making great, inimitable music. Antisemitism particularly in New Haven was real, palpable, and hurtful for the boy. He was frequently called terms like "kike" or "Christ-killer." More generally, he was ragged for being sensitive and "different," and for naively exulting at things that were new to him, like those schoolyard anthills (as "Columbus Arshawsky"). During this childhood, so different from Goodman's (Benny lived with a large, somewhat cushioning brood), Artie's parents argued like mad, as seen; and Shaw is wonderful on all that, and on his escape via the used sax he bought. Perhaps it was fortuitous that Artie started on that instrument, because his clarinet would later have a full sound somewhat like what emanates from a saxophone (versus BG, a clarinetist first and foremost from his early years). In sum, it was mostly an advantage that Artie had had quite a miserable childhood, again compared to Benny's. Those hurts helped make his copious band work so often soulful (think again of both his recordings of "Alone Together," among many others that were full of significant and lovely dollops of melancholia).

Artie shows in this memoir what a dogged autodidact he was, learning not from teachers but from others in the field, jamming with better, more seasoned players, and imbibing even from idiosyncratic unknowns like Floyd O'Brien, and from recorded fare by such as Armstrong or Beiderbecke; but also work by noted European composers of classical music. The memoir keeps getting interrupted by quite extended philosophical asides, but in a jazzy way, basically follows the chronology of its subject's "clawing upward" phase via this band and that, and finally his "Begin the Beguine" stardom. On balance this is certainly a fine autobiographical effort, and still would be to new readers interested in things AS.

And then in the early '50s came that last-gasp, splendid combo, with Hank Jones on piano and Joe Roland on vibraphone, fully into contemporary jazz trends, plus Tommy Potter, a Black bass player who'd worked with the bop god himself, Charlie Parker, along with Tal Farlow on electric guitar and Irv Kluger on drums (after Artie begged him to join up). I remember again when Shaw told me on the phone circa 1984 that the Book-of-the-Month Club was releasing a collection of that group's then recondite old work, and how pleasantly shocked I was by Artie's scampering here, there, and everywhere on his axe, remarkably and fully "progressive" by this time. Again, he seemed to have evolved far more than Benny Goodman. In fact, Goodman came to watch this last Gramercy edition in an intimate club atmosphere and just stared sullenly the whole night through, probably in shock, but obviously bleeding with envy, too, at his rival's last great, marvelously realized alterations on clarinet.

Interviewed in *Artie Shaw: Quest for Perfection*, one of the fine documentaries on Shaw, his pianist Jones emphasized how persistent Artie was even at that late point in making sure all tapings of songs were done right, sometimes extending to as many as 15 takes in the process. The soft-spoken Black pianist obviously admired his employer no end, and Artie, too, sounded gentle in retrospect, remembering that last great series of sounds he and his group had brought forth. Shaw himself played more quietly with this sextet than he had earlier in the Swing Era, positioning himself exceedingly close to the mikes. He also abandoned the Selmer clarinet he'd used for big band work in favor of a Buffet he called woodsier in tone. In this documentary he listens carefully and approvingly to his own superb work on "Don't Take Your Love from Me," in a kind of reverie hearing his old explorations on the clarinet. Jones also seems moved on listening to this unusual small-group contribution of the early '50s.[8]

However, would-be listeners might begin on the internet (where these recordings can now be found) with the combo's upbeat version of "How High the Moon," a grand recording, indeed. Here Artie starts off deceptively slowly and simply on that haunting melody, a real sleight of hand; and then without much warning he starts riffing all over the lot with skeins and spurls, and then simply flies (which he could do endlessly, off the cuff, and still at this point, in all keys!). Artie is more than "with it" here, throwing in some comic touches, too, yet anything but old hat or from some other day. The Roland vibes contributions also work well, as does Jones' piano, and when in ensemble, the whole contingent is wonderfully together as well.

That ensemble work glitters much more on the group's version of another standard, "Tenderly," initially taped in late '53. Here the mood is succinct, but terrific, with Roland's xylophone especially marvelous and the great Artie's clarinet sounding almost like an accordion in spots. It's as if he and the group in this entire set of recordings are shooting the rapids, just before the boat breaks up for good.

And then there's another great song they recorded that absolutely needs to be highlighted here, "Imagination," with the best version made in late '53 (there's another from '54). This is quite simply a lovely masterpiece that will remain in the listener's mind. Artie's sensual clarinet takes the fine melody from the top, and truly gives anyone with an ear and heart the chills! All his sensitivity and emotionalism are fully back on this standard, cum the most modern of the modern for that era. His reed work isn't at all "clever" on this "Imagination," nor is it distant and detached, as it too often sounded in the '49-'50 band. Here he's absolutely warm and sumptuous, sensitively spinning or weaving, and absolutely at one with that era of small-group jazz. Jones' piano plays the bridge, Farlow's electric guitar solo next claims the main melody, and then comes extended vibraphone commentary, and all again fitting well within that era of American jazz, if a bit proverbially, too.[9] But Artie, who regains the melody of "Imagination" nearer to the end, recapitulating his beginning, is still the group's centerpiece, and anything but ordinary here. His jazz sounds on "Imagination" go right to the heart, and stay inside a listener! No wonder today's internet is full of admiring comments on these last Shaw efforts, and from listeners as far away as Australia, equally surprised by how much all this can move current fans of different ages. We could mention other fine recordings that bunch made, too, but one last point should be reiterated and highlighted: great as this group was, it was only a small group, making for inevitable limitations that simply weren't there in the much more extensive, wider palettes provided by and for Shaw's great orchestras of the Swing Era. But this was truly a worthy and poignant send-off for Shaw in the recording realm, pushing the envelope, as he was so wont to do; while the crooners continued to dominate pop music, until rock became a major new competitor in that realm.[10]

Part of this last Shavian hurrah was a slight change when Artie went from sextet to quintet (a true Gramercy Five), with the departure of Roland on vibes, and Farlow replaced on guitar by Joe Puma. This altered group made far fewer tapings than the earlier one, most done at

## Seven. Toward Musical Retirement

Artie's expense, then handed to record companies, where they became particularly usable on LPs. As an example, from the earlier group's efforts came a gorgeous and quite extended "I Can't Get Started" (taped as many were after Artie's group finished its nightly gig at The Embers, a club in Manhattan). This "Started" is another of his beautiful offerings, with Artie very "slidey," but warm and melodic, while also effortlessly contemporary on that fine old tune. This version of the song ended up as the title tune of a Verve collection, included with other Gramercy items, an LP I bought back in the day and eventually (cf. baseball cards) gave away.

In terms of the "last last" Gramercy quintet, the standout among the few tapings done later in '54 is their version of "Too Marvelous for Words," a song which seemed most made for Sinatra's crooning, and which some will certainly know from Frank's evocative recording of the number. In Artie's small-group take, the clarinet virtuoso starts simply, and in a linear, accessible manner sets out the song's fine melody. But despite discreetly appropriate, perhaps overly terse solos from Puma on guitar and Jones on piano, Artie ends up the improvisational cynosure here, not scampering so much as sliding again, this time almost horizontally on his clarinet, with skeins of linked-up notes that finally end up as too much *art* on this number, as he might put it; or too much musical logorrhea, as I'd label it, and not enough entertainment, where beginning, middle and end generally work better. But this is still compelling combo jazz of the era, if a candidate for shortening (not that Artie would have cared, including financially, at this end point of his magnificent career).

Speaking of money, Shaw did get that altered Gramercy bunch into Vegas for a four-week gig starting in late April '54, and in good part for the cash, this in a town that was less raucous than it later became. Both Dorsey brothers came night after night—anything but snidely competitive the way Goodman was—to dig this marvelously new but last Shaw musical orientation. That group then moved to a stint in San Francisco, but by the fall of '54 Artie felt that the definitive end had indeed come. He thought of how Joe Louis had boxed till he could give no more, and he'd always admired Louis deeply. Artie now felt that he, too, could give no more at his own craft.

These combos probably took much out of him on clarinet (though he made it easier on himself by inveterately slurring and avoiding staccato); but they were now done with in both versions. There was only one last series of superficial, undemanding dates for Shaw to play in Australia (again, mainly for cash), and in the company of other musicians; plus stars like Ella Fitzgerald, whom he liked and valued, the comedian Jerry Colonna, and his old "traps" alumnus Buddy Rich, whom he increasingly disliked (though later attending his funeral). But that was it, and no recordings came from this tour. Shaw was now through with his main vocation, and would repeat quite often as justification that he'd gone about as high or far as he could in this field. Certainly in terms of small-group jazz of the time, Artie was more than cool and still current enough to influence even honchos of the period like the baritone sax player, Gerry Mulligan. However, this latest AS direction simply wasn't lucrative, compared to Shaw's more mainstream efforts of the high Swing Era. He was now certain that he never wanted to mount and run a band anymore, even as Ellington kept going, and as Basie also went into a kind of renaissance in his "April in Paris"–Big Joe Williams period.[11] But that peripatetic, demanding life was no longer for Artie, even if Basie himself begged him to reconsider his full retirement from music.

Artie Shaw with Doris Dowling in 1952. They were married that year and she became the mother of his second son, Jonathan; but unfortunately, that marriage also foundered within a few years (STARSTOCK/Photoshot/Avalon).

But Shaw had more than enough reasons to make it stick. One was that as much as he'd disdained popularity, a part of him always wanted to be part of the "center," and he knew that in the mid-'50s that center now belonged to such as Rosie Clooney, Johnnie Ray, Peggy Lee, Nat Cole, Tony Bennett et al. And yes, his old rival, Sinatra, now in the midst of a great comeback (think "Witchcraft" and so forth). Besides these crooners who had never been his dish but were now so central, Artie perhaps didn't see another musical revolution coming around the bend; but that something called rock 'n' roll would soon appeal too, and hugely, especially to the young, via Chuck Berry, Little Richard, Jerry Lee Lewis, and not least, a handsome gyrator from the South named Elvis.

Finally of course, the literary-intellectual life kept enticing Shaw, too. He'd been an autodidact in music and now wanted to make the same thing happen in a very different field or endeavor. However, the New York intellectuals didn't accept him with open arms, and a gaggle of short stories he already had available weren't easy to peddle in the aftermath of his congressional appearance, and with blacklisting now a significant phenomenon in America, not least in the entertainment world. His marriage to Ms. Dowling also fell apart, perhaps conveniently, and she put down separate roots in L.A. with their son, Jonathan, who would predictably have problems later in life[12]; while Shaw moved back to Manhattan but found he was restless there, too.

It's easy to excoriate the late Artie as a common denominator in all these breakups, and to chide him for his lack of paternal attention, too. He certainly said some cutting things re those sons, whom he saw only intermittently over the years. But there may have been some spite on the other side of the marital ledger, too. The old "hell hath no wrath" adage isn't perhaps appropriate to cite in our day; but when Artie recalled that Betty Kern and then Doris Dowling both kept their sons away from him, sons he'd at first loved having, some truth may be found there, too. In other words, the possibility remains of nuancing this sorry familial situation, sad especially for both offspring of the famous but now retired bandleader and clarinet player extraordinaire.[13]

# Eight

# The Long Coda

On yet another typical impulse, and with no marital or professional shackles now holding him back, Shaw decided to leave the conformist atmosphere of mid–'50s America behind, truly behind. In New York he opted to pack up and sail to Europe, pick up a car, then drive wherever, just as he'd done in late '39, when he ended up in Acapulco before it became a tourist mecca. Armed with elements of the language spoken there, and now set to live mainly on royalties, he stopped his odyssey this time around in Spain. There Artie had a beautiful cliffside home built to his fussy but remarkable specifications above the sea on the Costa Brava, before it also took off in popularity. The town where he lived was called Begur, and though the odd inhabitant there knew of this visiting virtuoso, Shaw's clarinet-playing days were definitively done, never to return. Woody Herman would often rue the fact that Artie turned his instrument, or at least one of them, into a lamp; and many others would consider this an inexplicable catastrophe, too. At the same time, some bandleaders also envied Shaw for giving it his all from early teenhood to middle age, then having the guts to leave that life completely and unambiguously at 44, devoting himself to other pursuits. Meanwhile, they grew older and more beaten down, and despite nostalgia, sometimes far from the mainstream (not of course the case with organizations like Basie's or some of Buddy Rich's big bands).

Artie would eventually find irksome downsides in Spanish mores and their mañana mentality, also discussed in Orwell's *Homage to Catalonia*; but at first he found this as liberating a retreat as the Mexican one had been a decade and a half earlier. And of course Shaw could fight, and did, for exactly what he wanted, tilting from the get-go against bureaucratic constraints, which many Americans have found a challenge in European countries. Frederick Morton remembers, for instance, that new homes over there in that era, even this sprawling abode built against a cliff, were supposed to have no more than two fireplaces. But Shaw's new house ended up with no less than seven![1]

## Eight. The Long Coda

Evelyn Keyes is the best source on Artie's time in Spain, and her initial memoir—at least the 70 pages or so on Shaw—is a fine one, indeed. It provides nitty-gritty, but in a way that's not vulgar or pandering. Artie had been up in Paris when he met her, first commenting on her haircut, which differed from what he recalled of the actress in old films (including *Gone with the Wind*). Keyes considered the man she bumped into shockingly intelligent, and they found it easy to talk their former woes and future hopes, though she never thought he'd invite her to be his housemate in Begur, then to become his eighth and last wife (marrying on a trip to Gibraltar during the fall of '57).

As was usual for him, Artie became ever more difficult in that relationship with the passage of months and years (about six in all) on foreign terrain. He now wanted to present the world with nothing less than a body of Hemingway-worthy literary work, maybe even the Great American Novel. But discipline in that realm came hard to him, and really, it was never his trade, despite the fact that he did belatedly publish a few volumes of his novellas and stories. Shaw was more and more a champion reader, too, eventually possessing some 15,000 books in his library when I talked to him.[2] But that growing library did not contain only high-minded fare. Keyes remembers that he had an overflowing spate of books simply on fishing of different kinds, and with varied species in mind. Shaw got plenty obsessed in that direction, too. (As a parenthetical aside, Goodman was also a fisherman, once invited to join a hall of famer in that department down in Florida, a fellow who could also hit baseballs quite adeptly, Ted Williams.) Every once in a while, a still restless Shaw just wanted to blow his Begur pop stand and drive somewhere where the trout or salmon awaited, and where Keyes could simply admire the stunning scenery.

On one such trip, however, as noted, he flew into a rage when the couple got to the French border and discovered that Keyes had unaccountably forgotten their passports (she wondering to herself why *he* couldn't have thought to bring them). But they made it to Paris, where the couple had met, for a kind of reunion of souls, and they had another reunion there, too: Artie went to hear his old rival, and when he saw Goodman in his bathrobe sipping tea before a concert, and doubtless booked to do the same in other places later on, he felt happy that he'd given up that life—truly vindicated, or so he felt. In Benny's case he could never understand till he passed how Artie could ever abandon the instrument on which both had become masters.

With Keyes, Shaw certainly bellowed a lot, partly due to his damaged ear, and dictated plenty, too. He wanted a familial atmosphere in Begur and forced a dog on Evelyn, despite her allergies, which he deemed psychosomatic. He wanted to eat better, so she dutifully ordered cookbooks from Paris, and on an outdated stove patiently crafted an initial lemon pie for Artie, only to have it ruined when he sprayed DDT all over it, killing off some flies she hadn't noticed! But he could be a vulnerable little boy, too, as when on one occasion he went outside alone, picked up a clarinet he had, played a little, then put it away again for good. Keyes felt very bad that he couldn't ditch his high standards and just have fun with it. But he knew he couldn't, and that was that. When Shaw decided, he decided.

Occasionally distinguished visitors came by, none more so in that era than Eddie Fisher and Elizabeth Taylor. Shaw managed to give them a sharp lecture on standing up for their rights with the media, as the big stars he acknowledged them to be. But when Eddie strode inadvertently through the clear glass leading to the balcony outside, due to his fears concerning Liz's boys on the terrace, he and Evelyn felt they'd hurt the "star" and his lovely lady of that time, too. Fisher was lucky, however, to emerge with nary a scratch.

Taylor of course had jumped from Mike Todd, after his sudden death, to Fisher, and Todd along with John Huston dominate the earlier parts of Keyes' first memoir. Like Shaw both were of course powerhouses, and when I saw Keyes interviewed circa 1977 by Carson on *The Tonight Show*, she admitted something she'd learned via analysis: that having lost her father at age three, she had glommed onto very strong men who would be certain to abandon her. On that show she spoke in an ersatz English-y accent I found offputting, but her book *Scarlett O'Hara's Younger Sister* is delightful, and she was more natural and splendid, too, in her extended interview with Brigitte Berman for *Time Is All You've Got*.

And so was the lady I ended up talking to once on the phone in the '90s. She gave me her address in L.A. (on Doheny Drive), and I duly sent her *the* short story I'd done on Shaw in the '80s (calling my fictional sax player Bunny Wald), and which I kept reworking later as well. It was based on my often hesitant phone calls to Shaw and our conversations. She liked it, she said, except for the title, "Killing the Buddha." How had I gotten that one? Well, one day on the phone with Shaw during the Me Decade or just after, he enjoined me yet again to be me and not idolize anyone. "You've read *If You Meet the Buddha on the Road, Kill Him!*, right?" I had to admit I hadn't picked up that particular self-help tome of the era (by Sheldon Kopp and originally published in 1972). In fact, I was rather surprised that Artie would mention it. He synopsized quickly, explaining that if you see the Buddha on the road, you do kill him (since he is undoubtedly not the true Buddha but merely an expression of your

## Eight. The Long Coda 161

longing). I, too, found that a grisly way of putting it, and altered the title in this short story I never actually tried to publish (to "Leaving the Buddha"). À propos of being oneself: after sending Shaw my periodical memoir of 1982, "Looking for Mr. Bellow," I remarked that now he perhaps knew more about that celebrated author. Instead, he said, and positively, that he'd really learned more about me. As seen, he was certainly one to help younger types self-actualize, no question.

Keyes published another memoir later on, with more on Artie; but it wasn't nearly as riveting as the first one. The parts on Shaw were really on her protective friendship with him in older age, and his grousing about prostate problems and other growing health troubles. Of course he still thought (as he expressed to me on several occasions) that he'd make it to at least 150! He'd even add "and that's a conservative estimate!"

Long before that, in 1960 or so, and at the dawn of the decade that would see so much change, Artie decided he was fed up with Spanish bureaucracy and ways, and even the language itself. Why, he wondered, did they have to use masculines and feminines (referring to their nouns and adjectives)? It felt like a waste of effort. On a trip to the U.S. he and Keyes had gotten a taste of exciting new trends in Manhattan, and of new talents like the writer Terry Southern and the mordant comic Lenny Bruce. Finally Artie decided in 1961 that they should flee his European haven and instead, buy a rambling home in Connecticut situated on a lake, one containing what felt to her like myriad rooms.

There he ordered his wife to cut her hair appropriately in order to fit in with WASP society of that Cheeveresque time and milieu, and to eschew cussing. Their marriage, however, began to flounder, as he wanted to see other women with impunity, lambaste her for anything and everything, and at the same time, even put her down for idolizing him! He simply didn't want to be considered God! So he once yelled out while driving. But Keyes did admire him greatly, and couldn't help being amazed by his large range of interests and hobbies, now including marksmanship, at which Shaw came to excel nationally; and in cold Connecticut winters, skating on the frozen lake by his home and even executing (to her astonishment) marvelous figure 8s. What couldn't the man do? So she'd wonder.

She did gently prod him back to his real trade, the world of music, but he spurned her efforts there. He simply had too many other pursuits and ambitions percolating inside, one of them being movie production and/or distribution. Even in the late '40s he'd thought that might be a way to go, but it hadn't happened back then. By the mid– '60s, however, via his Artixo Productions, a film distributing company he'd formed, Shaw grabbed onto a unique, artsy British film no one had signed on to distribute in the U.S. This *Séance on a Wet Afternoon* was certainly different, as I myself felt seeing it at age 20 or so in a mainstream theater; but not one that brought in a lot of money or made this particular watcher want to see it again. Shaw had, however, hoped—especially if Kim Stanley, its lead actress, won the Academy Award, which she didn't—that it might pave the way for him as an independent to rival the big studios in making movies. None of that panned out for him.[3]

Meanwhile, Artie's dictatorial tendencies became so pronounced that even Keyes' psychiatrist finally decided to ditch professional neutrality, and strenuously enjoin her to split from the former bandleader. That she basically did, but after a hiatus, she remained Artie's confidante and buddy for many years to come, while he went from one significant other to the next. Keyes' second memoir, again not as compelling as the first, did reveal that protective side she showed to advantage with the curmudgeonly, aging Shaw. The state of their marriage, however, remained in doubt even after his death, when Keyes pushed for a large slice of his estate, and eventually (for what remained of her own life) did well in that regard. She had certainly been the most open-minded and longest lasting of Shaw's ladies, open-minded for sure because despite his new involvements, he had an old-fashioned need for Evelyn to remain a port in the periodic personal storms he experienced, including with those two sons who wanted more from him than they could get. For Artie's part, he didn't consider it a real marriage from quite early on; but at the least, Keyes remained a wonderful friend to him.[4]

I certainly wouldn't call Shaw sociopathic, as some have done, and Keyes did love and value his gentle side, as she emphasizes in her interview with Berman; but at times he verged on extreme in the psychological department when relating to significant others. Even his driving, where he stubbornly did things his own way, taking too many chances, scared Keyes a lot, and with good reason. When he became friendly with jazz writer Gene Lees, Artie terrified him, too, driving the serpentine road from Lees' home in Ojai, California, to Shaw's. From then on Lees made sure to drive himself![5]

If Artie could be authoritarian in his personal relations, such as with Keyes and other women, he was also relentlessly didactic, and sometimes it was hard to know where the former quality left off and the latter took over. But the didacticism was, in part, a positive, beneficial trait in his personality, as many of his ex-sidemen would attest. In terms of the principal author of this book, here was a nobody calling out of the blue in the late '70s, and immediately, Shaw rhymed off those books by Halle, preeminently his *Out of Chaos*, which seemed to intellectualize the healthy cohesion Artie had wrought with his musical contingents. It was a book which taught this historian a good deal as well. Shaw then went on to speak to me (or *at* me) for years on end. As he instructed, I'd call at the peak hour of 2 p.m. or so (expensive in terms of long-distance costs back then), sometimes dialing to the last digit and hanging up, then getting my courage back and dialing fully again. Didactic? No question about that in Artie. Simply for openers, he preached the virtues of being psychoanalyzed to me. When about to sign off, he'd sometimes say something like: "Well, I have to get back to my manuscript. There is nothing else." He liked to repeat that phrase "there is nothing else." I.e., one's work—in his case, endless work on *The Education of Albie Snow*, a good 1,000 pages long and at one point slated for three separate volumes. (It was apparently inspired by Romain Rolland's 10-volume novel of the Belle Epoque, *Jean-Christophe*.) In any event Shaw was implying that all that should indeed be central in one's life.

In addition to being a teacher, sometimes to the point of holding forth almost *ex cathedra*, Shaw also had a great, unremitting regard for talent, including the embattled talent of frail human flowers like Marmarosa, and yes, Ms. Keyes, too. He didn't patronize the ugly (as in Dodo's case) or the down-at-heels if they had something unusual to give. He didn't patronize me either, though he could easily have done so back then. He could have shut me down for good when I published an article in part based on our conversations. In other words Keyes' shrink notwithstanding, one can see why she remained a part of his life for so long, and why Ava, too, consulted him a number of times after their breakup.

The didacticism even extended to the increasing prevalence of drugs. Shaw was disquieted (as well he should have been) by the vogue of hard ones that began hitting the jazz world big time in the mid–'40s and having tragic effects. But during that New York respite from Spain in the late '50s, he and Keyes attended a party, where he convinced her to try some mescaline with him. She would remark that as different colors kept multiplying inside her, and him, too, they enjoyed about their most peaceful month or so together!

Yes, Shaw would try to teach one about such things and experiences, but he also wanted people to self-actualize. He once told me a story, and approvingly, about a psychiatrist he knew who had a patient near the point of jumping from a window. Shaw asked the shrink what he did, and the answer was that "if the guy had wanted to jump, I'd have let him jump. It was his decision." In other words a person like Shaw with so much life experience to impart also wanted people to be themselves and make their own choices, including creative ones.

In his concentration on intellectual matters (when we spoke) he did verge sometimes on the self-help mania of that era (late '70s, early '80s). The odd time and only rarely would I mention his old records, and one of his responses was: "I don't want to discuss 'em—I graduated from that school a long time ago." He preferred to talk about books he was reading or his current, huge manuscript. Occasionally I'd ask roughly when he might finish that magnum opus in the making. But to him the process was everything, and who cared about the outcome or a potential audience? "Did Picasso care?" he once said. "Or Einstein? They just kept doing." He cited another writer of yore with allegiance to no government, needing no reward—his sole reward being the intensity he brought to his work. He also quoted Mozart to the effect that only rest could tire you out, not labor (in Mozart's case, composing).

We talked a bit about another idol of mine back then, Saul Bellow, whom I'd met a number of times and with whom I'd corresponded quite obsessively. And Shaw once said, despite the odd note or card Bellow dispatched to me every six months or so, "I'm sure you're quite peripheral to his concerns," a doubtless accurate view. One's own work (in that kind of league) was far more central, as he kept emphasizing. Shaw did find it odd that I'd reread some of Bellow's novels quite a number of times. For rereading he felt it better to stick with the classics. "If I were going to a deserted island," he told me on one occasion, "and had one book to take, I'd choose something like Plato's *Republic*. That would keep a person busy," he smiled over the phone (or so it felt). In the early '80s when I reread Bellow's *The Dean's December*—not one of his best—several times, Shaw, too, read it and thought Bellow had given in to some intellectual snobbery there. Regarding other Bellow books, he noted the adverse effect on that author of having won a Nobel Prize, but also with a certain empathy, given how celebrity had impacted his own life and trajectory.

Mostly when Artie answered the phone, he seemed to have time for a conversation, mainly one-sided, to be sure. Occasionally, however, he'd snap that he was very busy (even in mid-afternoon, when he was done writing for the day), and would hang up peremptorily, and without his trademark "Take care of yourself," his usual sign-off. He did unburden intermittently about wrestling with his huge autobiographical novel, trying to decide what he could cut to make it more manageable. As I understood it, even the first part on a young genius of sorts was super-voluminous. Once I even broached the idea of trying my callow hand at editing, and, unbelievably to me, Shaw said in his impulsive manner that we could meet for a "bite" and discuss it. This obviously on the strength of my "Becoming an Intellectual: The Strange Saga of Artie Shaw," which I'd squirreled away in a rather obscure academic journal, but which a German friend of his drew to Shaw's attention. (Shaw chided me, and correctly, for pilfering from his conversations there, then seemed to get over it.) Maybe my memoir on Bellow also gave me some cred, as I knew he would have liked to be up in that author's literary league. But I was simply too idolatrous, fearful of a Southern California I didn't really know, and lacking in ready cash to fly down there and take Shaw up on a task that would have certainly overwhelmed me (along with most other humans!).

Another time I tried to tell him simply to finish his purported masterwork, instead of making like Sisyphus ad infinitum; and he remonstrated that the problem would then be starting another project, i.e., a new creative albatross of sorts. He'd talk of "squeezing the water" out of such enterprises, but without convenient limitations presented by the old 78s, he never quite arrived when it came to this literary effort. At all events I knew that Shaw tried to work at his desk through each morning, as many authors have done. So I made sure never to call him before two or so, which unfortunately was peak time cost-wise in those days. Shaw seemed to like this morning work routine of his, and once cited Irving Wallace, a friend of sorts (or so it sounded), to the effect that keeping that sort of regimen put a "spine" in one's day.

Once in a while I'd hear the blonging of a doorbell—on several occasions journalists had apparently come to do a story on him or conduct an interview. In the same period I was more surprised when a youngish female voice answered Shaw's phone, and in a warm, replenishing manner, almost that of a natural nurse. This was a significant other named Jennifer, whom Shaw subsequently lauded for her brightness exceeding her years (late twenties or so?). But however intelligent she was, Artie told me it was necessary as usual to fill in her educational gaps, as he'd done before with others like Ava Gardner. One time he told me he'd had Jennifer read Somerset Maugham's autobiographical novel *Of Human Bondage*. Locating some unwonted chutzpah, I remonstrated to Artie that the greatest of Maugham's short stories ("The Alien Corn," "The Human Element," etc.) would do better, along with that writer's essays on El Greco, etc. Shaw also had to explain to this Jennifer who figures like Tagore were.

In that era, too, Artie told me he was taking a break from his literary labors and going off to the mountains for a satori, on which I myself felt hotly ignorant (not knowing then what such a thing involved). But near to the time I stopped calling, was Shaw perhaps becoming more

**Artie Shaw (right) and Dick Johnson. Artie had Johnson direct a reformed AS band in the '80s and play the clarinet parts as he wished (courtesy Donna Pau).**

human, seen, for example, in how he finally formed a revived AS band in late '83, soon letting Dick Johnson lead it and play the clarinet parts as he wished? Was Artie also perhaps trying to find some spiritual solace as old age claimed him? Perhaps. In one of our phone conversations he even used music, enduringly great music, to prove the existence of God. He declared that if J.S. Bach could compose a masterpiece like the B Minor Mass, then there *had* to be a deity. On a lighter note, he didn't mind repeating Mel Brooks' jokes on child-rearing re my own travails in that department, though I found Brooks, another of his acquaintances, snide regarding Shaw when he dropped his name into an interview with Johnny Carson circa 1974. Artie also repeated a few times how he'd spurn those huge advances promised for a tome on his intimate life of yore, which apparently on moral grounds, he refused.

Certainly by the '70s and '80s the "generation gap" was affecting Shaw, and not only in relations with significant others like Jennifer. On *The Tonight Show* and at other times he did try to dress in splashy, contemporary style; and Ms. Keyes mentioned that his jeans were faded just so in that period, but he'd also churlishly comment about certain young people and trends that eluded or confounded him. He felt they didn't read and try to understand things the way he did. One day on the phone he complained to me about "this kid Spielberg" getting a lot of money to make a film he considered a dud (*1941*). It seemed to make him angry. I once asked whether young people could teach him anything, and he said that some lady of the boomer generation he met in Vegas had said something that "blew him away," but that mostly it was all "déjà vu."

And of course he kept talking in interviews (though not with me) about the Beatles wrecking popular music, and records becoming simply too loud, which of course certain boomers once they aged would ironically confirm. He disliked the growing anger in rock 'n' roll, as did Benny Goodman. Shaw even denied rock as authentic music at all, though he considered some of its players as more than decent. But stars as diverse as Elvis Presley and the '70s icon John Denver, along with popular groups like Fleetwood Mac, did little for him. Neither did country music. Meanwhile, even jazz, Shaw's original field, had become ever more arcane, too, he felt. And yet Artie didn't want to live in the past, either, taking curmudgeonly refuge in Swing Era nostalgia or more generally, in that period's mores. À propos here, he once asserted to me that the present world is a pile of crap, but it's the only crap game in town.[6]

But again re music, I mostly (and purposely) avoided the subject in my conversations with Shaw. However, the odd time I'd make a faux pas of sorts, as when I came back from a trip to Manhattan in the early '80s and lauded Woody Allen's clarinet work I'd heard there at his usual haunt on a Monday night, as I recall. I thought his was a fine Dixieland group, indeed, and that a sober, but adept Woody more than kept up on his instrument. I wish I could remember Shaw's exact response on the phone, but suffice it to say that he sounded derisive and downright dismissive, even sardonic. How *could* I bring him such a detail regarding a rank amateur, albeit a very famous one? It was beneath contempt. In terms of other clarinet players, he was fairly positive regarding Acker Bilk's chalumeau parts on the hit recording of "Stranger on the Shore," but completely put off by Bilk's sorties there into a higher register.[7]

Basically, I didn't poke much into the lion's cage of sorts, remaining for the most part an intellectual mendicant with Shaw, probably one reason he talked so much to me and at such length. I was willing to take the course, so to speak. And as the loner he'd sometimes call himself, he could at least discuss what interested him, and where he was then at. In addition, the man did have a truly generous side to him. More, he was such a compulsive perfectionist about his pursuits in life that he would drive himself somewhat crazy at all of them, whether it was fly-fishing, marksmanship, home repair and decoration, or far from least, professional music-making. Given that unwieldy novel he kept wanting to make better and better, his talks with me (and others) perhaps constituted a welcome form of relaxation, or repose.

But what of my own motivations here? I guess I simply thought, and quite wrongly back then, that I could transpose keys, so to speak—that I'd get the same lush Shaw as found in his music via that rather gruff expatiator he'd become in these private conversations. Which of course wasn't possible. And maybe Artie had a point, too, about him being a substitute father-figure of sorts to go with my own, both from roughly the same generation, the imposing "Greatest Generation," or so it seemed back then to this baby boomer.

Then, too, there was an adage that Artie put in his own terms somewhere, to the effect that the neurotic goes out in the world to find what will keep the neurosis going! My own growing-up period had been a difficult one in an overwhelming milieu, with strong but confusing, chameleon-like parents; and so I guess I kept on searching for the difficult in life. And Artie was certainly difficult! One observer had it right that just when you thought you knew such a man, you really didn't. But I had developed a lot of patience in my young life and was still in the process of completing the development of an adult persona, and there it is: I went repetitively to this larger-than-life type who had already confounded all sorts of people, but pleased them greatly, too.

And despite the fact that some cattily labeled him pretentious, Artie truly did put together an imposing humanistic and even scientific culture, too. There was plenty to learn from him. And he was certainly the antithesis of gaudily-degreed academics, many of whom (in a well-known adage) kept focusing in their research on more and more about less and less. Artie knew and imparted a great deal, indeed.

And so this neurotic kept taking the course of sorts even after he'd graduated, making too much of a meal of it all, self-punishing (because pretty well every time I dialed there was a certain fear in me, manifested, too, in how I'd sometimes go to that last digit a number of times, then start again, before actually following through). And wondering myself just what I was seeking or getting from all this.

There is much more one could add on this "long coda" in Artie's life, including how this handsomest of all bandleaders during the Swing Era ceded to the passage of time as a bald, owlish, if wise-looking older gentleman. But that isn't our main event here. I should perhaps note that well after I'd stopped calling (circa 1985)—simply because I was on to other concerns, not due to any antipathy from either side of the equation—I impulsively got in touch around 2000 or so with a seasoned agent I didn't know at all re an idea I had for an as-told-to book with Shaw. And this agent, Nat Sobel, surprised me by being very interested.

I then wrote Shaw about the idea on January 22, 2001, though I hadn't talked to him on the phone for over a decade. His reply came back dated May 23, oddly enough on his 91st birthday. I don't know if there was any significance in that. Via my research I once knew a famed French general, who in retirement said he had no birthdays, no Christmas or New Years, no holidays of any sort, and that all he did was work all year long (including on quite a few books). Perhaps Shaw was that way about his own birthday. He did seem self-astonished that five months had gone by since he'd received my missive.

His reply came on letterhead showing his address as 2127 Palos Court, Newbury Park, California, to which he'd migrated from his previous L.A. residence. (Newbury Park is part of Thousand Oaks in Ventura County.) Showing a lukewarm interest in my book idea, Shaw did, however, want a sense of how much of an advance he'd get, and with a favorable split in his direction, given that his own verbiage would be the main focus. He did say he'd read the Truffaut-Hitchcock book I'd mentioned as a kind of role model for our own potential work; but unlike in that book, he felt that a problem in this case was a distinct lack of equality, given that Artie Shaw was a well-known quantity, but this Singer wasn't. He also cited other books in print on his life and career, and the fact that he was then thinking of giving full agreement and participation to Tom Nolan for his projected biography, given that he admired Nolan's previous book on Ross Macdonald. He said all that constituted a kind of "glut." Shaw signed off with a signature that deserves a bit of analysis, too. The "A" in "Artie" had no bar or line across its width and looked simply like a thumb or small rocket. This to me reflects a person who had no time to waste in life (time, in his aphorism used by Berman in her documentary, being "all you've got").

From my end I, too, soon came to my senses, feeling that I'd been trying via this proposal to step back myself into Heraclitus' proverbial river. At that time I was very thronged in academe with big projects on the go and teaching duties, so I simply abandoned the idea. Had I thought it through before proposing it to the agent and Shaw, I would also have reminded myself that since retiring from music-making, Artie had been a prolix, ubiquitous, but often fascinating interviewee, and that in my listening-to tome there would undoubtedly be a certain duplication, much more than a little! This was especially true regarding his "regret trope" re leaving his primary calling. He kept repeating, with variations, grisly analogies like the one about missing his gangrenous arm (that had had to be lopped off).[8]

Still, I kept listening to his old music, which of course was his greatest contribution in life, but thought no further about getting in touch again with this nonagenarian. However, I was surprised and even shocked to hear of his death at the end of December 2004, the news coming to me just as I was noodling along on my amateur clarinet (amateur indeed!) against one of Shaw's slower records of the swing epoch. From a logical point of view his demise shouldn't perhaps have constituted such a shock. The man was after all 94 and a half. He'd outlived pretty well all the other old-time bandleaders, becoming among the last survivors in the Swing Era pantheon. Additionally, health issues had been really plaguing him, as was inevitable. For instance, he'd once taken a German shepherd he'd just acquired for a walk, holding the leash, and another dog got its attention. His dog ran after the other one, and Artie was pulled down onto the pavement, breaking a leg and affecting the hip as well. As all know, that alone can be the beginning of the end, along with the terrible problems he was also experiencing from diabetes (including loss of eyesight), and other health issues he was enduring.[9]

But Shaw's death constituted the passing of a true giant of American music. As an epitaph he would have preferred, or so he'd often express, something like: "He did the best he could with the materials at hand." But when appearing before students at USC, he shortened it to the pithier "Go away!"[10] He of course repeated that elsewhere, too. More of Shaw being characteristically arresting and in this case, comical? Not totally. He did put (in his view) much selfishness into his obsession with making a great number of polished, beautiful, and unique records during a golden era of sorts. And so many of us today can reap so much from all that effort and dedication. Unlike many "icons" today, some of whom feel scarcely more than pygmies in terms of their contributions, Artie was anything but famous simply for being famous, to cite Daniel Boorstin's old adage. He created a veritable *oeuvre* with a distinct, significant place in musical history, a very large footprint, indeed.

One hopes this guide of sorts may help orient people in this regard, particularly a bevy of younger listeners truly starved for good, melodious, emotionally satisfying fare, now so lacking in contemporary American music. And maybe another beneficial plus of connecting with Artie's great work of the Swing Era would be for budding musicians, who could learn much from his plentiful tricks of the trade. For Shaw was and is truly worth emulating, and not only for woodwind players.

Of course any book-length attempt to describe or analyze this major figure's work along with aspects of his life is bound to end up with problems. Including ours! All sorts of readers may well have "taste" issues here, and some will inevitably note lacunae, no question of that. This may sound vain, but it reminds one somewhat of how Artie in later years was repetitively enjoined to pick up the clarinet and just have fun on it. And he'd look serious and a bit miffed, and reply that there was anything but fun in this pursuit for someone like himself who wanted to make wonderful, finished products on the instrument, along with what came from those accompanying him. And to be truthful, the present effort also started out more pleasurably than it ended up. It was wonderful to switch on so much fine music and simply dig it. But a book is a very different matter, as so many authors know.

All that notwithstanding, we hope that our attempt to at least somewhat steer listeners through Artie's great and extensive group of recordings will be beneficial. We emphasize that this is more an essay cum memoir elements than a scholarly tome. But our main job was somehow to try and convey that powerful fragility which can still draw listeners into the deep intimacy of Artie's solos, so often reflecting his real feelings and self, and made against orchestral backgrounds he shaped as his own, almost as one does raising a family. We reiterate our humility in this enterprise, hoping that were he still alive, Mr. Shaw wouldn't have been too put off by the interpretations we've proffered here. (Not that he ever really needed them!)

# Chapter Notes

## Introduction

1. Tony Oppedisano (with Mary Jane Ross), *Sinatra and Me: In the Wee Small Hours*.

2. On Shaw's evolution from music to the intellectual realm, see Barnett Singer, "Becoming an Intellectual: The Strange Saga of Artie Shaw." There is also some discussion of this in Singer, "Recalling Artie Shaw: The Last of the Swing Virtuosos."

3. After retirement Shaw did rather like another crooner, Tony Bennett, but found him too unintrospective about his occupation. See Ted Panken, "For Artie Shaw's 104th Birthday Anniversary, Two Uncut Interviews from April 2002."

4. Morton is interviewed on Shaw's Spanish period in Brigitte Berman's wonderful documentary of 1985, *Artie Shaw: Time Is All You've Got*. (The title came from one of Artie's aphorisms.)

5. Barnett Singer, "Looking for Mr. Bellow." That memoir was used quite extensively in both major biographies of Bellow that came out in the 2000s.

6. Vladimir Simosko, *Artie Shaw: A Musical Biography and Discography*.

7. John White, *Artie Shaw: His Life and Music*.

8. Tom Nolan, *Artie Shaw, King of the Clarinet: His Life and Times*.

9. Robert Lewis Taylor, "Middle-Aged Man Without a Horn."

10. Artie Shaw, *The Trouble with Cinderella: An Outline of Identity*.

11. There is footage of Poli's Palace in another superb documentary put together by Russell Davies in 2003, *Artie Shaw: Quest for Perfection*, which can be found on YouTube in seven parts.

12. Shaw's interview segment on Armstrong is in *ibid.*, part 1.

13. The best and clearest guides to Shaw's development in this era are Simosko, chapters 1–3, Nolan, chapters 1–8, and relevant parts of Shaw's *The Trouble with Cinderella*, 22–291, if interrupted by many philosophical divagations.

14. In a number of interviews, Shaw stresses this constant learning process from those who were generally older and more seasoned, until graduating to the next level and upward, including toward eventual bandleading. See, for example, his interview with Panken of April 2002. On the "Columbus Arshawsky" story, see Shaw, *The Trouble with Cinderella*, 28–32.

15. A fundamental source on this and what it felt like remains Shaw, *The Trouble with Cinderella*, 291–301. See also Simosko, 43–44, Nolan, 59–62, and White, 53–55. Secondary authorities like White dispute Shaw's memory of having only the one number to replay, averring that his group also played another. On that concert and Shaw's innovative piece, one could also consult Gerald W. Ringe, "The Historical Importance and Resulting Arrangement of Artie Shaw's Third Stream Composition Interlude in B-Flat," a fine piece of work.

16. Schuller defined "Third Stream Music" in Gunther Schuller, *Musings: The Musical Worlds of Gunther Schuller*, 119, and the whole concept as seen in this Shaw piece is extensively treated in Ringe, *passim*, who considers Shaw pioneering in that regard.

17. The best and most thorough guide

to the fortunes of this first Shaw band is Simosko, chapter 4, but see also the relevant pages of Shaw's *The Trouble with Cinderella* and Nolan, 62–76.

18. See Robinson's interview segments in *Time Is All You've Got*, and also his quotations in Burt Korall's superb liner notes for the 1976 release *The Complete Artie Shaw* Vol. I, 1938-1939 (with the new and soon-famous band to come). There would be seven volumes in the series, each containing two LP records.

19. In *Time Is All You've Got*, Shaw emphasized in retrospect how onerous all this was, dealing with or getting rid of drunk sidemen, polishing and repolishing (as well as discarding) arrangements, etc. And yet Lee Castle, who was also interviewed in this documentary of the '80s, thought that Artie really knew his direction right from the time he organized his first non-lucrative band with strings, and that he always had a musical trajectory in mind.

20. The fullest and best treatment of the 1937 band's evolution, and then of how Shaw moved toward what became the "Beguine" band, is in Simosko, chapter 5; but also fundamental are appropriate parts of Shaw's *Trouble with Cinderella*, chapters 40–42 and Max Kaminsky (with V.E. Hughes), *My Life in Jazz*, chapter 7.

## Chapter One

1. Best is interviewed in Berman's *Time Is All You've Got*, and Privin is quoted in Korall's liner notes for *The Complete Artie Shaw* Vol. I, 1938-1939.

2. Quite often this Shaw band netted $30,000 a week in a period when money could buy so much more than today, and was little taxed. See Taylor, 76. In later interviews Artie would even amend that to $60,000, but often perhaps meaning gross. As, for example, in *Time Is All You've Got*, discussing these astronomical sums that did make him feel somewhat guilty.

3. On this Boston riot of sorts, see, among others, Taylor, 79–80, and more generally, on the price of being a new celebrity, Shaw, *The Trouble with Cinderella*, chapter 43.

4. In *Time Is All You've Got*.

5. Artie opened up pithily but memorably on this phenomenon to Burt Korall, in Korall's liner notes to *The Complete Artie Shaw* Vol. I, 1938-39.

6. For aspects of this issue, see Gene Lees, "Artie Shaw: The Anchorite." Lees does cavil a bit omnisciently here with Shaw's estimates of his mother (although types like Ava Gardner, who knew her and her influence, did not!).

7. The arrangement here (not to mention execution) improved upon an earlier one created for the previous and less "finished," though powerful and popular, 1937 band, persisting into early '38. That band being Art Shaw and His New Music. See *Inventory of the Artie Shaw Collection, 1910–2005*.

8. Comparative downsides Holiday found in Shaw included the fact that before celebrity brought him big money, he paid her less than Count Basie had done. She also found him at times rather snobby (including overly bookish?). See Robert G. O'Meally, *Lady Day: The Many Faces of Billie Holiday*, 128.

9. On her period with Shaw, see Helen Forrest (with Bill Libby), *I Had the Craziest Dream*, chapters 4–7.

10. Ibid., 94, 95, 98, 105. For more on Forrest's time with Goodman, see chapters 8–9.

11. I spoke to Griffin in conjunction with an article I was preparing on Goodman: Singer, "How Did Benny Goodman Get to Carnegie Hall?" Like Forrest, he much preferred Artie as a person to Benny.

12. Again, the arrangement went back to one for the 1936 band, which lasted into early spring '37, the first of course containing strings and not as good as the '37 edition; and both bands inferior to the first great Shaw aggregation under discussion here, including this topflight, definitive recorded version of his theme song. See *Inventory of the Artie Shaw Collection*.

13. Among others, his tenor sax player Hank Freeman used this "voice" analogy for Shaw's playing, cited in Burt Korall's liner notes to *The Complete Artie Shaw* Vol. I, 1938-1939.

14. This was absolutely certain in the case of Romberg, who rang up Shaw, in-

forming him that he believed "Softly..." better in the version provided by Artie's band than his original song! Shaw related this anecdote to Terry Gross of NPR during the '80s. See "100 Years of Jazz Clarinetist Artie Shaw."

15. The newspaper editor citation (by Shaw) is found in Korall's liner notes for *The Complete Artie Shaw* Vol. IV, 1940-41. Shaw repeats his emphasis on the bandleader as an editor of sorts in Panken. On Buddy Rich's life and his ascent to the Shaw band, see Pelle Berglund, *Buddy Rich: One of a Kind (The Making of the World's Greatest Drummer)*, chapters 1-4, and Mel Tormé, *Traps, the Drum Wonder: The Life of Buddy Rich*, chapters 1-8; and on Rich's techniques and Artie's attempts to rein him in, *ibid.*, chapters 10-11.

## Chapter Two

1. See Shaw, *The Trouble with Cinderella*, chapter 41.
2. Privin quoted in Korall's liner notes to *The Complete Artie Shaw* Vol. II, 1939.
3. For the chronology of Shaw band gigs mentioned here, Simosko, 68-69 remains clearest and best.
4. Simosko expressed this in a single conversation with Singer, but also notes the slim number of Shaw takes on recordings in his book, *passim*.
5. He called Sinatra's singing, even presumably including his ever evolving work of the '50s and '60s, boring in an interview with Panken.
6. The Buddy Rich and Shaw interviews (the latter on Goodman's reaction) are in *Time Is All You've Got*, and Rich is also quoted on the band being voted number one for 1938 in Burt Korall's liner notes to *The Complete Artie Shaw* Vol. II, 1939. In his fine biography of Goodman, Ross Firestone notes that by the latter stages of his musical career Benny had to a degree burned psychological bridges with a lot of sidemen he considered hiring, even on a temporary basis. See Firestone, *Swing Swing Swing: The Life and Times of Benny Goodman, passim*.
7. Noted by Forrest in conversation with Burt Korall in his liner notes to *The Complete Artie Shaw* Vol. II, 1939.

8. For the concluding, improvised "Surrender..." cadenza—drawn, according to Shaw, from sonata form—see his remarks to Bruce Talbot in "Artie Shaw: NEA Jazz Master." Shaw refers, as we do a number of times here, to the absolute necessity and centrality in jazz of the element of surprise. *Ibid.*, 53. On wanting to drop this great band for good, Shaw's most definitive statements came in an interview with Dave Dexter, Jr., in mid-October '39. See Dexter, "Artie Shaw Fed Up with Music Racket," where Artie sounds off about autograph hounds, piranha-like reporters, and so forth.

9. See, among others on this, Taylor, 80, quoting Shaw, who of course also told the story elsewhere.

10. Shaw even called that band (along with all his bands) a kind of instrument he fashioned out of a variety of players under his cohesive grip and vision. See his interview with Panken.

11. Shaw very often found audiences of any kind a necessary annoyance, and sometimes hoped there would be rain so he and his bandmates could play exactly as they wanted, unimpeded. See his quotations in Taylor, 80.

12. For the preceding, see, among others, *ibid.*, 84, and Nolan, 128-130, as well as Lees citing the Sammy Cahn story in "Artie Shaw: The Anchorite." Helen Forrest claimed that she was the "last to leave" Shaw's room, still trying to get him to reconsider his decision. Forrest, 90. And on the whole run-up from the previous spring to Shaw's great escape, see Simosko, chapter 7.

13. Artie declared that he called Glenn Miller about Gray being right to arrange for that band, thereby taking some credit for its popular success. Shaw quoted in White, 77.

## Chapter Three

1. See Lana Turner, *Lana: The Lady, the Legend, the Truth*, 48-50, 57-59, 62-66. Those into Hollywood history will know that Betty Grable blew her top to Silvers when Shaw eloped, having seen her own marriage with the bandleader as a probability; and so, more dangerously, did Judy Garland, whom he considered

only as a good friend and a sister of sorts, but who spun into a deep depression when she saw news of the sudden marriage in the papers. See Tom McGee, *Betty Grable: The Girl with the Million Dollar Legs*, 75–76, and Gerald Clarke, *Get Happy: The Life of Judy Garland*, 125–29.

2. On Shaw's arranger Still, see Catherine Parsons Smith, *William Grant Still: A Study in Contradictions*.

3. See Les Robinson on this "singing" quality, quoted in Korall's liner notes for *The Complete Artie Shaw* Vol. IV, 1940-41.

4. On the etiology of this original work, including the fact that Shaw only hatched a name for it while in the recording studio, see Freddie Johnson, "Freddie Johnson Interviews: Artie Shaw on KPCC FM."

5. Shaw told the story to Burt Korall for the latter's liner notes in *The Complete Artie Shaw* Vol. IV, 1940-1941.

6. Shaw liked this song's melody and how it reflected a part of his own personality. He recorded it several times—the first one being this most well-known and original version in 1940; but also on the Musicraft label late in 1945, then with another, more boppish band in 1950, and even with his last small group in 1954. See Marc Myers, "Artie Shaw: Love of My Life."

7. Butterfield had a sound like no other on trumpet in that period, and Shaw went to an entirely different kind of arrangement (worked out with Lennie Hayton) on this "Star Dust" in order to take full advantage of Billy's verve. Artie was of course an inveterate coacher and shaper of his players, but he averred to Robert Lewis Taylor that Butterfield needed no advice whatsoever. Taylor, 82. However, the valuable first trumpeter was mercurial about staying in bands, and apt to quit abruptly. So Shaw gave him generous pay, but put half into an account Butterfield couldn't touch till year's end. See Talbot interview of Shaw and also Mike Zirpolo's article "'Star Dust' (1940) Artie Shaw, with Billy Butterfield and Jack Jenney." Shaw also had to rein in Butterfield's penchant for alcohol. Re Artie's well-worn story of finding Chuck Peterson's previous trumpet work in the '38-'39 band vitiated by marijuana use and Artie experimenting with it himself to show the effect it had, the best version is in a tape of Shaw made by Aram Saroyan, used in Saroyan's article "Artie Shaw Talking," 3–6.

8. As Samantha Wright notes from her own experience, this Shaw contribution on "Star Dust" is "probably one of the most difficult clarinet solos ever..." See "Artie Shaw" on her blog of May 16, 2019. In her "Artie Shaw and Stardust" post of Dec. 4, 2021, she mentions the "insane altissimo B in bar 14." Artie declared that he was partly pushed into playing very high to have his clarinet heard against the brass, and in certain environments where he and his bands gigged. See Talbot interview of Shaw.

9. Shaw had used Conrad cane reeds through 1939, and in 1940 moved to Enduro plastic reeds. During World War II, French cane reeds were hard to come by (cane was needed for military purposes), especially after France fell to the Nazis in June 1940. Shaw found plastic reeds fine for a goodly swath of his music-playing life. There are different internet postings on this subject, including by Simosko.

10. Re the number analyzed here, Jesse Read considers the very title of "Prelude in C Major" a kind of joke, given that it is actually in C# major (or Db), confirmed in Mike Zirpolo, "'Prelude in C Sharp Major' (1940) Artie Shaw."

11. Shaw's acquaintance with the klezmer idiom may have been there from early on, but never placed in the foreground, not least by him! He later found his "Dr. Livingstone, I Presume" rather inane, and never wanted to be subsumed within the klezmer genre at all. See Eric Seddon, "Artie Shaw and the Altissimo." And of course as much as many of his solos had real and earthy Jewish plaintiveness in them, Shaw also wanted very much to distance himself from the Jewish past and its recent immigrants in America; not least his father, who spoke most of the time in Yiddish and made Shaw ashamed (and much later ashamed for *being ashamed*), particularly in New Haven, Conn., versus his very early years in New York. See his discussion of all this in *The Trouble with Cinderella*, 135–139.

12. Artie was partly being saucy here. After a song plugger pushed "When the Swallows Come Back to Capistrano" on him, Artie surprised him on the radio with this odd, but certainly inventive departure from the original tune, one he apparently didn't like. Simosko also notes the comedic aspects of this Shaw piece of work, but one with unusual switches (see Simosko, 91). Jesse Read calls the solos here among the happiest and most inventive of the era, and the entire record quite remarkable for the contours and range that almost defy gravity and logic.

13. One should not overly accentuate the autodidactic, off-the-cuff aspects of Shaw's work on the licorice stick. He also learned, and at times disseminated information about, which exercises and even equipment were most useful for aspiring jazz players on the instrument. For this period under discussion, see Artie Shaw and Arnold Brilhart, *Artie Shaw Clarinet Method: A School of Modern Clarinet Technic*. Of course he kept on fiddling with his own techniques as well. Re his "Concerto for Clarinet," on which Shaw was so modest, Gunther Schuller also played it down in his *The Swing Era: The Development of Jazz, 1930–1945*. But through his entire section on Shaw, Schuller keeps giving with one hand and taking with the other, and the book seems at its worst in this part, churlish, patronizing, and not as reliable a "guide" as it purports to be. See *ibid.*, 692–714, and specifically on "Concerto for Clarinet," 705. Brian Rust is also rather patronizing toward Shaw, and brief in his *My Kind of Jazz*, 89–91.

14. Butterfield and Robinson are quoted in Burt Korall's liner notes to *The Complete Artie Shaw* Vol. 4, 1940-41. And for this whole period, see Simosko's short but informative chapter 8 (85–92) and relevant pages of Nolan in chapters 21–25.

## Chapter Four

1. Shaw cited in Korall's liner notes for *The Complete Artie Shaw* Vol. V, 1941-42.

2. The interviews of Shaw and ex-sidemen are included in *ibid*. See also Kaminsky, 124–127.

3. But there are those who stress the importance and pioneering quality of Shaw's "Third Stream" attempts, including Ringe, who goes back to his "Interlude in B-Flat" to establish a lineage there. See Ringe, "The Historical Importance," *passim*; and John Wilson, "Artie Shaw Rarities Come to Light."

4. Peggy sometimes found Goodman's demands onerous, but she is charitable to him in her autobiography, even if noting his frequent absent-mindedness, and also (without much apparent rancor) his commandeering of royalties for songs the band cut but which her vocals made into hits. See Peggy Lee, *Miss Peggy Lee: An Autobiography*, 15–16, 103.

5. Simosko's chapter 9 (93–98) on this band and period is most useful for chronology, especially of live AS events. Nolan's chapter 25 has more human-interest material.

## Chapter Five

1. On Shaw's state of mind prior to enlisting, including his wrangle with the attorney Andrew Weinberger, see Taylor, 84, 86.

2. See for the foregoing *ibid.*, 91–92, among others, and for the entire wartime era, Nolan, chapter 27, Simosko, chapter 10, Kaminsky, chapter 9, and Shaw's account in *The Trouble with Cinderella*, chapter 47.

3. Shaw was always positive about this first heavy stint of psychoanalysis, which also helped him adapt to a changing musical world. See, for example, Taylor, 92.

4. It should be noted that the term "bebop" wasn't actually coined till Dizzy Gillespie did so at a recording session of January 9, 1945. But the phenomenon was already going strong. See Chuck Haddix, *Bird: The Life and Music of Charlie Parker*, 73, and Scott DeVeaux, *The Birth of Bebop: A Social and Musical History*. For the bop influence on Woody Herman, see Gene Lees, *Leader of the Band: The Life of Woody Herman*, 97–99 and *passim*. Kaminsky notes the oedipal disdain of boppers in the late '40s for even great old jazz players like Hot Lips Page. Kaminsky, 192, 211.

## Chapter Six

1. Including in interviews with Korall in Korall's liner notes for *The Complete Artie Shaw* Vol. VI, 1942–45.

2. Ava said her best period with Shaw was the one (pre-marriage) that included following Artie and his band on the road, whether in California, Chicago or New York, and savoring their innovative music. See Peter Evans and Ava Gardner, *Ava Gardner: The Secret Conversations*, 206. She had long enjoyed big band music, including that made by Artie, who in her view influenced her future paramour, Frank Sinatra, with his long-held musical phrasing. *Ibid.*, 208. On her deep admiration of Shaw musically, see also Ava Gardner, *Ava: My Story*, 89. She enjoyed the eight months or so of dating cum much talking, dancing, etc., but *not* the increasing put-downs of her intellectually. On the chess story, see *ibid.*, 93–94.

3. See Nolan, 196–197, and on Eldridge and the plunger story, Artie's interview segment in *Time Is All You've Got*, among other places.

4. On the classical elements here and possibly yet another "Third Stream" attempt at melding jazz and "longhair"-type music, see Mike Zirpolo, "Repost Number One: 'Summertime' (1945) Artie Shaw / Eddie Sauter" and Dave Radlauer, "Artie Shaw: A Journey of Self-Discovery."

5. Bigard's view is quoted in a number of places including in Lees, "Artie Shaw: The Anchorite." Being in the same difficult line of work, Bigard put Shaw above Goodman in that regard, despite the latter's own greatness on clarinet.

6. See Simosko, 108.

7. Saxophonist Les Clarke quoted in Burt Korall's liner notes to *The Complete Artie Shaw* Vol. VI, 1942–1945.

8. Among other places, the anecdote is cited in Simosko, 87.

9. Shaw uses that adjective, for instance, when discussing the later band with Korall. See Korall liner notes, *The Complete Artie Shaw* Vol. VII, 1939–1945 Retrospective.

10. See, among others on this, Taylor, 79. The name of this boy who was bonkers for the Shaw sound on clarinet was Lenny Lewis. When Lewis grew up, he himself played and led an orchestra, before taking a job as one of Shaw's band managers!

11. See Simosko, 109, and for some other aspects noted here, Nolan, chapters 29–31, *passim*.

## Chapter Seven

1. For this period, including personnel in Shaw's orchestras and recording dates, Simosko's discography is vital in Simosko, 200–203.

2. Tormé spoke reverentially about Shaw as an idol to him when growing up in Chicago and in how he helped shape him once he came into Artie's postwar employ. See his comments in Berman, *Time Is All You've Got*, and also in Mel Tormé, *It Wasn't All Velvet: An Autobiography*, 88.

3. Artie's increasing use of cutting remarks had driven Ava ever more toward the use of booze, but she still tried to understand him, including the tortured relationship he had with his mother, whom Ava called "crazier than a quilt." See Evans and Gardner, *Ava Gardner*, 201, and on her drinking, 204, as well as the IQ test she took to prove her intelligence, 203. Shaw constituted "one of the deep hurts of my life" and "yet Artie and I remained close for years, and I can't say anything against him." Gardner, *Ava: My Story*, 97–98. She said she admired the clarinetist and bandleader the most of her three famed husbands. *Ibid.*, 98. In unseemly fashion, Artie would later repeat her intimate evaluations of Sinatra as too much on the distaff side for her, and these found their way into other book-length accounts, such as John Brady's *Frank & Ava: In Love and War*, 101–102.

4. A high point was his participation with 85 members of the New York Philharmonic Orchestra in "Music Under the Stars" at Ebbets Field, where he played Mozart's famed Clarinet Concerto (but never at Carnegie Hall, as some have averred). Over 31,000 were on hand for this benefit concert for the infant State of Israel at the Dodgers' home base. See, among other sources, C.H., "'Music

Under the Stars' Held at Ebbets Field for Benefit of Palestinian Institutions." On the story that he supposedly but didn't actually play the Mozart Clarinet Concerto with the New York Philharmonic in Carnegie Hall under the conductorship of Leonard Bernstein, see, among others, David Mullis, "Artie Shaw."

5. As usual Simosko's book, *passim* is a valuable reference work for dates of recordings, labels, soloists, etc. The internet also helps a good deal there.

6. A version of the story is found, among many other places, in Brady, *Frank & Ava*, 78–79.

7. Footage is seen among other places in Davies' documentary, *Artie Shaw: Quest for Perfection*, part 5.

8. Footage in *ibid.*, part 6.

9. One critic gave the group a two-edged compliment by calling it "George Shearing with a clarinet." Cited by David Johnson in "Shaw Sounds Final: Artie Shaw, 1949–54."

10. It's important to note that both "Tenderly" and "Imagination," each taped near the end of 1953, had conventional time limits of three minutes or so, due to the demands of two small record labels, Bell and Clef. There are longer versions in the more copious clutch of tapings done from the latter part of February through early March 1954. See Simosko, 208–209. But my preference is for the ones presenting more of a beginning, middle and end, where the proverbial "less is more" is demonstrated. Shaw's "How High the Moon"—which, however, is right for a longer skein of musical explorations—comes from the latter group of tapings, as do more forgettable reworkings of "Begin the Beguine," "Frenesi," and other old Shavian chestnuts. Shaw could, however, see the handwriting on the wall, given how modern jazz was becoming more and more a series of technical exercises that could appeal less and less to mass audiences. But he also thought his last clarinet work was up with his very best. See his interview with Panken.

11. Shaw knew both of these icons, but considered Basie the more substantial and Ellington very good, even unique when good, but more inconsistent and (unjustly) more adulated. See Talbot interview of Shaw.

12. There are a number of interviews with Jonathan, easily located on the internet. He certainly had some of his father's philosophical bent and proclivity for searching, and he always looked a lot like that celebrated dad, too, one who mostly spurned him. See, for example, Justin Joffe, "Tattoo Artist Jonathan Shaw on Brawling with Bukowski and Other Wild Tales."

13. Shaw expresses his side of the matter in Davies' *Artie Shaw: Quest for Perfection*," part 5.

## Chapter Eight

1. Morton interviewed in Berman's documentary *Time Is All You've Got*.

2. Shaw was generally a "neatnik," as Ava Gardner, among others, learned in her relationship with him; but books were, or at least became, another matter. When Vladimir Simosko visited him at his California home in the early '90s, he saw books everywhere, and not only in cases, but piled on the floors beside chairs and even on the staircase. Simosko, 140. Another visitor in the same period saw tomes loading down a baby grand piano, tables, etc. See Frank J. Prial, "Literary Life, After Ending the Beguine."

3. On Shaw and this 1964 movie and his hopes for it, see his interview segments in Tony Mastroianni, "Artie Still Swings on Another Beat," published on February 16, 1965, when the film was about to open in this city where Shaw had once lived and worked.

4. See Evelyn Keyes, *Scarlett O'Hara's Younger Sister: My Lovely Life in and out of Hollywood*, chapters 51–68, *passim*; interview of Keyes in Berman, *Time Is All You've Got*; and Evelyn Keyes, *I'll Think About That Tomorrow*, part 4, "Old Husband, New Friend," and part 5, "Trying a New Point of View." After a long hiatus, Artie called her in 1985 to discuss the Berman documentary and also his new band, and they started having marathon phone calls (mostly made from his end), dinner dates, and even family time with his son Jonathan and his wife and infant son. The well-known story about Artie crying on learning he was a grandfather

is in *ibid.*, 243–245. Keyes even babysat Artie's dog. On taking care of him while he was in hospital, and cleaning his fridge at his home while he was there, see *ibid.*, 285–306.

5. See Lees, "Artie Shaw: The Anchorite."

6. On the Beatles obsession, see Singer, "Recalling Artie Shaw," 175. On Elvis, Fleetwood Mac, and John Denver not impressing, see Lees, "Artie Shaw: The Anchorite," based on a talk he had with Shaw. On rock not really being music at all, see Talbot interview of Shaw. And on jazz growing inaccessible, and too much patronizing by critics of players like Stan Getz (because he became popular), see *ibid.*, 63.

7. For Shaw on Bilk, see "The James A. Drake Interviews: Artie Shaw" (from his meeting with Shaw in 1974). Shaw was also more than decent with Dick Johnson, when he took over a re-formed Shaw band in the '80s and played the old clarinet solos. Artie's idea was to let Johnson be who he was even on well-known numbers like the 1940 "Star Dust." See Chip Deffaa's 1985 article on Shaw in Deffaa, *Swing Legacy*. I should add re Woody Allen playing clarinet in Manhattan that I impulsively gave him a copy of my "Looking for Mr. Bellow," one reason perhaps that he put Bellow into his movie *Zelig* of that period? There is of course no way to authenticate that.

8. See Prial article in the *New York Times*, where Shaw mentions missing the arm, but at least being able to live the way he wanted to do. Howard Reich of the *Chicago Tribune* heard roughly the same thing from Artie in the early '90s. Cited in Reich, "Enigmatic Shaw: Marching to Sound of His Own Clarinet." Shaw of course had many other iterated themes he'd retail in different ways and right to the end, including on his old rival Goodman's putative one-dimensionalism and stupidity! See, for instance, Talbot interview of Shaw.

9. At least Shaw had long since given up a terrible smoking habit that, had it persisted, would surely have shortened that long life of his. He told Gene Lees (before their eventual breakup) that in his salad days he'd sometimes gotten up to as many as seven packs a day. Lees, "Artie Shaw: The Anchorite." Lees originally published this segment in his *Jazzletter*, June–August 2004. Nolan, chapter 57, is fullest on Shaw's health problems near the end of his life.

10. Cited among other places in "Artie Shaw," an obituary in Swingmusic.net, 6.

# Bibliography

"Artie Shaw." Obituary. Swing Music Net, n.d. www.swingmusic.net/Shaw_Artie.html.

Berglund, Pelle. *Buddy Rich: One of a Kind (The Making of the World's Greatest Drummer)*. Lavallette, NJ: Hudson Music, 2019.

Berman, Brigitte (director). *Artie Shaw: Time Is All You've Got*. Documentary film. Toronto: Bridge Film Productions, 1985.

Brady, John. *Frank & Ava: In Love and War*. New York: Thomas Dunne, 2015.

C.H. "'Music Under the Stars' Held at Ebbets Field for Benefit of Palestinian Institutions." *New York Times*, June 17, 1949, 26. https://timesmachine.nytimes.com/timesmachine/1949/06/17/84271678.html.

Clarke, Gerald. *Get Happy: The Life of Judy Garland*. New York: Random House, 2000.

Davies, Russell (director). *Artie Shaw: Quest for Perfection*. Documentary film. London: BBC Four, 2003. https://www.youtube.com/watch?v=CnGAxyuezWY&ab_channel=JohnFerguson.

Deffaa, Chip. *Swing Legacy*. Metuchen, NJ: Scarecrow Press, 1989.

DeVeaux, Scott. *The Birth of Bebop: A Social and Musical History*. Berkeley: University of California Press, 1997.

Dexter, Dave, Jr. "Artie Shaw Fed Up with Music Racket." *Downbeat*, October 15, 1939.

Drake, James A. "The James A. Drake Interviews: Artie Shaw." Mainspring Press (blog), April 11, 2022. https://78records.wordpress.com/2022/04/11/the-james-a-drake-interviews-artie-shaw/.

Evans, Peter, and Ava Gardner. *Ava Gardner: The Secret Conversations*. New York: Simon & Schuster, 2013.

Firestone, Ross. *Swing Swing Swing: The Life and Times of Benny Goodman*. New York: W.W. Norton, 1993.

Forrest, Helen (with Bill Libby). *I Had the Craziest Dream*. New York: Coward, McCann & Geoghegan, 1982.

Gardner, Ava. *Ava: My Story*. New York: Bantam Books, 1990.

Haddix, Chuck. *Bird: The Life and Music of Charlie Parker*. Urbana: University of Illinois Press, 2013.

Henning, Amy. "Artie Shaw." Big Band Swing & more (blog), n.d. https://www.touchoftonga.com/DavidMulliss/artie-shaw.html.

*Inventory of the Artie Shaw Collection, 1910–2005*. University of Arizona School of Music, n.d. http://collections.music.arizona.edu/artieshaw/collection/MMS5Shaw.pdf.

Joffe, Justin. "Tattoo Artist Jonathan Shaw on Brawling with Bukowski and Other Wild Tales." *The Observer*, March 29, 2017. https://observer.com/2017/03/jonathan-shaw-interview/.

Johnson, David. "Shaw Sounds Final: Artie Shaw, 1949–54." Night Lights (blog), Indiana Public Media, May 19, 2021. https://indianapublicmedia.org/nightlights/shaw-sounds-final-artie-shaw-194954.php.

Johnson, Freddie. "Freddie Johnson Interviews: Artie Shaw on KPCC FM." YouTube, n.d. https://www.youtube.com/watch?v=TxcxSdMDjkk&ab_channel=FreddieJohnson.

Kaminsky, Max (with V.E. Hughes). *My Life in Jazz*. New York: Harper & Row, 1963.

Keyes, Evelyn. *I'll Think About That Tomorrow*. New York: Dutton, 1991.

———. *Scarlett O'Hara's Younger Sister: My Lively Life in and Out of Hollywood*. Secaucus, NJ: Lyle Stuart, 1977.

Korall, Burt. Liner notes for *The Complete Artie Shaw*, Volumes I–VII. RCA, 1976–1981.

Lee, Peggy. *Miss Peggy Lee: An Autobiography*. New York: Donald Fine, 1989.

Lees, Gene. "Artie Shaw: The Anchorite." Jazz Profiles (blog, Steven A. Cerra), June 1, 2019. https://jazzprofiles.blogspot.com/2019/06/artie-shaw-anchorite-parts-1-3-complete.html.

———. *Leader of the Band: The Life of Woody Herman*. New York: Oxford University Press, 1995.

Levinson, Peter J. *Tommy Dorsey: Livin' in a Great Big Way—a Biography*. Cambridge, MA: Da Capo Press, 2005.

———. *Trumpet Blues: The Life of Harry James*. New York: Oxford University Press, 1991.

Mastroianni, Tony. "Artie Still Swings on Another Beat." *Cleveland Press*, February 16, 1965. http://www.clevelandmemory.org/mastroianni/tm333.html.

McGee, Tom. *Betty Grable: The Girl with the Million Dollar Legs*. Vestal, NY: Vestal Press, 1995.

Myers, Marc. "Artie Shaw: Love of My Life." JazzWax (blog), December 5, 2019. https://www.jazzwax.com/2019/12/05/index.html.

Nolan, Tom. *Artie Shaw, King of the Clarinet: His Life and Times*. New York: W.W. Norton, 2011. First published as *Three Chords for Beauty's Sake: The Life of Artie Shaw*. Norton, 2010.

O'Meally, Robert. *Lady Day: The Many Faces of Billie Holiday*. New York: Arcade, 1991.

"100 Years of Jazz Clarinetist Artie Shaw." *Fresh Air*, National Public Radio, WBUR, May 19, 2010. https://www.wbur.org/npr/126972706/100-years-of-jazz-clarinetist-artie-shaw.

Oppedisano, Tony (with Mary Jane Ross). *Sinatra and Me: In the Wee Small Hours*. New York: Scribner's, 2021.

Panken, Ted. "For Artie Shaw's 104th Birthday Anniversary, Two Uncut Interviews from April 2002." Today Is the Question: Ted Panken on Music, Politics, and the Arts (blog), Word Press, May 23, 2014. https://tedpanken.wordpress.com/tag/artie-shaw/.

Prial, Frank J. "Literary Life, After Ending the Beguine." *New York Times*, August 18, 1994. https://www.nytimes.com/1994/08/18/garden/at-home-with-artie-shaw-literary-life-after-ending-the-beguine.html.

Radlauer, Dave. "Artie Shaw: A Journey of Self-Discovery." Jazz Rhythm (blog), n.d. http://www.jazzhotbigstep.com/215.html.

Reich, Howard. "Enigmatic Shaw: Marching to Sound of His Own Clarinet." *Chicago Tribune*, January 5, 2005.

Ringe, Gerald W. "The Historical Importance and Resulting Arrangement of Artie Shaw's Third Stream Composition Interlude in B-flat." Doctoral dissertation, University of North Texas, August 2016.

Rust, Brian. *My Kind of Jazz*. London: Elm Tree Books, 1990.

Saroyan, Aram. "Artie Shaw Talking." *Los Angeles Times*, August 6, 2000. https://www.latimes.com/archives/la-xpm-2000-aug-06-tm-65218-story.html.

Schuller, Gunther. *Musings: The Musical Worlds of Gunther Schuller*. New York: Oxford University Press, 1986.

———. *The Swing Era: The Development of Jazz, 1930–1945*. New York: Oxford University Press, 1989.

Seddon, Eric. "Artie Shaw and the Altissimo." The Jazz Clarinet (blog), December 30, 2011. http://thejazzclarinet.blogspot.com/2011/12/artie-shaw-and-altissimo.html.

Shaw, Artie. *The Trouble with Cinderella: An Outline of Identity*. Santa Barbara: Fithian Press, 1992. First published 1952.

Shaw, Artie, and Arnold Brilhart. *Artie Shaw Clarinet Method: A School of Modern Clarinet Technic*. New York: Robbins Music, 1941.

Simosko, Vladimir. *Artie Shaw: A Musical Biography and Discography*. Lanham, MD: Scarecrow Press, 2000.

Singer, Barnett. "Becoming an Intellectual: The Strange Saga of Artie Shaw." *Biography* 4 (Fall 1981), 326–339.

———. "How Did Benny Goodman Get to Carnegie Hall?" *American History* 36 (April 2001), 22–28.

———. "Looking for Mr. Bellow." *Jewish Dialog* (Hannukah 1982), 2–38.

———. "Recalling Artie Shaw: The Last of the Swing Virtuosos." *Contemporary Review* 287 (September 2005), 171–175.

Smith, Catherine Parsons. *William Grant Still: A Study in Contradictions*. Berkeley: University of California Press, 2000.

Talbot, Bruce. "Artie Shaw: NEA Jazz Master (2005)." Interview, October 7–8, 1992. Archives Center, National Museum of American History, Smithsonian Institution. https://www.si.edu/media/NMAH/NMAH-AC0808_Shaw_Artie_Transcript.pdf.

Taylor, Robert Lewis. "Middle-Aged Man Without a Horn." *The New Yorker*, May 19, 1962, 47–98.

Tormé, Mel. *It Wasn't All Velvet: An Autobiography*. New York: Viking, 1988.

———. *Traps, the Drum Wonder: The Life of Buddy Rich*. New York: Oxford University Press, 1991.

Turner, Lana. *Lana: The Lady, the Legend, the Truth*. New York: Dutton, 1982.

White, John. *Artie Shaw: His Life and Music*. New York: Continuum, 2004. First published 1998.

Wilson, John. "Artie Shaw Rarities Come to Light." *New York Times*, October 28, 1984. https://www.nytimes.com/1984/10/28/arts/artie-shaw-rarities-come-to-light.html.

Wright, Samantha. "Artie Shaw." Samantha Wright (blog), May 16, 2019. https://samanthawright.co.uk/blog/f/artie-shaw.

———. "Artie Shaw and Stardust." Samantha Wright (blog), December 4, 2021. https://samanthawright.co.uk/blog/f/artie-shaw-and-stardust.

Zirpolo, Mike. "'Prelude in C Sharp Major' (1940) Artie Shaw." Swing & Beyond (blog), March 25, 2016. https://swingandbeyond.com/2016/03/25/88.

———. "Repost Number One: 'Summertime' (1945) Artie Shaw/Eddie Sauter." Swing & Beyond (blog), October 11, 2016. https://swingandbeyond.com/2016/10/11/reads-and-re-reads-the-protean-mr-gershwin/.

———. "'Star Dust' (1940) Artie Shaw with Billy Butterfield and Jack Jenney." Swing & Beyond (blog), October 21, 2017. https://swingandbeyond.com/2017/10/21/star-dust-1940-artie-shaw/.

# Index

Aaronson, Irving 13, 14
"Absent Minded Moon" (song) 107
Acapulco 73, 158
"Acc-Cent-Tchu-ate the Positive" (song) 116
Adams, Pepper 48
"Adios Marquita" (song) 76
"Aesop's Foibles" (song) 149
alcoholism 14, 110
"All Alone" (song) 19
"All in Fun" (song) 69
"All the Things You Are" (song) 34, 69–70
Allen, Dorothy 125
Allen, Gracie 96, 97
Allen, Red 99
Allen, Woody 167
"Alone Together" (song) 47, 48, 49, 95, 96, 152
alto saxophone 99
American Federation of Musicians, Local 802 16
"And the Angels Sing" (song) 79
anti–Semitism 90, 152
"Any Old Time" (song) 28, 30, 51
"April in Paris" (song) 79–80, 132, 156
Arlen, Harold 78, 101, 116
Armstrong, Louis: at benefit concert 16; music resembling style of 51, 54; Pastor, T. compared to 36; Shaw, A. compared to 102; Shaw, A. contact with 14; Shaw, A. influenced by 152
Arshawsky, Harold (Artie Shaw's father) 12, 26, 75
Arshawsky, Sarah (Artie Shaw's mother) 12, 13, 16, 26, 75
*Artie Shaw* (Simosko) 9–10
*Artie Shaw* (White) 10
*Artie Shaw, King of the Clarinet* (Nolan) 10
*Artie Shaw Plays Cole Porter* (LP) 141

*Artie Shaw Plays Cole Porter and Irving Berlin* (LP) 141
*Artie Shaw: Quest for Perfection* (documentary) 153
*Artie Shaw: Time Is All You've Got* (documentary) 120, 160
artists, observations concerning 8
Arus, George 18, 36, 37, 60
Astaire, Fred 81
"At Sundown" (song) 39, 40–41, 56
Atlas, James 42
Auld, Georgie: as improviser 56; Pastor, T., comparison to 55; Pastor, T. upstaged by 27, 37, 51; Pastor, T. *versus* 58; Rich, B. attitude toward 54, 56; as saxist 39, 60, 62, 65, 67, 117; in Shaw band, 1938–1939 40, 41, 43, 45, 73; in Shaw band, 1941–1942 99, 102, 103, 106–107, 108; as tenor soloist 53, 59, 60, 69, 71
"Autumn in New York" (song) 80, 132
Avola, Al 18

baby boom generation 128, 137, 167
Bach, J.S. 166
"Back Bay Shuffle" (song) 27
Baker, Chet 48
bandleaders: old-time surviving 170; prominent 63; Shaw, A. compared to other 74, 78, 93; wartime fiddles added by 82
bar mitzvah 90
Barbour, Dave 141
baritone saxophone 100
Bartee, John 149
Bartok, Bela 145
Basie, Count: in later years 158; musical adapting by 112; renaissance period 156; Shaw, A., comparison with 78, 119; sophistication of 103; trumpeters playing with 116

**185**

# Index

Bassey, Bus 80
Beatles: changes in 74; fame, price of 24; impact on popular music 138, 167; popularity of 50; swing musicians compared to 93, 138
"Beau Night in Hotchkiss Corners" (song) 91
bebop (bop): invention 112; musicians influenced by 115, 121; in Shaw, A. band (1949–1950) 149; swing mixed with 118–119, 128, 129, 146
"Bedford Drive" (song) 117
Beethoven, Ludwig van 75
"Begin the Beguine" (song): band prior to 65; era of 81; hits, other compared to 53, 76; as innovative piece 82; making and impact of 23, 24, 153; as masterpiece 22; music, other in contrast to 43, 78; music in aftermath of 32; musicians maturing with band of 55; Shaw interpretation of 19; songs, other in addition to 27; tinkering with 21; updated versions of 104
Beiderbecke, Bix 14, 152
Bellow, Alexandra 37, 44–45, 126
Bellow, Saul: biography 42; low-ceiling and high-ceiling literature referred to by 83; Shaw, A. comments concerning 164; Shaw, A., dealings with 8–9, 144–145; Shaw music played for 37, 44–45, 126; writings on 161, 165
Bennett, Tony 156
*The Benny Goodman Story* 4
Berezowsky, Nicolai 145, 146
Berigan, Bunny 14, 16, 18, 41, 108
Berlin, Irving 58, 141
Berman, Brigitte 15, 26, 57, 120, 160, 162
Berry, Chuck 157
Best, John: "Beguine" impact noted by 24; Miller, G. band joined by 59, 66; Shaw, A.'s wartime band joined by 110; as trumpeter 18, 36, 62
"Between a Kiss and a Sigh" (song) 36
"Beyond the Blue Horizon" (song) 103
big bands: at benefit concerts 16; prelude to 19; twilight of 150
Bigard, Barney 118, 122, 128
Bilk, Acker 167
"Bill" (song) 46
Black musicians: in Goodman band 100, 120; in Gramercy Five 81; influence of 14, 16; in Shaw band, early 1950s 153; in Shaw band, 1938–1939 22, 27, 28, 30; in Shaw band, 1941–1942 99, 100, 101, 104, 107–108; in Shaw band, 1944–1945 115, 126; *see also under individual musician*
"Blue Skies" (song) 19
"Blues in the Night" (song) 101
"Body and Soul" (song) 21, 44, 94
"Boogie Woogie" (song) 108
"booting" (term) 54
"bop" (term) 112
Boyer, Anita 83, 84, 85, 91
Brooks, Mel 166
Brown, Les 120
Brown, Vernon 80, 92
Bruce, Lenny 161
Bryan, Mike 102, 103
Burness, Les 27
Burns, George 96, 97
*Burns and Allen* (radio show) 81, 83
"But Not for Me" (song) 119–120
Butterfield, Charles William "Billy": in ensemble 82, 83, 89, 90; in films 81; as lead trumpeter 93, 94, 95, 96, 97; migration of 96; Shaw, A. hiring of 80; Shaw band breakup, reaction to 97; "Stardust" melody played by 86, 87

Cahn, Sammy 72–73
"The Calypso" (song) 91
Campbell, Glen 71
"Can't Help Lovin' That Man" (song) 117
Cantor, Joe 13
"The Carioca" (song) 46
Carle, Frankie 70
Carleton, John 138
Carmichael, Hoagy 86, 97, 101–102
"Carnival" (song) 107
Carson, Johnny 45, 160, 166
Carter, Benny 99
Casa Loma Orchestra 16
*Casablanca* (film) 106
Castle, Lee 102, 151
Catlett, Sid 41, 108
Cavallaro, Johnny 12–13
chamber music, music resembling 77, 127–128, 133
Charles, Ray 97
Cherry, Don 151
Christian, Charlie 81
Clapton, Eric 81
Clar, Arden 148
clarinet: classical 17; "Fred's Delight" 148; Goodman, B. on 3; learning 13, 16; Miller, G., sound resembling 49; saxes, doubling with 131–132; Shaw, A. on (*see* Shaw, Artie [b. Arthur Arshawsky] on clarinet)
clarinet players 167

# Index

classical music:
Clinton, Larry 93
Clooney, Rosie 156
clothing and dress, past and present musicians compared 67
Cohen, Paul 116, 120, 121
Cohn, Al 146, 147
*The Cold War as History* (Halle) 6
Cole, Nat 156
Coleman, Harry 148
Colonna, Jerry 156
"Comes Love" (song) 59
"Comin' On" (song) 27
Commanders (music group) 13
Como, Perry 114, 141
*Complete Artie Shaw* 57
*The Complete Arty Shaw* (series of LPs) 4–5
"Concerto for Clarinet" (piece) 91–92, 122, 146
"Confessin' (That I Love You)" (song) 99
Conniff, Ray: arrangements 118, 125, 150; migration of 96; music composed by 107; Shaw, A. hiring of 80; in Shaw band, 1941–1942 102, 103, 104, 117; singers 142; songs by 126; on trombone 114
"Copenhagen" (song) 38
Copland, Aaron 145
Coslow, Sam 51, 67

Dameron, Tadd 147, 148
"Dancing Co-Ed" (film) 57, 64
"Dancing in the Dark" (song) 93–94, 96
"Dancing on the Ceiling" (song) 132
"Danza Lucumi" (song) 84
Darin, Bobby 71
Day, Doris 120
"Day AFTER Day" (song) 36
"Day In, Day Out" (song) 64
*The Dean's December* (Bellow) 164
Debussy, Claude: compositions by 145; Shaw, A. influenced by 16, 60; songs resembling music of 105, 129, 130, 142
"Deep in a Dream" (song) 36
"Deep Purple" (song) 52–53, 58
"Delightful Delirium" (song) 50
DeNaut, Jud 80, 82, 89, 91, 95
Denver, John 167
Depression 3, 14–15, 16, 41
DeRose, Peter 52
"Deuces Wild" (song) 104
Diamonds (music group) 53
DiMaggio, Joe 22
D'Isere, Guy 16–17
divorce during Swing Era 68

"Do I Love You" (song) 70
"Dr. Livingstone, I Presume" (song) 89–90
Dodds, Johnny 51
Domino, Fats 89
Donahue, Sam 110
Donaldson, Walter 89
"The Donkey Serenade" (song) 46
"Don't Blame Me" (song) 134, 136–137
"Don't Take Your Love from Me" (song) 153
Dorsey, Tommy: bandmembers 18, 24, 69, 141, 142, 143; at benefit concert 16; imitations of 22; Jenkins, L. compared to 39; Jenney, J. compared to 87; Rich, B. relationship with 46; Shaw, A. criticism of 54; Shaw, A. music imitated by 82; Shaw, A. playing with 14; singers working for 108; songs 32; "Stardust" version by 86; trombone playing by 27
Dorsey band, singers for 89
Dorsey brothers: as bandleaders 15, 63; career in 1950s 155; enduring hits of 93; rise of 17; Shaw, A. compared to 78
Dowling, Doris 151, 157
"Down South Camp Meeting" (song) 4
drug use 67, 74, 163
Duke, Vernon (Vladimir Dukelsky) 79, 132, 133, 136

"Easy to Love" (song) 122–123, 124
"Easy to Say" (song) 61
"The Education of Albie Snow" (Shaw) 6, 119, 163
Egstrom, Norma *see* Lee, Peggy (Norma Egstrom)
Eldridge, Roy: in Gramercy Five ensemble (reconstituted) 138, 139; as lead trumpeter 124, 137; open-horn solo by 126; in Shaw band, 1944–1945 115, 117, 119; trumpet solos by 120, 121, 127, 131, 133
electric guitar 114; as new instrument 81; Shaw, A. band (1940–1941) 89, 90; Shaw, A. band (1941–1942) 102; Shaw, A. band (1949–1950) 148; Shaw, A. band, early 1950s 153, 154
Ellington, Duke: alums of 108; as bandleader 63; career, 1950s 156; clarinetist working for 118; Goodman music praised by 30; Shaw, A. attitude toward 93, 137–138; Shaw, A. music compared to that of 32
Elman, Ziggy 30, 79
Ertegun, Ahmet 53
ethnic revolution, 1960s 90

# Index

Evans, Bill 48
"Evensong" (song) 105
expressionism, musical equivalent of 88

*The Fabulous Dorseys* (film) 146
Farlow, Tal 153, 154
Faso, Tony 118
*The Father* (Strindberg) 77
Fatool, Nick: as drummer 92, 95; in ensemble 82, 89; migration of 96; Shaw, A. hiring of 80, 141
female singers: attitudes toward 106; treatment of 28, 30
feminism 68
*Fiddler on the Roof* (musical) 136
Fields, Dorothy 134
film industry, music industry compared to 63
films: emotion-laden 66; music themes similar to 79; romantic era in 39, 79; World War II era 84–85, 106
Fisher, Eddie 160
Fitzgerald, Ella 155
*The Fleet's In* (film) 107
Fleetwood Mac 167
"A Foggy Day" (song) 124–125
*Forever Amber* (Winsor) 134, 143, 144
Forrest, Helen: Boyer, A. compared to 83; evaluation of 36; Goodman, B. recalled by 28–29; as Goodman, B.'s singer 69, 73; as James, H.'s singer 106; memoirs 10; pop songs featuring 38; Shaw, A., announcement of split, reaction to 72–73; Shaw, A., relations with 61; as Shaw, A.'s singer 7, 39, 40, 50, 54, 61, 62, 64, 66, 67, 68, 69; as Shaw, A.'s singer: "Bill" 46; as Shaw, A.'s singer: "Comes Love" 59; as Shaw, A.'s singer: "Deep Purple" 52, 53; as Shaw, A.'s singer: "I Didn't Know What Time It Was" 71; as Shaw, A.'s singer: "I Poured My Heart into a Song" 58, 63; as Shaw, A.'s singer: "I Want My Share of Love" 49; as Shaw, A.'s singer: "I'm in Love with the Honorable Mr. So and So" 51; as Shaw, A.'s singer: "A Man and His Dream" 60; as Shaw, A.'s singer: "My Reverie" 39
Forrestal, James 109
Four Brothers band 119
Four Freshmen 133, 142
Frankel, Victor 90
"Fred's Delight" (song) 148
"freebooting" (term) 54
Freeman, Hank 18
"Frenesi" (song) 75, 76, 77–78, 80, 82, 88

Friml, Rudolf 46
Fromm, Lou 138

Gardner, Ava: books recommended to 6, 165; literary interests 134, 143; marriage 11, 42, 61, 113–114, 134, 139; memoirs 10; music inspired by 126, 131, 134; musical tastes 128, 130, 147; Shaw, A., acquaintance with 30; Shaw, A. music described by 27; Shaw, A., post-marital relations with 63, 163; Sinatra, F., relations with 30, 114, 146, 151
Garland, Joe 62
Garland, Judy 17, 30, 32, 73
Geller, Harry 59, 66
generation gap 166–167
"The Gentle Grifter" (song) 138
Gentry, Charles 116, 130, 141
*George White's Scandals* (film) 91
"Georgia on My Mind" (song) 97
Gershwin, George: "But Not for Me" 119, 120; death 128; "A Foggy Day" 124; Jewish background 136; "The Man I Love" 45, 125; "Oh, Lady Be Good!" 64; "Our Love Is Here to Stay" 128; *Rhapsody in Blue* 136; "Someone to Watch Over Me" 129; "Summertime" 122, 126; "They Can't Take That Away from Me" 127
Gershwin, Ira 33; "But Not for Me" 119, 120; "A Foggy Day" 124; Jewish background 136; "Oh, Lady Be Good!" 64; "Our Love Is Here to Stay" 128; "Someone to Watch Over Me" 129; "They Can't Take That Away from Me" 127
"Get Out of Town" (song) 142
Gibson, Fredda (*later* Georgia Gibbs) 106, 107
Gillespie, Dizzy 112
*The Girl from Utah* (stage musical) 131
Glow, Bernie 118, 120
"Go Fly a Kite" (song) 60
Goddard, Paulette 81
*The Goldwyn Follies* (film) 128
Goodman, Benny: acolytes of 53; as bandleader 15, 63, 73; Black musicians working for 100, 120; childhood compared to Shaw, A. 90, 152; classical music played by 145; competitive nature of 155; films devoted to 146; Forrest, H. recollections of 28–29; influence and legacy 3–4, 22; influences on 13; in later years 159; medical problems 80; recorded and live music compared 38–39; rise of 17;

rock, opinion of 167; Shaw, A. attitude toward 93, 137–138; Shaw, A. compared to (as bandleader) 28–29, 30, 42, 43, 81, 108; Shaw, A. compared to (music) 8, 10, 19, 27, 31, 32, 33, 34, 37, 39–40, 45, 49, 68, 78, 88, 118, 138, 145, 153; Shaw, A. competition with 24, 33, 57–58; Shaw, A. criticism of 39, 88; singers 69, 73, 79; "Stardust" version by 86; trumpeters 102, 138

Gramercy Five ensemble: "Dr. Livingstone, I Presume" 89–90; end of 134; explorations by 92; forming 81–82; "Keepin' Myself for You" 83; music, other compared to 103; "When the Quail Come Back to San Quentin" 90–91

Gramercy Five ensemble, reconstituted (1945) 138–139

Gramercy Five ensemble, reconstituted (1953–1954) 151, 154–155

Gray, Glen 16

Gray, Jerry 17, 21, 52, 73

"Greatest Generation" 168

Green, John 94

Griffin, Gordon "Chris" 30, 138

Griselle, Thomas 101

Guarnieri, Johnny: in ensemble 82, 83, 89, 90; migration of 07; as piano soloist 88, 91, 95; Shaw, A. hiring of 80; in Shaw band, 1941–1942 99, 100, 102, 103, 108

"Guilty" (song) 142

Hackett, Bobby 81

Halle, Louis 6, 7, 133, 163

Hammerstein, Oscar 37, 44, 69, 117

"A Handful of Stars" (song) 85

Harding, Buster 117

Harry James Orchestra 106

Hart, Lorenz 71, 126, 132

Hawkins, Coleman 54

Haymes, Dick 151

Hays Code 76

Hayton, Lennie 85, 95, 107

Hemingway, Ernest 6, 8

Henderson, Fletcher 22, 27, 108

Henderson, Skitch 79

Hendrickson, Al 80–81, 82

Hendrix, Jimi 81

Herfurt, Skeets 141

Herman, Woody 112, 119, 128, 131, 158

Higginbotham, J.C. 99

"Hindustan" (song) 107

Hines, Earl "Fatha" 13

Hitler, Adolf 24, 61

Holiday, Billie: clarinet resembling voice of 62; "I Cover the Waterfront" 94; in Shaw band, 1938–1939 28, 30, 51; "Time on My Hands" 124; tribute to 116

Hollywood 13

*Homage to Catalonia* (Orwell) 158

Horne, Lena 99

"The Hornet" (song) 140

House Committee on Un-American Activities 151–152

"How High the Moon" (song) 153–154

Huizinga, Johan 148

Huston, John 160

"I Ask the Stars (and They Agree)" (song) 103

"I Can't Believe That You're in Love with Me" (song) 31

"I Can't Escape from You" (song) 137

"I Can't Get Started (with You)" (song) 80, 132–133, 155

"I Could Write a Book" (song) 126

"I Cover the Waterfront" (song) 94, 95, 96, 122, 149, 150

"I Didn't Know What Time It Was" (song) 71

"I Don't Want to Walk Without You" (song) 106

"I Get a Kick Out of You" (song) 150

"I Got the Sun in the Morning and the Moon at Night" (song) 142

"I Poured My Heart into a Song" (song) 58, 63

"I Surrender Dear" (song) 65, 66

"I Want My Share of Love" (song) 49

"I Was Doing All Right" (song) 128–129

"If I Had You" (song) 96, 97

"If What You Say Is True" (song) 68

*If You Meet the Buddha on the Road, Kill Him!* 160–161

"I'll Never Be the Same" (song) 116–117

"I'll Never Smile Again" (song) 93, 143

"I'll Remember" (song) 62

"I'm Coming Virginia" (song) 53

"I'm Getting Sentimental Over You" (song) 32

"I'm in Love with the Honorable Mr. So and So" (song) 51

"Imagination" (song) 154

impressionism, musical equivalent of 88, 89

"In the Mood" (song) 39

"In the Still of the Night" (song) 142

"Indian Love Call" (song) 21–22, 27

"Innuendo" (song) 147

"Is It Taboo? (to Fall in Love with You)" (song) 103
"It Had to Be You" (song) 40, 97
"It's All Yours" (song) 50
"I've Got You Under My Skin" (song) 142

James, Harry: as bandleader 108; biographies 145; Forrest, H. as singer for 36, 69; Forrest, H. romance with 28; Goodman, B.'s band, departure from 43; Griffin, G. playing with 30; orchestra 106; in Shaw band, 1941–1942 102; Shaw, A. music imitated by 82
jazz: classical influence on *see* classical music: jazz influenced by; improvised 100; post-swing progressive 129, 130, 167; revolution in 112
jazz piano 80, 117
Jenkins, Gordon 151
Jenkins, Les 39, 54
Jenney, Jack 80, 87, 95, 96, 150
Jerome, Jerry: migration of 96; in Shaw band, 1940–1941 80, 84, 88, 92, 94, 97
Jewish influence on music 33, 37, 44, 68, 136
Jewish musicians 14, 33, 37, 68, 136
jitterbug 38, 62–63, 65, 66, 70, 124
Johnson, Dick: as clarinetist 49, 78–79; in reformed Shaw orchestra 7, 92, 149, 166; on Shaw, A.'s clarinet skill 35; Singer, B. dealings with 9
Johnson, Wendell 7
Jones, Allan 46
Jones, Hank 153, 154, 155
Jordan, Paul 105, 107
jungle, music suggesting 89–90
"Just Floating Along" (song) 133
"Just Kiddin' Around" (song) 104

Kahn, Roger Wolfe 14
Kallen, Kitty 142
Kaminsky, Max 19, 100, 110, 111
Kardiner, Abram 9, 144
"Keepin' Myself for You" (song) 83, 127
Kelly, Paula 104, 105
Kenton, Stan 112
Kern, Elizabeth "Betty" 11, 109, 139, 157
Kern, Jerome: classical influence 78; daughter of 11; death 117; Jewish background 136; Sauter arrangement of songs by 131; Shaw, A. songs, opinion of 89; songs, Shaw, A. versions of 33, 34, 35, 69
Kessel, Barney 114, 118, 128, 138–139
Keyes, Evelyn: marriage 11, 42, 134, 159–160, 161–162; memoirs 10, 61, 159, 160, 161, 162; Shaw, A. appearance, comments on 166; Shaw, A., post-marital relations with 63, 162, 163
"Kind of a Drag" (song) 105
"King of the Clarinet" (title) 10, 27, 43
Kitsis, Bob 54–55, 60, 65, 69
Klein, Manny 14, 75, 141
Kluger, Irv 153
Kopp, Sheldon 160
Korall, Burt 57
Krupa, Gene 41, 43, 46, 114, 148
Kyser, Kay 93

La Centra, Peg 17
"Lady Day" (song) 116
*The Last Analysis* (Bellow) 144–145
"The Last Two Weeks of July" (song) 64
Lee, Peggy (Norma Egstrom) 108, 114, 141, 148, 156
Leeman, Cliff 18
Lees, Gene 26, 162
"Let's Dance" (song) 32
"Let's Walk" (song) 140
Levinson, Peter 145
Lewis, Jerry Lee 157
Linn, Ray 141
"Little Darlin'" (song) 53
"Little Jazz" (song) 119
Little Richard 157
*The Lives of a Cell* (Thomas) 7, 133
Loesser, Frank 106
Lombardo, Guy 93, 143
"longhair" music 18, 78, 98, 143, 145, 150
Louis, Joe 35, 155
"Love for Sale" (song) 142
"Love Is Here" (song) 68, 69
"Love Me a Little" (song) 99
"Love of My Life" (song) 84–85
"Love Walked In" (song) 126
"Lover Come Back to Me" (song) 44, 45
Lynn, Imogene 117

Macdonald, Ross 169
Magidson, Herb 91
"The Maid with the Flaccid Air" (song) 129–130, 131
"The Maid with the Flaxen Hair" (song) 129
"Mamas and Papas" 133
"A Man and His Dream" (song) 60
"The Man I Love" (song): mood of 44, 45, 46, 48; songs, other compared to 127; versions compared 125, 126
Mandel, Johnny 147
Mann, Herbie 48
*Man's Search for Meaning* (Frankel) 90

mariachi effects 77
"Marie" (song) 22
"Marinella" (song) 84
Marmarosa, Michael "Dodo": background and hiring by Shaw 114–115; "Dancing on the Ceiling" 132; "Don't Blame Me" 137; in Gramercy Five ensemble (reconstituted) 138, 139; "I Can't Get Started" 133; "I'll Never Be the Same" 117; "The Maid with the Flaccid Air" 130; "No One But You" and "They Didn't Believe Me" 131; Shaw, A. relationship with 163; in Shaw band (1944–1945) 120–121; in Shaw band (1949–1950) 147; "Summertime" 122; "These Foolish Things" 125
Marsala, Joe 41
masculine-feminine interplay 129
Maugham, Somerset 165
McHugh, Jimmy 134
McKimmey, Ed 102
McRae, Teddy 27, 60
"Melancholy Mood" (song) 62
*Melody & Madness* (radio show) 38, 50
Mel-Tones 141–142
Mercer, Johnny 84–85, 101, 107, 116
Meredith, Burgess 81
Milhaud, Darius 122
Miller, Glenn: in Air Force 109; band-members 59, 66, 73; clarinet sounds resembling 49; films devoted to 146; music predating 39; popularity of 89; popularity *versus* A. Shaw 25, 93, 100; Shaw, A. criticism of 7, 35; songs 32; summit not reached by 43
Modern Jazz Quartet 133
Monroe, Vaughn 123
*Moonglow* (Shaw, LP) 4, 94
"Moonglow" (song) 94–95, 96, 122
"Moonlight Serenade" (song) 32
"Moonray" (song) 61, 62
Morton, Frederick 8, 158
Mozart, Wolfgang 145, 164
Mulligan, Gerry 156
Mundy, Jimmy 108, 116, 120
musical revolution 156–157
Musicraft 139–140, 141
"My Blue Heaven" (song) 89
"My Reverie" (song) 39
"Mysterioso" (song) 139

"Needlenose" (song) 107
New England Puritanism 68
Nichols, Red 14
"Nightmare" (song) 32–33, 91, 139

Nimitz, Chester 109, 110
"No One But You" (song) 130–131
"Nocturne" (song) 101
Nolan, Tom 10, 121, 142, 169
Noone, Jimmie 13
"Not Mine" (song) 107
"Now We Know" (song) 79

Oakland, Ben 91
Oberstein, Eli 130
O'Brien, Floyd 152
*Of Human Bondage* (Maugham) 165
"Oh Lady Be Good!" (song) 64–65
"Ol' Man River" (song) 34
"One Foot in the Groove" (song) 55, 56
"One Night Stand" (song) 54–55, 56
"Orinoco" (song) 149
Orwell, George 158
"Our Love Is Here to Stay" (song) 128
*Out of Chaos* (Halle) 6, 7, 133, 163
"Out of Nowhere" (song) 58, 94

Page, Oran "Hot Lips" 100, 101, 104, 107–108
Palladino, Don 150
Parker, Charlie 112, 153
Pastor, Tony: in Art Shaw and His Orchestra 17; as AS bandleader (temporary) 57, 72; Auld, G. compared to 55; band led by 69, 73; lack of musicians resembling 33; in Shaw Band, 1938–1939 22, 28, 36, 37, 50, 54, 59, 60, 64, 68; solos by 45, 58, 70; tenor sax 30; tenor sax solos by 23, 51, 62; upstaging of 27
Pearl Harbor, attack on 96, 98, 104–105, 106
*People in Quandaries* (Johnson) 7
"persistence" (term) 34
Peter Pan Novelty Orchestra 12
Peterson, Chuck 18, 55, 62
Phillips, John 133
"Pick Yourself Up" (song) 7
Pied Pipers 54, 86, 142, 143
Plato 164
Platters 89
Plumb, Neely 80
popular culture, romantic era in 61, 79
popular music 128, 138, 167
Porter, Cole 19, 21, 70, 123, 141
Potter, Tommy 153
Poulenc, Francis 145
Powell, Mel 108
"Prelude in C Major" (song) 87, 88, 89
Presley, Elvis 23, 157, 167
Privin, Bernie: best displaced by 36; as

Shaw, A. bandmember 24, 39; as trumpeter 44, 45, 47–48, 54, 55, 58, 59, 60
"Prosschai" (song) 51–52
Puma, Joe 154, 155
Puritanism 68
"Put That Down in Writing" (song) 64

Quenzer, Arthur 67, 69

racial discrimination 28, 115, 126
radio shows 38, 50, 81, 83
radio work 14, 15, 38, 83, 91
Raney, Jimmy 146, 148, 150
Raskin, Milt 141
Ravel, Maurice 16, 60, 105, 122
Ray, Johnnie 156
Rayman, Morris 138
Read, Jesse: Shaw band music (1940–1941) evaluated by 93; Shaw band music (1941–1942) evaluated by 103, 105; Shaw band music (1944–1945) evaluated by 117–118, 120, 122, 125, 131–132, 133, 137; Shaw band music (1949–1950) evaluated by 148, 149; Shaw music (1946) evaluated by 142
*The Red and the Black* (Stendahl) 121
*Republic* (Plato) 164
Reynolds, Herbert 131
*Rhapsody in Blue* (musical composition) 136
Rich, Buddy: Auld, G., attitude toward 56; background and Shaw, A. band joined by 41; as bandleader 158; as Dorsey, T. bandmember 69; as drummer 44, 46, 49, 50, 51, 54, 55, 59, 60, 61, 62, 64, 65, 70; influences on 108; Shaw, A. band influenced by 40; Shaw, A. relations with 156; Shaw, A. win recalled by 57
Rich, Fredy 14
Robinson, Les: after Shaw band breakup, 1939 73; after Shaw band breakup, 1941 97–98; migration of 96; saxes led by 37; Shaw, A. hiring of 80; in Shaw band, 1938–1939 18; in Shaw band, 1941–1942 99, 102, 103, 104; in Shaw orchestra (1946) 141; Shaw orchestra described by 95, 132
rock 'n roll: adaptability required for 137–138; advent of 154, 157; anger, growing in 167; Darin, B. views on 71; immersion in 53; musicians, drug use by 74; revolution 68
"Rockin' Chair" (song) 101–102
Rockwell, Tommy 72
Rockwell-O'Keefe Theatrical Agency 17

Rodgers, Harry 18
Rodgers, Richard 71, 126, 132, 136
Roland, Joe 153, 154
Romberg, Sigmund 37, 44, 78, 136
"A Room with a View" (song) 39, 40
"Rosalie" (song) 44
"Rose Room" (song) 48–49
Rosenlund, Ralph 119, 120, 125, 132
Ruderman, Morton 77
Russin, Babe 141
Russo, Sonny 147

"'S Wonderful" (song) 117–118, 150
"St. James Infirmary Blues" (song) 104
Sanicola, Hank 151
Saroyan, William 144
Sauter, Eddie: Goodman, B., arrangements for 108; Shaw, A., arrangements for 120–121, 122, 126, 127, 129, 130, 131
saxophone: "Absent Minded Moon" 107; "Alone Together" 47; "April in Paris" 79; "Back Bay Shuffle" 27; clarinet compared to 13, 83, 152; clarinets, doubling with 131–132; "Concerto for Clarinet" 92; "Confessin' (That I Love You)" 99; "Deep Purple" 52–53; "Don't Blame Me" 136; "Easy to Love" 122–123; "I Didn't Know What Time It Was" 71; "I Surrender, Dear" 65; "If I Had You" 96, 97; "I'll Never Be the Same" 117; "Indian Love Call" 22; "It's All Yours" 50; "Keepin' Myself for You" 127; learning 12; "Love Is Here" 69; "Love of My Life" 84; "Lover, Come Back to Me" 44; "The Maid with the Flaccid Air" 130; "Man I Love" 45; "Moonglow" 95; "No One But You" 131; "Oh, Lady Be Good" 64; in postwar era 142; "Rockin' Chair" 102; "Rose Room" 49; "September Song" 118; in Shaw band, 1940–1941 80; in Shaw band, 1941–1942 100, 107; "So Easy" 148; "Somebody Nobody Loves" 106; "Someone's Rocking My Dreamboat" 106; "Star Dust" 86; "These Foolish Things Remind Me of You" 125; "They Can't Take That Away from Me" 127; "Time on My Hands" 124; "What Is This Thing Called Love?" 35; "Yesterdays" 34
*Scarlett O'Hara's Younger Sister* (Keyes) 160
Schuller, Gunther 17
*Séance on a Wet Afternoon* (film) 162
*Second Chorus* (film) 81, 84–85, 91
Second Herd 119

segregation 28
Seinfeld, Jerry 63
self-help trend 160, 164
"Sentimental Journey" (song) 120
"September Song" (song) 118–119
*"September Song" and Other Favorites* (LP) 118
"Serenade to a Savage" (song) 62, 63
sexual revolution 51
"Shadows" (song) 70
Shaw, Artie (b. Arthur Arshawsky): accident and pedestrian death 14; ambition, views on 6–7; Bellow, S. recollections of 9; birth 11–12; childhood 8, 11–12, 15, 16, 90, 152; Communist associations 117, 143, 145, 146–147, 151–152; death 170; didactic bent 162–163; early career 12–14; education 13, 15, 72; fame, price of 9, 23–26, 32, 71; as father 11, 29–30, 75, 112, 157, 162; father, relationship with 12, 26, 75; films, work in 57, 64, 81, 84–85, 161–162; generation gap impact on 166–167; Goodman, B., dealings with 57–58; health problems 56–57, 150, 151, 170; hearing damage 110–111; instruments played by (other than clarinet) 12, 13, 21, 152; Jewish background 15, 26, 37, 44, 90, 134, 143, 152; legacy 170, 171; literary and intellectual interests 5–7, 72, 108, 113, 140, 144, 157, 159, 164; mother, relationship with 12, 13, 16, 26, 75; in Navy 109–112; psychoanalysis undergone by 40, 144–145, 163; in radio 14–15, 38, 83, 91; retirement 5–7, 35, 39, 45, 59, 92, 135–136, 137, 155–157, 158–160, 161–169, 170–171; rock, relationship with 137–138; singers, attitude toward 7, 141, 143, 147; spiritual leanings 165–166; women, relationships with 26, 29–30, 31–32, 42, 54, 61, 75, 78, 93, 114, 126, 129, 152, 162, 165, 166
Shaw, Artie (b. Arthur Arshawsky) on clarinet: achievements, limit to 155; analysis and critique of 45; as authentic artist 21; in band, 1949–1950 149; in band, early 1950s 153; clarinetists, other compared to 35–36, 153; "conversations" played by 40; in ensemble 81, 83, 84; evaluation of 56; evolution 43, 78–79, 152; film work 84; Jewish influence 44; learning 13, 16; notes range 50; with orchestra, 1946 142; progress made on 19; sadness in solos 15; talent 34
Shaw, Artie (b. Arthur Arshawsky) on clarinet, songs: "Alone Together" 47, 95–96; "Back Bay Shuffle" 27; "Begin the Beguine" 23; "But Not for Me" 119–120; "Concerto for Clarinet" 91–92; "Confessin' (That I Love You)" 99; "Copenhagen" 38; "Dancing in the Dark" 93; "Dancing on the Ceiling" 132; "Deep Purple" 52, 53; "Dr. Livingstone, I Presume" 89–90; "Donkey Serenade" 46; "Easy to Love" 122–123; "Frenesi" 77; "The Gentle Grifter" 139; "Georgia on My Mind" 97; "I Ask the Stars" 103; "I Can't Escape from You" 137; "I Can't Get Started with You" 133; "I Cover the Waterfront" 94, 150; "I Was Doing All Right" 128; "If What You Say Is True" 68; "I'll Never Be the Same" 116, 117; "Imagination" 154; "Indian Love Call" 22; "Keepin' Myself for You" 127; "Love Is Here" 69; "Moonglow" 94–95; "Moonray" and "I'll Remember" 62; "My Reverie" 39; "Nightmare" 33; "No One But You" 131; "Nocturne" 101; "Not Mine" 107; "Oh, Lady Be Good" 64–65; "One Foot in the Groove" 55; "Out of Nowhere" 58; "Prelude in C Major" 88; "Rockin' Chair" 102; "Rose Room" 48, 49; "September Song" 118; "Shadows" 70; "Somebody Nobody Loves" 107; "Someone to Watch Over Me" 129; "Someone's Rocking My Dreamboat" 106; "Soon" 126–127; "Stardust" 86, 87; "Suite No. 8" 105; "Summertime" 126; "These Foolish Things Remind Me of You" 125; "They Can't Take That Away from Me" 128; "Time on My Hands" 124; "Too Marvelous for Words" 155; "Traffic Jam" 60–61
Shaw, Artie (b. Arthur Arshawsky) marriages 61, 63, 71, 91, 145; biographical treatment of 10–11; Gardner, A. 133–134, 139, 143; Kern, E. 109, 112, 113; Keyes, E. 151, 159–160, 161–162; overview of 33; Turner, L. 76–77; Winsor, K. 143–144
Shaw, Artie music (general): assessment of 87–88; books on 10; collectors and collecting 4–5, 7–8; imitations of 82; overview of 4
Shaw, Artie (b. Arthur Arshawsky), musical influences on: Armstrong, L. 14; as budding musician 15–16, 17; classical 77–78, 145–146, 152; Goodman, B. 4, 22; Jewish composers 136;

## Index

Mexican 76, 77, 79; swing bands, other 18
Shaw, Artie (b. Arthur Arshawsky) sources: biographies 9–10, 11, 19, 120, 121, 169; documentaries 15, 23, 120, 153, 160; memoirs 19, 159, 161, 162
Shaw, Artie (b. Arthur Arshawsky) writings: autobiography 10, 14, 15–16, 19, 25, 47, 90, 144, 151, 152–153; "Education of Albie Show" 6, 119, 163; memoir 10, 152–153; novel, work on 164–165, 167–168; novellas and stories 159
Shaw, Jonathan Dowling 157
Shaw, Steven Kern 11, 112, 157
Shaw band (thru 1937) 16, 17–18, 19
Shaw band (1938–1939) 21–26; band, 1944–1945 compared to 115, 125; beginning/formation of 18–19; breakup of 59, 69, 70–73, 74; evaluation of 27–28, 31–39, 40, 43–44, 46–51, 57, 58, 64–66; members 41–42; orchestra, 1940–1941 compared to band, 1938–1939 81; production and scheduling demands 53–54; "Star Dust" version by 150
Shaw band (1940–1941) 84–89; achievements 93–96; band, 1944–1945 compared to 115, 132; breakup of 92–93, 96, 97–98; evaluation of 96–97; orchestra description and members 75–76, 78–79, 80–81; overview 74; *see also* Gramercy Five ensemble
Shaw band (1941–1942) 98, 99–104, 105–108, 130
Shaw band (1942–1943): Rangers 109–110, 111
Shaw band (1944–1945) 115–123, 124–134; bebop played by 146; breakup of 134, 139–140; evaluation of 135; formation of 112, 113
Shaw band (1945) 48
Shaw band (1946): Art Shaw and His Orchestra 141–142, 143
Shaw band (1949–1950): band, early 1950s compared to 154; band, 1944–1945 compared to 125, 130, 135; evaluation and critique of 147–150
Shaw band, early 1950s 153–156
Shaw band, reconstituted (1980s): assembling of 7, 149, 166; clarinet parts in 49, 78–79, 92
Sherwood, Bobby 76, 79, 117
"Shine On, Harvest Moon" (song) 39
Shostakovich, Dmitri 78, 145
"Similau" (song) 148
Simosko, Vladimir 9–10, 19, 53
Sims, Zoot 146, 150
Sinatra, Frank: career, 1950s 156; crooning 155; as Dorsey band singer 88–89, 142, 143; Gardner, A. attitude concerning music of 124; Gardner, A. relationship with 30, 114, 146, 151; "I'll Never Smile Again" sung by 93; musical influences on 27, 30; on his own 141; Shaw, A. criticism of 7, 54; "Stardust" version performed by 86; works on 8
Singer, Barnett: childhood 168; Johnson, D. playing heard by 92; musical interests 3, 9, 37, 44–45; Shaw, A. contact and conversations 5–9, 11, 119, 135–136, 160–161, 162–163, 164–165, 166–170; Shaw music preferences 87–88, 89, 91, 93; writings 8–9
singers and singing as lower pursuit 141, 143
Siravo, George 126, 127, 128–129, 130–131, 133, 136
Smith, Willie "The Lion" 14, 16, 92
"Smoke Gets in Your Eyes" (song) 89
"So Easy" (song) 148
Sobel, Nat 168
"Softly, as in a Morning Sunrise" (song) 36–37, 38, 44
"Solid Sam" (song) 104
"Somebody Nobody Loves" (song) 106
"Someday Sweetheart" (song) 19
"Someone to Watch Over Me" (song) 129
"Someone's Rocking My Dreamboat" (song) 106
"Sometimes I Feel Like a Motherless Child" (song) 107
"Song of India" (song) 108
"Soon" (song) 126–127
Southern, Terry 161
Spain 158–159, 161
Spielberg, Steven 167
Stacy, Jess 27
Stafford, Jo 54, 86
Stanley, Kim 162
"Star Dust" (song) 85–87; early *versus* recorded version, 1940 39; instrumentals/contingent 101, 106; songs, other compared to 88, 95; success of 93; updated versions of 104, 149, 150
Stendahl 121
Stevens, April (Carol LoTempio) 53
Steward, Herbie 114, 119, 147
Still, William Grant 77
"Stranger on the Shore" (song) 167
Stravinsky, Igor 16, 105, 122
Strindberg, August 77

# Index

"A String of Pearls" (song) 73
strings: clarinet adapted to 43; orchestra with, pre-1942 16, 17, 80, 84, 93–94, 96; orchestra with, 1946 141, 142; section, band with 75, 77, 78, 79, 82, 84; Shaw band, 1941–1942 102, 103
Styne, Jules 106
Suesse, Dana 67
suffering, art stemming from 75
"Suite No. 8" (song) 105
"Summertime" (song) 120–122, 126, 129, 130, 131
"Summit Ridge Drive" (song) 82, 83
swing bandleaders: old-time surviving 170; Shaw, A. compared to other 74, 78, 93
swing bands: polls 57; Shaw, A. borrowing from other 18; Shaw, A.'s band compared to other 17, 30, 31, 36, 39
Swing Era: bands near end of 98; clarinetists of 28; dawn of 3–4; divorces during 68; jazz after 129, 130; music after 142; musical expectations in 17–18, 32, 60–61; nostalgia regarding 146, 167; peak of 19, 42; survivors of 170; twilight of 4, 114, 118, 130, 134, 140

"A Table in the Corner" (song) 67–68
"Take the 'A' Train" (song) 32
"Take Your Shoes Off Baby (and Start Runnin' Through My Mind)" (song) 104
"talent" (term) 13, 34
Taylor, Elizabeth 160
Taylor, Robert Lewis 10
"Tea for Two" (song) 120
Tempo, Nino 53
"Temptation" (record) 83–84
"Tenderly" (song) 154
"Thanks for Everything" (song) 36
"These Foolish Things Remind Me of You" (song) 124, 125
"They Can't Take That Away from Me" (song) 127–128
"They Didn't Believe Me" (song) 131, 132
"Third Stream Music" (term) 17, 105
"This Is It" (song) 50
Thomas, Lewis 7, 133
Thornhill, Claude 14
Tilton, Martha 79
"Time on My Hands" (song) 122, 124
"To a Broadway Rose" (song) 104
Todd, Mike 160
"Too Marvelous for Words" (song) 155
Tormé, Mel 4, 33, 141–142, 143, 144

Tough, Dave 8, 99, 102, 103, 108, 110
"Traffic Jam" (song) 60–61, 62, 63
*The Trouble with Cinderella* (Shaw) 10, 15–16, 47, 90, 151, 152–153
Turner, Lana 11, 42, 57, 76–77, 134
"Two in One Blues" (song) 107–108

vaudeville 41

Wallace, Irving 165
Walton, Jon 117, 127, 128, 132, 136–137
*The Waning of the Middle Ages* (Huizinga) 148
Weill, Kurt 118
Weinberger, Andrew 72, 109
Weiss, Sid 62
"West End Blues" (song) 14
"What Is This Thing Called Love?" (song) 35, 36
"When Buddha Smiles" (song) 4
"When Love Beckoned (on 52nd Street)" (song) 70
"When the Quail Come Back to San Quentin" (song) 90–91
White, John 10
"Who Blew Out the Flame?" (song) 39
"Who's Excited?" (song) 87
"Why Shouldn't I?" (song) 97
"Wichita Lineman" (song) 71
Williams, Cootie 55, 108, 121
Wilson, Brian 133
Wilson, Ollie: "But Not for Me" 120; "Easy to Love" 123; "The Maid with the Flaccid Air" 130; in Shaw band, 1944–1945 114, 118; "Someone to Watch Over Me" 129; "These Foolish Things Remind Me of You" 125; "They Didn't Believe Me" 131
Wilson, Teddy 16, 116–117
Winsor, Kathleen 11, 134, 143, 144, 145
"Without a Dream to My Name" (song) 67
women, song lyrics depictions of 68, 69
"work" (term) 34
World War II 43, 79, 90, 143; era 148
Wright, Samantha 61
Wrightsman, Stan 77
Wylie, Austin 13

"Yesterdays" (song) 33, 34, 35
"Yolanda" (song) 134
"You Go to My Head" (song) 125
"You're a Lucky Guy" (song) 70

Zarchy, Zeke 141
Zito, Fred 150